International Perspectives on Knowledge and Quality

Reinventing Teacher Education

Series Editors: Marie Brennan, Viv Ellis, Joce Nuttall, Peter Smagorinsky

The series presents robust, critical research studies in the broad field of teacher education, including initial or pre-service preparation, in-service and continuing professional development, from diverse theoretical and methodological perspectives. It takes an innovative approach to research in the field and an underlying commitment to transforming the education of teachers.

Advisory Board

Beatrice Avalos (University of Chile, Chile)
Ann Childs (University of Oxford, UK)
Lauren Gatti (University of Nebraska, USA)
Mary Hill (University of Auckland, New Zealand)
Elizabeth Kahn (Northern Illinois University, USA)
Yang Xiaowei (East China Normal University, PRC)
Clare Kosnik (Ontario Institute for Studies in Education, University of Toronto, Canada)
Adam Lefstein, (Ben Gurion University of the Negev, Israel)
Janet Orchard (Bristol University, UK)
Anne Phelan (University of British Columbia, Canada)
Anja Swennen (VU University, the Netherlands)
Tom Are Trippestad (Western Norway University of Applied Sciences (HVL), Norway)

Also available in the series

Developing Culturally and Historically Sensitive Teacher Education: Global Lessons from a Literacy Education Program, edited by Yolanda Gayol Ramírez, Patricia Rosas Chávez and Peter Smagorinsky

Navigating Teacher Education in Complex and Uncertain Times, Carmen I. Mercado

Forthcoming in the series

Secondary English Teacher Education in the United States, Donna L. Pasternak, Samantha Caughlan, Heidi L. Hallman, Laura Renzi, and Leslie S. Rush

The Promise and Practice of University Teacher Education: Insights from Aotearoa New Zealand, Alexandra C. Gunn, Mary F. Hill, David A.G. Berg and Mavis Haigh

The Struggle for Teacher Education, edited by Tom Are Trippestad, Anja Swennen, and Tobias Werler

Transforming Teacher Education with Mobile Technologies, edited by Kevin Burden and Amanda Naylor

International Perspectives on Knowledge and Quality

Implications for Innovation in Teacher Education Policy and Practice

Edited by
Brian Hudson, Niklas Gericke,
Christina Olin-Scheller and Martin Stolare

BLOOMSBURY ACADEMIC
LONDON • NEW YORK • OXFORD • NEW DELHI • SYDNEY

BLOOMSBURY ACADEMIC
Bloomsbury Publishing Plc
50 Bedford Square, London, WC1B 3DP, UK
1385 Broadway, New York, NY 10018, USA
29 Earlsfort Terrace, Dublin 2, Ireland

BLOOMSBURY, BLOOMSBURY ACADEMIC and the Diana logo are trademarks
of Bloomsbury Publishing Plc

First published in Great Britain 2022
This paperback edition published in 2023

Copyright © Brian Hudson, Niklas Gericke, Christina Olin-Scheller, Martin Stolare
and Bloomsbury, 2022

Brian Hudson, Niklas Gericke, Christina Olin-Scheller, Martin Stolare and Bloomsbury have
asserted their right under the Copyright, Designs and Patents Act, 1988, to be identified
as Author of this work.

For legal purposes the Acknowledgements on p. xxi constitute an extension of
this copyright page.

All rights reserved. No part of this publication may be reproduced or transmitted in any form or
by any means, electronic or mechanical, including photocopying, recording, or any information
storage or retrieval system, without prior permission in writing from the publishers.

Bloomsbury Publishing Plc does not have any control over, or responsibility for, any
third-party websites referred to or in this book. All internet addresses given in this book were
correct at the time of going to press. The author and publisher regret any inconvenience caused
if addresses have changed or sites have ceased to exist, but can accept no responsibility for
any such changes.

A catalogue record for this book is available from the British Library.

A catalog record for this book is available from the Library of Congress.

Names: Hudson, Brian, 1951- editor. | Gericke, Niklas, editor. | Olin-Scheller,
Christina, editor. | Stolare, Martin, 1969-editor.
Title: International perspectives on knowledge and quality: implications for innovation in teacher
education policy and practice / edited by Brian Hudson, Niklas Gericke, Christina Olin-Scheller
and Martin Stolare.
Description: First Edition. | New York; London: Bloomsbury Academic, 2022. |
Series: Reinventing Teacher Education / series editors: Marie Brennan, Viv Ellis, Joce Nuttall,
Peter Smagorinsky | Includes bibliographical references and index. |
Identifiers: LCCN 2021035355 (print) | LCCN 2021035356 (ebook) |
ISBN 9781350178403 (Hardback) | ISBN 9781350178410 (PDF) | ISBN 9781350178427 (eBook)
Subjects: LCSH: Teachers–Training of–Cross-cultural studies. |
Education–Standards–Cross-cultural studies. | Knowledge, Theory of.
Classification: LCC LB1707.I578 2022 (print) |
LCC LB1707 (ebook) | DDC 370.71/1–dc23/eng/20211104
LC record available at https://lccn.loc.gov/2021035355
LC ebook record available at https://lccn.loc.gov/2021035356

ISBN: HB: 978-1-3501-7840-3
PB: 978-1-3502-2678-4
ePDF: 978-1-3501-7841-0
eBook: 978-1-3501-7842-7

Series: Reinventing Teacher Education

Typeset by Deanta Global Publishing Services, Chennai, India
Index by Betts Indexing, UK

To find out more about our authors and books visit
www.bloomsbury.com and sign up for our newsletters.

We dedicate this book with our appreciation to all the teachers, students and those working to support them who participated in the studies included in this book.

Contents

List of Illustrations ix
List of Contributors xi
Series Editors' Preface xiv
Volume Editors' Preface xvi
Foreword *Sirpa Tani* xix
Acknowledgements xxi

1 Powerful Professional Knowledge and Innovation in Teacher Education Policy and Practice
   Martin Stolare, Brian Hudson, Niklas Gericke and Christina Olin-Scheller 1
2 Reinventing Subject Teaching in Integrated Teacher Education Programmes for Primary School in Norway
   Lise Iversen Kulbrandstad and Lars Anders Kulbrandstad 23
3 Teacher Education and History Teachers' Powerful Professional Knowledge *Mikko Puustinen* 45
4 Embedding Epistemic Quality in the Pedagogy of Student Geography Teachers *David Mitchell and Alex Standish* 63
5 Epistemic Literacy as an Aim for Religious Education and Implications for Teacher Education
   Alexis Stones and Jo Fraser-Pearce 87
6 Investigating Literature as Knowledge in School English
   Larissa McLean Davies, Lyn Yates and Wayne Sawyer 109
7 Transforming Circular Economy Principles into Teachers' Powerful Professional Knowledge *Kalle Juuti and Niklas Gericke* 127
8 Teachers as Curriculum Makers for School Mathematics of High Epistemic Quality *Brian Hudson* 145
9 Establishing Links to Specialized Knowledge in Social Studies Teaching *Ann-Christin Randahl and Martin Kristiansson* 167

10	Supporting Teachers' Professional Development in Social Studies Education *Martin Stolare, Gabriel Bladh and Martin Kristiansson*	185
11	From a Personal to a Pedagogically Powerful Understanding of School Mathematics *Cosette Crisan*	205
12	Implications of Powerful Professional Knowledge for Innovation in Teacher Education Policy and Practice *Martin Stolare, Brian Hudson, Niklas Gericke and Christina Olin-Scheller*	225

Index 243

Illustrations

Figures

1.1	The didactic triangle	8
1.2	Subject didactics in Sweden pre-2010: A vaguely delimited field of knowledge in teacher education	13
1.3	Subject didactics in Sweden post-2010: A field of knowledge in teacher education with boundaries	13
4.1	Curriculum making model	71
4.2	The didactic triangle	71
4.3	A Visual representation of systematic and regional geography	74
4.4	Planning for student progress – step 1	74
4.5	Concept map of population	80
4.6	Student teacher A: Planning the progression of the concept 'migration'	80
5.1	The didactic triangle	100
8.1	The pedagogical relation in the didactic triad	149
8.2	The didactic relation in the didactic triad	149
8.3	The didactic triad within the wider school and societal context	150
8.4	Mapping Shulman's categories onto the didactic triad	161
8.5	Mapping the emerging themes onto Shulman's categories and the didactic triad	163
9.1	The semantic plane	171
9.2	Semantic profiles	172
9.3	Turns distributed in the semantic plane	176
9.4	Semantic wave	178
9.5	Low flat line	179
9.6	High flat line	180
10.1	Adaptation of the 3-T model PD research	189
10.2	The model of *didaktical* reconstruction	190
10.3	Migration and the selection of specialized knowledge	195
10.4	The model for explaining processes of migration	197
10.5	Migration and the transformation of specialized knowledge	200

11.1	Domains of mathematical knowledge for teaching	207
11.2	Graphs of $f(x) = x^2$ for different domains of definitions	218
12.1	Mapping Shulman's categories onto the didactic triad	227
12.2	Mapping the emerging themes onto Shulman's categories and the didactic triad	236

Tables

2.1	Norwegian Teacher Education Programmes for Compulsory School 1980–2017	30
2.2	The Teacher Education Subject of Norwegian 1980–2017	32
4.1	Secondary Geography Initial Teacher Education Curriculum, UCL IOE	66
7.1	Circular Economy Strategies Adopted in Teacher Education	134
9.1	Analytical Tool	174

Contributors

Gabriel Bladh is Professor in Social Science Education at Karlstad University, Sweden. His research focus is on Geography Education. He is a co-director of the Center for Social Science Education (CSD) and part of the ROSE (Research on subject specific education) research group.

Cosette Crisan is Associate Professor (teaching) in Mathematics Education at the UCL Institute of Education, University College London, UK, where she co-leads the Subject Specialist Research Group (SSRG). She is particularly interested in how key practices of the discipline of mathematics can be better promoted and incorporated into the teaching and learning of school mathematics.

Kalle Juuti is Associate Professor of Digital Learning at School in the Department of Education at the University of Helsinki, Finland. He chairs a faculty digitalization group. His research interests focus on learning in digital environments, education for sustainability and science education.

Martin Kristiansson is Senior Lecturer in Civics at Karlstad University, Sweden. He is a member of the Research on Subject-Specific Education (ROSE) group and a senior researcher at Centre for Social Science Education (CSD).

Lars Anders Kulbrandstad is Emeritus Professor in Norwegian at the Inland Norway University of Applied Sciences, Norway and Senior Professor in Swedish as a Second Language at Karlstad University, Sweden,

Jo Fraser-Pearce is Associate Professor (Teaching) at the UCL Institute of Education, University College London, UK. She is faculty head of Postgraduate Taught Provision. Her main research interests lie in the areas of religious and spiritual education.

Niklas Gericke is Professor in Science Education and Director of the SMEER (Science, Mathematics and Engineering Education Research) Research Centre at Karlstad University, Sweden, and a guest professor at NTNU in Trondheim, Norway.

Brian Hudson is Guest Professor in the Department of Educational Studies at Karlstad University, Sweden, and Emeritus Professor of Education at the University of Sussex, UK. He is a Fellow of the Institute of Mathematics and its Applications, an honorary member of EERA Network 27 Didactics – Learning and Teaching and was awarded a National Teaching Fellowship in 2004.

Lise Iversen Kulbrandstad is Professor in Norwegian at the Inland Norway University of Applied Sciences, Norway, where she is head of the PhD programme in Teaching and Teacher Education. She has been a member of the ROSE group at Karlstad University, Sweden.

Larissa McLean Davies is Associate Professor for Languages and Literacies Education at the University of Melbourne, Australia. She is the lead chief investigator of the ARC Discovery Project, *Investigating Literary Knowledge in the Making of English Teachers*: a monograph arising from this project was published in 2021.

David Mitchell currently co-leads a geography initial teacher education programme at the UCL Institute of Education, University College London, UK. His research interests are the teacher's role and agency in the geography curriculum, particularly in relation to education for sustainability. David is the PI of the EU-funded 'GeoCapabilties 3' project, completed in September 2021.

Christina Olin-Scheller is Professor in Educational Work, and director of the CSL (Centre of Language and Literature in Education) Research Centre and ROSE (Research on Subject-Specific Education) Research Group at Karlstad University, Sweden. She coordinates the Swedish National Literacy Network and participates in the Nordic QUINT (Quality in Nordic Teaching) research centre.

Mikko Puustinen is a history and social studies teacher in upper secondary school and a researcher in the Research Group for Social Studies Education at the University of Helsinki, Finland. His research interests include history and social studies didactics and teacher education.

Ann-Christin Randahl is Senior Lecturer in Swedish with a specialization in didactics at the Department of Swedish at Gothenburg University, Sweden. Her main research interests are writing, professional development, and social media. She is part of the ROSE and the LCT Nordic networks.

Wayne Sawyer is Emeritus Professor in Education at Western Sydney University, Australia. His research interests include secondary English teaching, including issues around knowledge in the teaching of literature; literacy policy, and effective teaching – the latter especially in low SES contexts.

Martin Stolare is Professor in History at Karlstad University, Sweden. He is a co-director of the ROSE (Research on Subject-Specific Education) research group and a senior researcher at CSD (Centre for Social Science Education) at Karlstad University, Sweden,

Alexis Stones is Subject Lead for the Postgraduate Teacher Education Programme (PGCE) in Religious Education at the UCL Institute of Education, University College London, UK. Her teaching and research interests are religion and science, sacred art, and peace education.

Alex Standish is Associate Professor of Geography Education at the UCL Institute of Education, University College London, UK. He works in teacher training, supervises postgraduate students and is researching the nature of disciplinary knowledge in the school curriculum. He is a co-editor of *What Should Schools Teach? Disciplines, Subjects and the Pursuit of Truth*.

Lyn Yates is Redmond Barry Distinguished Professor Emerita of Curriculum at the University of Melbourne, Australia.

Series Editors' Preface

Teacher education continues to be one of the most pressing and topical issues in the field of educational practice and research. In a range of countries around the globe, there is strong interest in how teachers are prepared, in the content of their pre-service education and training programmes and in measuring and monitoring their effectiveness. These interests are often framed by commitments to nation-building; policy commitments to productivity, 'levelling-up' or social justice; or even political desires to foster and perpetuate 'culture wars'. Fundamentally, there is a questioning of the role and function of what makes up the 'good' or successful teacher in society in order to reproduce or transform the 'good' society. There are questions about the place of ethical and moral judgements in teachers' practice, about the introduction of and corporate methods and the role of teachers in innovation. Associated with such questions, government policy agenda around the world address whether and how teachers should be educated or trained as teaching comes to be seen, in some jurisdictions, as a short-term mission rather than as a professional career.

For some time now there has been an international concern to reform programmes of pre-service (or initial) teacher education. This movement has been driven by a belief that raising standards in education and raising attainment in schools will only be managed effectively if teacher quality is improved. The best way to reform the teaching profession is through changing their teacher education programmes. However, as these reforms are being enacted, contradictions in policy, practice and curriculum design in pre-service teacher education are increasingly apparent in different national settings. These contradictions are, in part, related to the underlying cultural identity of teaching (as a profession, for example) as well as the distribution of wealth within and across these different societies. In some countries, teacher education is seen as a vital tool in the building of national educational, scientific, cultural, technological and economic infrastructures. In others, teacher education has become a means by which those countries' human capital can be improved, economic competitiveness leveraged and status as knowledge economies ensured. Yet, while many of the drivers are common across these contexts, the direction of policy and how policies are enacted in practice varies considerably, and the role of higher education in teacher preparation is often a significant source of diversity across countries.

The series presents robust, critical research studies in the broad field of teacher education, including initial or pre-service preparation, in-service education and continuing professional development, from diverse theoretical and methodological perspectives and from different national perspectives. The series has an underlying commitment to transforming the education of teachers and aims to support innovative approaches to research in the field.

International Perspectives on Knowledge and Quality: Implications for Innovation in Teacher Education Policy and Practice presents a sequence of chapters related to the Swedish Research Council-funded *KOSS* project, authored by research groups across Sweden, Finland, Norway, the UK and Australia. The research underlying the chapters focuses directly on some of the most topical issues in teaching and teacher education currently: the place of knowledge in teaching and learning; the epistemological distinctions and their pedagogical implications for school subjects; the definition of quality in the preparation of subject teachers; and the nature of the power that knowledge has for the transformation of the individual person and the societies they are part of.

The researchers draw on a number of strong traditions of educational theorizing and, notably, integrate the northern European tradition of subject didactics with English interests in the sociology of knowledge and the promising concept of epistemic quality. Theoretically, therefore, this is an important and timely book. Practically, though, the various chapters offer a way of thinking about knowledge in teaching and teacher education that moves beyond pat social media spats about 'knowledge-rich' teaching versus a barely defined binary alternative. Instead, taken together, the chapters argue for the importance of subject-based disciplinary communities of professional practice and for developing teachers' knowledge of subject-specific expertise alongside other domains of professional knowledge. Fundamentally, the authors argue for a re-invigoration of teacher professionalism through a very serious engagement with one of the key aims of education – the growth of knowledge. The book makes a significant contribution to how we understand innovation in teacher education.

Viv Ellis, Peter Smagorinsky,
Marie Brennan & Joce Nuttall
Series Editors

Volume Editors' Preface

This book arises from the work of the KOSS Network *Knowledge and Quality across School Subjects and Teacher Education* funded by the Swedish Research Council (2019–22). The network brings together cross-disciplinary educational research groups from Sweden, England and Finland specializing in different school subjects. The research groups involved are *ROSE* (Research on Subject-specific Education) at Karlstad University in Sweden, *SSRG* (Subject Specialism Research Group) at the University College London in the UK, and *HuSoEd* (Research Community for Humanities and Social Sciences) at the University of Helsinki in Finland. Central aims of the KOSS research programme are to study how content knowledge in different school subjects is defined and transformed and to consider the implications for innovation in teacher education policy and practice. The book focuses on the latter aspect and has been developed parallel to a second book published simultaneously by Bloomsbury Academic entitled *International Perspectives on Knowledge and Curriculum: Epistemic Quality across School Subjects* (Hudson et al. 2022).

The application made to the Swedish Research Council built on prior collaboration between the research groups and was developed in some detail at a seminar held in Apertin, Sweden, in February 2018. The grant was awarded in November 2018 and the first meeting of the network took place in Stockholm in May 2019. The majority of chapters in this book are based on papers first presented at symposia at the European Conference on Educational Research (ECER) and the Nordic Conference on Teaching and Learning in Curriculum Subjects (NOFA). In particular, most of these papers formed contributions to symposia on *Powerful Knowledge across School Subjects* as part of ECER 2018 at the University of Bolzano in September 2018, on *Powerful Knowledge, Epistemic Quality and Transformations* as part of NOFA7 at Stockholm University in May 2019, and on *Powerful Knowledge and Epistemic Quality across School Subjects and Teacher Education* as part of ECER 2019 at the University of Hamburg in September 2019. Several other chapters arose from the development of the KOSS network's wider activities during this period of time.

The network is hosted by the ROSE group at Karlstad University, which designated it a strong research group in 2016. The group has developed from three subject-specific research centres at Karlstad University which focus on subject-specific research in close cooperation with teachers, students, teacher educators and a range of other stakeholders. The SSRG group at the UCL Institute of Education has specific interest and expertise in all areas of curriculum, pedagogy and assessment, especially the role of knowledge in school teaching. The HuSoEd group at Helsinki University has specific interest in subject didactics of different school subjects and in the humanities and social sciences particularly. The groups within the network share their expertise and interests in exploring and developing aspects of powerful knowledge, epistemic quality and transformation processes and how these hold implications for innovation in teacher education policy and practice.

The primary forms of collaboration in the network are workshops and research mobility, supplemented by webinars, joint conference presentations and publications. The network's first workshop took place in Stockholm following the Nordic Conference on Teaching and Learning in Curriculum Subjects (NOFA7) at Stockholm University in May 2019. The second workshop was hosted by the HuSoEd group at Helsinki University in October 2019 while the third one was hosted by the SSRG group in London in March 2020. This pattern has continued with workshops in Karlstad, Helsinki and London during the second half of 2020 and in 2021.

The book is arranged as twelve chapters featuring contributions from Australia, England, Finland, Norway, Scotland and Sweden that address the teaching of a range of subjects and cross-curricular contexts, including subject teaching in general, social studies, economics and the teaching of English, geography, history, mathematics and religious education. It is structured so as to reflect the continuum of teacher education from initial teacher education that is the focus of the earlier chapters to continuing professional development in the later ones. The first chapter by Martin Stolare, Niklas Gericke, Brian Hudson and Christina Olin-Scheller is entitled *Powerful Professional Knowledge and Innovation in Teacher Education Policy and Practice*. This reflects a focus on teachers' *powerful professional knowledge* (Furlong and Whitty 2017) the consideration of which builds on work reflected in (Hudson et al. 2022). The latter is based on a theoretical framework that draws on the themes of *powerful knowledge* (Young 2014), *transformation* processes (Gericke et al. 2018) and *epistemic quality* (Hudson 2018). In drawing attention to the importance of disciplinary knowledge in professional contexts, Furlong and Whitty (ibid.) stress that this does not exclude the importance of other kinds of knowledge and that there is a crucial pedagogical element in professional education. We go further, however, by arguing there is also a crucial *didactical* dimension and also a need to recognize the significance of subject didactics as disciplines in their own right, as occurs in most Scandinavian countries. We see a key challenge for professional disciplines such as teacher education being the need to establish precisely how disciplinary knowledge, which is epistemologically strong, functions together with other forms of knowledge and thereby influences practice. In turn, we recognize the importance of Furlong and Whitty's (2017: 49) question, 'How can disciplinary knowledge and other external knowledges be brought together with professionals' reflective practice and practical theorising in professional arenas to produce really powerful professional knowledge and learning?' We hope this book goes some way to answering this question and to promoting a broader debate within the professional community.

References

Furlong, J. and Whitty, G. (2017), 'Knowledge Traditions in the Study of Education', in G. Whitty and J. Furlong (eds), *Knowledge and the Study of Education: An International Exploration*, 13–57, Oxford: Symposium Books.

Gericke, N., Hudson, B., Olin-Scheller, C. and Stolare, M. (2018), 'Powerful Knowledge, Transformations and the Need for Empirical Studies across School Subjects', *London Review of Education: Special Issue on Knowledge and Subject Specialist Teaching*, 16 (3): 428–44. UCL IOE Press. DOI: 10.18546/LRE.16.3.06

Hudson, B. (2018), 'Powerful Knowledge and Epistemic Quality in School Mathematics', *London Review of Education: Special Issue on Knowledge and Subject Specialist Teaching*, 16 (3): 384–97. UCL IOE Press. DOI: 10.18546/LRE.16.3.03

Hudson, B., Gericke, N., Olin-Scheller, C. and Stolare, M. (2022), *International Perspectives on Knowledge and Curriculum: Epistemic Quality across School Subjects*, London: Bloomsbury Publishing plc.

Young, M. (2014), 'Powerful Knowledge as Curriculum Principle', in M. Young, D. Lambert, C. R. Roberts and M. D. Roberts (eds), *Knowledge and the Future School: Curriculum and Social Justice*, 65–88, 2nd ed., London: Bloomsbury Academic.

Brian Hudson, Niklas Gericke,
Christina Olin-Scheller and Martin Stolare

Foreword

This book and the work of the network *Knowledge and Quality across School Subjects and Teacher Education* (KOSS) in general tackle one of the main issues that teacher education is facing: the role of knowledge in today's world where information can be acquired from not only official sources but also, more and more frequently, from the social media. The question of what kinds of knowledge and skills young people need in the digitalized and globalized world, where rapid changes require people to be flexible, is increasingly important. Abilities to collaborate and to interact with others, and to critically evaluate information to solve complex problems, are essential. These needs can be connected to the ideas of twenty-first-century skills, which have made many educationalists stress learner-centric approaches. When learning has been conceived as an active and constructive process, teaching has often been thought to represent an old-fashioned idea where a teacher delivers knowledge for passive receivers, the students. This is, of course, a crude generalization, but – based on my own experiences – it can easily be observed in many policy documents and academic studies where constructivist ideas of learning have been highlighted. This has often been done at the expense of discipline-based teaching. What is the role and status of teaching then in current and future schools? What do school subjects have to offer for young people? These questions are explored by KOSS researchers.

KOSS has brought researchers of subject education together to delve into the role and status of discipline-based teaching in this day and age. The network started its work by exploring the concept of powerful knowledge and its potential in the context of school subjects represented in the network. 'Powerful knowledge' is understood as a specialized knowledge, which is based on academic disciplines and their ways of comprehending phenomena that are investigated. It is also different from the everyday knowledge that students (and teachers) bring with them into the school. One of the most important aspects for me in the concept of powerful knowledge is its dynamic character: knowledge is not thought to be stable, but always open to be challenged and developed further. For me as a geographer and teacher educator, it has been eye opening to listen to the researchers of other school subjects, and their views of what 'powerful knowledge' could mean in their own field of interest. Complex relationships between academic disciplines, discipline-based school subjects and teaching have been discussed not only with colleagues coming from the same field of interest, but also across subjects.

Teachers have to balance between different types of knowledge in their work: the disciplinary knowledge that is based on their academic education, pedagogical knowledge and everyday knowledge, which is brought to their classrooms by their students. KOSS is interested in exploring these complex relations and understandings, having its focus on the teachers' role in the process. What kind of knowledge is powerful? How can disciplinary knowledge be transformed to fit the educational aims of teaching? What kinds of similarities and differences are there between different school subjects in their ways of dealing with knowledge? This edited volume by KOSS researchers explores these questions and poses some additional enquiries that are important for everyone who is interested in the future of education.

Sirpa Tani
Professor of Geography and Environmental Education
University of Helsinki, Finland

Acknowledgements

The editors are particularly grateful for the support from the Swedish Research Council received between 2019 and 2022 by the KOSS Network: 'Knowledge and Quality across School Subjects and Teacher Education' through the award of the Educational Sciences network grant (2018-03603).

We are also grateful to the ROSE research group (Research On Subject Specific Education) at Karlstad University, Sweden, for its support in general and also for supporting many of the studies included in this book.

We thank Murray Bales for his careful work in the language editing process.

In addition, we thank the following for permission to publish or adapt figures for which they hold the copyright:

Figure 1.1 *The didactic triangle (Hudson 2022)*
Brian Hudson is the copyright holder

Figure 4.1 *Curriculum making model (Geographical Association 2020)*
Our thanks to the Geographical Society for permission to use this figure.

Figure 4.2 *The Didactic Triangle (Hudson 2022)*
Brian Hudson is the copyright holder

Figure 4.4 *Planning for student progress – step 1 (QCA, cited in Gardner et al. 2015)*
Our thanks to the Geographical Society for permission to use this figure.

Figure 5.1 *The didactic triangle (developed from Hopmann 1997) (Gericke et al. 2018: 437)*
Creative Commons Attribution to: Gericke, N., Hudson, B., Olin-Scheller, C. and Stolare, M. (2018), 'Powerful Knowledge, Transformations and the Need for Empirical Studies across School Subjects', London Review of Education, 16 (3): 428–44. https://doi.org/10.18546/LRE.16.3.06

All content published by ScienceOpen is under the Creative Commons licence CC-BY 4.0

https://creativecommons.org/licenses/by/4.0/#

Figure 8.1 *The pedagogical relation in the didactic triad*
Brian Hudson is the copyright holder

Figure 8.2 *The didactic relation in the didactic triad*
Brian Hudson is the copyright holder

Figure 8.3 *The didactic triad within the wider school and societal context*
Brian Hudson is the copyright holder

Figure 9.2 *Semantic profiles (adapted from Maton 2013: 13)*
Our thanks to Karl Maton for permission to adapt and use this figure.

Figure 10.1 *Adaptation of 3-T model PD research (Prediger et al. 2017, 2019b)*
Our thanks to Susanne Prediger for permission to use this figure.

Figure 10.2 *The model of* didaktical *reconstruction (adapted from Kattman et al. 1997)*
Our thanks to Michael Komorek for permission to use this figure.

Figure 10.3 *Migration and the selection of specialized knowledge*
Our thanks to Michael Komorek for permission to use this figure.

Figure 10.5 *Migration and the transformation of specialized knowledge*
Our thanks to Michael Komorek for permission to use this figure.

Figure 11.1 *Domains of mathematical knowledge for teaching (Ball et al. 2008: 403)*
Our thanks to Deborah Loewenberg Ball for permission to use this figure.

1

Powerful Professional Knowledge and Innovation in Teacher Education Policy and Practice

Martin Stolare, Brian Hudson, Niklas Gericke and Christina Olin-Scheller

Introduction

Teachers' ability to teach subject content has been identified as a major factor influencing students' knowledge acquisition in the debate arising in the wake of international student assessments (Vollmer 2014). This book focuses on the ability to teach a specific subject matter, something that can thus be perceived as the core of teachers' professional knowledge. In every sense, this is a classical educational question difficult to avoid for researchers interested in the processes of teaching and learning (Shulman 2004). Still, in this chapter teachers' subject teaching ability is discussed in light of the social realism perspective and the associated 'powerful knowledge' framework. The concept of powerful knowledge has gained strong momentum since first being introduced just over ten years ago. With expressions like 'bringing knowledge back in', the English educational sociologist Michael Young argued for students' entitlement to encounter the specialized knowledge that has proven particularly powerful for understanding the present, and for preparing to face the possible challenges of the future. 'Powerful knowledge provides more reliable explanations and new ways of thinking about the world and can provide learners with a language for engaging in political, moral, and other kinds of debates' (Young 2008: 14). To date, this approach, based on powerful knowledge, has mainly been connected to construction of the school curriculum. With this book, we aim to broaden the discussion by linking the social realism perspective and the powerful knowledge approach to the issues of teachers' professional knowledge as well as the structure and focus of teacher education. In this way, attention is drawn to the fact that a knowledge perspective may indicate that teacher education needs to be improved in relation to both policy and practice.

The perspective of this book is international and comparative. As a result, social realism and the powerful knowledge approach are considered in relation to the German-Nordic traditions of didactics, which since the nineteenth century have shaped the view of teachers' professional knowledge in continental Europe (Kansanen 2009). Thus, the book is a contribution to the ongoing conversation between representatives of the curriculum and didactics research traditions (Gericke et al. 2018; Bladh et al. 2018; Deng 2018; Qvortrup et al. 2021). We claim that in important respects the ability to teach is specific to our understanding; that is, teaching mathematics is different from teaching history. What is to be taught is intimately associated with how it is to be taught. Namely, there is a field of knowledge that lies between curriculum and pedagogy, a field that in the didactics traditions is defined as subject didactics (*fachdidaktik*) (Vollmer 2021; Bayrhuber et al. 2017). This book should be seen as an argument for strengthening subject didactics perspectives in both research and teacher education as a prerequisite for qualifying teachers' ability to teach.

The ambition with this book is to help develop an understanding of how educators and education systems can ensure that school-based knowledge-building reaches its transformative potential. In the same way as outlined in Gericke et al. (2022), the conceptual framework underlying the studies presented in this book draws upon the concepts *powerful knowledge, transformation processes* and *epistemic quality*. We especially focus on the implications for policy and practice in teacher education. Further, we relate to what is described as *powerful professional knowledge* (Furlong and Whitty 2017) and do so by linking social realism to a didactical perception of teaching and learning a content knowledge. This book seeks to contribute to meeting the needs of future citizens by producing new knowledge about educational processes that hold the potential to improve education by exploring what may constitute the *powerful professional knowledge* required for teacher education in particular.

There are reasons to relate the development of teachers' professional knowledge to the structure and organization of teacher education. The need for a coordinated and coherent system of teacher education from initial teacher education (ITE), through continuing professional development (CPD), is highlighted in the agenda of the European Union (EU) for Improving Teacher Quality (European Commission 2010).

A burning issue of the last decade, which directly relates to this book's focus, concerns how the relationship between theory and practice should be addressed within ITE. This is the 'eternal' question for teacher education, gaining new relevance in the light of the much greater emphasis on accountability in recent years. In this discourse, a university-based education is not necessarily recognized as a must for a good teacher education; on the contrary, it is in practice that student teachers are given the opportunity to develop into teachers. In this sense, a 'practice-turn' permeates the discussion of how ITE should be organized (Cochran-Smith 2016). This view has been particularly strong in the United States, the United Kingdom and Australia. Some leading critics of an overly theoretically oriented teacher education may be found in the political system. The policy changes implemented have meant a questioning of the role universities play in ITE. In this respect, the developments in the UK do stand out. Over a twenty-year period, a state-market system has been established while the number of institutions offering teacher education more than doubled, from 95 to over 240 (Hulme et al. 2021). However, this trend is not unequivocal. In other countries and education systems, such as Scotland, Germany, Ireland, Finland and Sweden, university-based teacher education has been able to defend its position despite being challenged by more school-based teacher education developments such as 'Teach First' (see Menter et al. 2016).

It is a given that the relevance of ITE must be constantly monitored and evaluated. Yet, we do not recognize the de-academization of ITE as a solution since that would completely undermine the efforts to build a knowledge base that can be characterized as powerful professional knowledge. Instead, the way forward is to establish and strengthen a field of knowledge that connects theory and practice. We understand that subject didactics can be such a field, namely, that is the argument we are making here. Subject didactics, identified as a field of research and practice between the 'mother' discipline(s) of the school subject and pedagogy, is to be regarded as central to the development of teachers' professional knowledge. With this potential, subject didactics should be the core of teacher education in both ITE and CPD. The nature of the subject didactics field requires that it is linked to the practice in school. Otherwise, subject didactics cannot provide answers to questions perceived as relevant by those who represent the school's practice. It is at the same time essential to ensure that subject didactics does not develop into a field where proven experience and short-term goal fulfilment have superseded critical scholarly perspectives.

The role of subject didactics in teacher education and the role of universities are difficult to ignore when the character of teachers' powerful professional knowledge is a theme. Still, this does not imply that the subject didactics perspective should be identical regardless of the focus of the ITE. In primary school, interdisciplinary thematic approaches are traditionally more prominent, a fact that ought to have an impact on the concrete representation of the subject didactics perspective in ITE for primary teachers.

Scope of the Book and Theoretical Background

ITE and CPD are addressed from various viewpoints in this book. The approach is comparative; examples are drawn from various countries, parts of the education system and across subjects. By using the theoretical concepts of powerful knowledge, transformation processes and epistemic quality, the research studies presented in the different chapters focus on how these concepts form knowledge of importance for the field of subject didactics and suggest how this knowledge might be developed within teacher education. More precisely, the chapters explore crucial characteristics of teachers' powerful professional knowledge and associated implications for teacher education policy and practice. This explorative book has arisen through invited responses to the following three key questions:

1. How can the nature of powerful knowledge and epistemic quality in different school subjects be characterized?
2. How can the transformation processes related to powerful knowledge and epistemic quality be described?
3. How can the nature of teachers' powerful professional knowledge be characterized and what are the implications for teacher education policy and practice?

The chapters in this book address research question 3 in particular, while questions 1 and 2 are the main foci of a complementary book focused on *International Perspectives on Knowledge and Curriculum: Epistemic Quality across School Subjects*. The latter is based on parallel research and published by Bloomsbury Academic (Hudson et al., 2022).

Powerful Knowledge and Teachers' Professional Knowledge

The concept of powerful knowledge underscores the role of knowledge in the curriculum and focuses on what is taught and learned (Young 2009). This book aims to take the next step and relate the concept of powerful knowledge to teacher education and teachers' knowledge base. And, as already indicated, we view teachers' subject didactic knowledge as a possible way to frame teachers' professional knowledge.

A basic idea behind the concept of powerful knowledge is that of boundaries. Powerful knowledge is specialized because it is linked to a restricted object of knowledge, and the production of knowledge is carried out in a specific manner (Young 2013). The division into disciplines is an expression of this specialization. The boundary does not imply that specialized knowledge is permanent and unquestionable; on the contrary, specialized knowledge is fallible and open to challenge. The second boundary is between specialized knowledge and everyday knowledge. The position is here that the former, unlike the latter, it is not tied to a specific context. Specialized knowledge is potentially powerful precisely because it can be used in different contexts (Young 2013).

Teacher education is a complex form of vocational education in which knowledge and perspectives are linked to different and, in some cases, conflicting, epistemological points of departure. This epistemological complexity is expressed in the organization and structure of teacher education programmes where academic disciplinary studies are combined with practical pedagogical courses. In the latter, the content is often valued relative to the idea of proven experience. The role of proven experience in teacher education puts the notion of boundaries between different types of knowledge to the test, an idea so central to the concept of powerful knowledge. In the challenge of dealing with different knowledge traditions in teacher education, there is a parallel with other types of vocational education. Wheelahan (2015) stresses the importance of vocational students encountering specialized, powerful knowledge to enable them to gain a broader and more profound understanding of the knowledge that permeates the professional practice they are to engage in. As referred to earlier, the organization and structure of teacher education are today under debate in several European countries. Yet, following Wheelahan's arguments, neglecting specialized knowledge in vocational education will lead to excessively contextually restricted teacher education that weakens teachers' ability to adapt to future changes of the education system. This means that the role of specialized, powerful knowledge in teacher education must be defended. The question is simply: what is that knowledge? – a straightforward question, easy to ask, yet difficult to answer.

One way to address this theme is to relate to Young and Muller's (2010) discussion of three different curriculum futures. They link their model of the three curriculum futures to the role of knowledge in the two curriculum traditions dominating the educational debate. In what Young and Muller call Future 1, knowledge is considered eternal and given, closely related to the classic disciplines. In Future I, knowledge is understood as independent of the context from which it was generated. In contrast to Future 1, Future 2 involves knowledge that is so dependent on its social context that it cannot be separated from that context or from the person who created it. As a result of this perception, it is argued that knowledge in Future 2 has been placed in the background of the curriculum, while there has been a much greater emphasis on skills and competencies. Young (2015a, b) thus sees a problem in both positions on the knowledge expressed in Future 1 ('under-socialized') and Future 2 ('over-socialized'). From the perspective of social realism, knowledge is perceived as created in a social context, but cannot be reduced to the specific situation. For this reason, an alternative is formulated in which knowledge is placed at the centre of the curriculum – referred to as Future 3. While such knowledge is related to the disciplines, that does not mean this disciplinary knowledge is not fallible and impossible to question (Young and Muller 2010).

Young and Muller's (2010) model of curriculum futures captures three positions with regard to the role of knowledge in curriculum, in English but also in international educational research. The three futures constitute a compelling rhetorical model, and here, it has its strength. The desirable future to Young and Muller is Future 3, but what it represents concretely is not entirely clear-cut. Morgan et al. (2019) addressed the pedagogical challenge to make the distinction between Future 1 and 3 clear. To do so, they emphasize the importance of stressing the dynamics of the disciplines. Not updating the understanding of the disciplines brings an imminent risk that Future 3 will become Future 1 as the content knowledge in the curriculum might be perceived as settled, and in a sense 'eternal'. This slippage is also likely if too few groups in society have input on the formation of the disciplines and the design of the curriculum. These processes need to be inclusive (Morgan et al. 2019). We recognize their views as central if the powerful knowledge approach is to defend its legitimacy.

The powerful knowledge approach is not undisputed (Alderson 2020; White 2012). One point of criticism has been described as the dichotomy between disciplinary and everyday knowledge. Catling and Martin (2011) argue convincingly, from the perspective of primary school, that dimensions of students' everyday knowledge (in geography) may be characterized as powerful knowledge. They point to an issue that we have also highlighted earlier (Gericke et al. 2018). In this context, we claim that a possible solution or at least approach to the problem that Catling and Martin stress is to relate powerful knowledge and Future 3 to the tradition of didactics. By looking at powerful knowledge through didactical lenses, the student becomes part of the picture without giving up on the idea that content knowledge is fundamental to teaching and learning processes (Jank and Meyer 2018). Perhaps even more important in this context – addressing the teacher's professional knowledge – is the didactics tradition effort to maintain a relationship to practice-generated knowledge (Hordern 2018b).

The teacher needs to be familiar with the knowledge of the discipline (or disciplines) to which the school subject is linked, as well as having an insight into how this disciplinary knowledge is generated. Still, this is not enough; the teacher also needs to have the ability to make significant disciplinary knowledge relevant to the students. This is a notion central to the perspective of subject didactics, expressed through the didactic triangle (Figure 1.1). An increased focus on the subject matter and the knowledge addressed in teaching, consequently, indicates that the role of subject didactics in teacher education has to be safeguarded. Indeed, it might even be a prerequisite for Young's and Muller's (2010) vision of a Future 3 curriculum to be realized.

Transformation Processes

In the collaborative studies underlying this book, we have sought to develop the concept of powerful knowledge in two important ways, as discussed by Gericke et al. (2018). First, rather than regarding powerful knowledge only as a concept related to educational practices, we have addressed its use as a tool in educational research related to subject education. More specifically, in line with Deng (2015), we advocate alignment of the curricular concept of powerful knowledge with the European research tradition of didactics in general, and subject didactics in particular. Second, we have developed the concept of powerful knowledge by refuting the dichotomization implied by Young (2015b, 104) that curriculum ('what to teach') can be separated from pedagogy ('how to teach'). Instead, we view these two aspects as being interrelated in didactical research. We recommend expanding the concept of powerful knowledge by incorporating the analytical concept transformation in descriptions of powerful knowledge related to different disciplines, institutions and school subjects.

Transformation is a crucial issue in various European didactical research traditions. It refers to an integrative process through which specialized knowledge, developed in subject disciplines, is restructured and re-presented in educational environments – by various processes outside and within the education system at individual, institutional and societal levels – as bodies and forms of knowledge to be taught and learned. Such transformation processes are apparent in concepts associated with a number of frameworks, including 'transposition' (Chevallard 2007), 'omstilling' (Ongstad 2006) and 'reconstruction' (Duit et al. 2012), and are reflected in the work of Bernstein (1971) relative to 're-contextualization' within the curriculum tradition. A school subject is never a simple reduction of the corresponding discipline, and disciplinary knowledge is always transformed to fit the educational purpose of teaching. Hence, in order to study the concept of powerful knowledge within school subjects, we need to study its transformation processes, address the 'why' question, and also the 'what' and 'how' questions.

The didactic tradition involves a dynamic perception of the relationship between the didactical questions: why? what? how? and for whom? These questions, framing the classroom activities, can work as guiding posts while planning and analysing teaching. From a didactic perspective, it is necessary to work with the didactical questions simultaneously since the answer to one question affects the response to another. This relationally dynamic approach is represented by the didactic triangle, described as the foundation of subject didactics (Uljens 1997: 167) and illustrated in Figure 1.1 from Hudson (this volume).

Although the different elements of the didactic triangle, represented by the corners and sides (Hopmann 2007), are in relation to each other, is it not insignificant where the planning or analysis of the educational process has its starting point. If the process starts with a 'for whom-what'-input, it might lead to a slightly different understanding of how the subject matter should be organized than if the take-off point is 'why-what'. While we embrace the need to follow

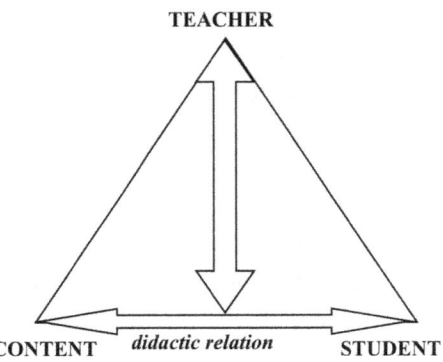

Figure 1.1 The didactic triangle (Hudson 2022).

Wolfgang Klafki's argument about the 'primacy' of the content and the 'why-what' question, it is how the content is related to other parts of the didactic triangle, and the interplay of the various didactical questions, that shape the representation of the subject matter (Klafki 1985/2001). In this sense, a didactical approach will help highlight the complexity and nuances of the transformation process.

Epistemic Quality

The idea of epistemic quality arose from a perspective informed by concepts drawn from the field of subject didactics (Hudson et al. 2015) and is seen as a way of thinking that helps to articulate aspects of what we mean by 'powerful knowledge' in different subjects. It was developed as a theoretical outcome of research in the field of mathematics education, but regarded as highly relevant for other subject domains. Fundamental to this idea is the recognition that school subjects have too often become a normative aspect of schooling and are treated as 'taken for granted *givens*' (Goodson and Marsh 1996), especially on the policy level. A key concept to influence the idea of epistemic quality's evolution is that of 'didactic transposition', which as outlined by Chevallard (2007) draws from the wider field of French didactics. This is a transformation process based on the principle that knowledge is not something that is to be taken as simply given and to be explained but 'knowledge is potentially encapsulated in situations, and it is in going through those situations that the student, or whoever, can learn' (2007). This view of learning as 'learning from the situation' is a central principle of French didactics, which sees knowledge as built up and transformed or *transposed* in didactic situations. The concept epistemic quality is developed further in Hudson (2022) by considering it with respect to the idea of *epistemic ascent* (Winch 2013) in the evolution of subject expertise. This is based on a continuum that reflects a trajectory in the development of expertise from that of the novice towards that of an expert in the subject. The framework developed by Winch (2013: 129) is based on three distinct, yet interrelated, kinds of knowledge: first, *knowledge by acquaintance*; second, propositional knowledge or *knowledge that*; and, third, procedural knowledge or *knowledge how*. In relation to powerful knowledge, there is a correspondence between *knowledge by acquaintance* and Young's (2013) use of the term 'everyday knowledge'. With regard to *knowledge that*, Winch (2013) considers that this is embedded within a conceptual structure which is itself embedded within further related propositions. Accordingly, he stresses that it is important to make inferences (Brandom 2000) by drawing on the concepts embodied within the subject matter. Further, it is necessary to be able to distinguish between claims that can be counted as knowledge and those that are simply beliefs, which reflects aspects discussed in relation to mathematical fallibilism (Hudson 2022). Finally, in relation to *knowledge how*, this is considered as an *epistemic capacity* that is linked to *knowledge by acquaintance* and *knowledge that* based on the recognition that knowing how to do something usually requires elements of the other two kinds of knowledge.

The process of beginning to learn a subject therefore involves beginning to use the language associated with the concepts of that subject and that a central dimension of learning about a subject is learning to participate in conversations and discussions that employ those concepts.

Powerful Professional Knowledge in the Context of Didactic Tradition

The three aspects of *powerful knowledge, transformation processes* and *epistemic quality* hold implications for teacher education policy and practice. In line with what has been stated so far in this chapter, we understand that it is fundamental to address teacher education from a knowledge perspective. We also believe it is relevant to use an empirical approach to explore the social realism approach and the role that Young, Muller, Wheelahan, Hordern and others assigns to specialized knowledge in teacher education. Given the ambition that students should encounter specialized, possibly powerful, knowledge, this places demands on the teacher's knowledge base and the focus and organization of teacher education.

The powerful knowledge approach has been implicitly associated with the secondary school curriculum. Primary school researchers also note the difficulties of relating powerful knowledge and disciplinary issues to the school's primary phase (Roberts 2014; Catling and Martin 2011). We agree that challenges exist in this respect. The primary school curriculum is often more interdisciplinary, meaning the role played by disciplinary and specialized knowledge is different to that in secondary school. Yet, this does not imply that disciplinary and, above all, specialized knowledge should not form part of the primary school curriculum and, consequently, of primary teachers' education. Having said that, a relevant question in this context is: how should teacher education (both ITE and CPD, both primary and secondary school) be organized to link subject matter in school to specialized knowledge? The intention is to address this question in the concluding chapter of the book, where the reasoning can be based on the various empirical studies presented. In this chapter, we focus more on the concept of teachers' professional knowledge.

The term 'powerful professional knowledge' was introduced by Furlong and Whitty (2017), who based their thinking on the powerful knowledge approach. Their discussion of the concept is brief; a clear substantive definition is not given. In that respect, the concept might generate more questions than answers. Nevertheless, powerful professional knowledge, embedded as it is in social realism, gives a rough, but still important, idea of how to perceive the character of teachers' professional knowledge. Teacher education has, however, generally strong connections to the academy – to TEIs (teacher education institutions) because being a vocational professional education part of the preparation to become a teacher is place-based. According to Furlong and Whitty (2017), the logic of knowledge, how it is generated and legitimized, varies in these two main parts of teacher education. They show that the relationship between TEIs and practice has been central in shaping the different educational knowledge traditions. Following Bernstein, they claim it is problematic if generic perspectives are allowed to determine the content and organization of teacher education. This could lead to erosion of the teachers' professional knowledge base. Further, they argue (Furlong and Whitty 2017) that this can leave knowledge open to manipulation by governments and employers, thereby potentially destroying the identities and autonomy that professionals traditionally acquire through immersion in disciplinary knowledge. This would then result in a shift from professional education to professional training, which may just as well be undertaken 'on the job' like in many academic settings.

By referring to powerful professional knowledge, the focus is on ensuring that specialized knowledge has a role in teacher education. Similarly, Hordern (2019) is on the same track when he reasons about teacher education and the different pathways for teachers' professionalization development. He points to the importance of a field of knowledge, embodying a part in teacher education, that lies between academia and practice. In this respect, he recognizes a difference between England and Germany.

> What England lacks perhaps, in contrast to Germany, is a distinct disciplinary tradition of specifically educational thought powered by educational concepts that can have resonance in practice. The lack of an offer of compelling educational concepts around which higher education research and practitioner thinking can gather and iterate has left 'practice' ripe for redefinition by governments and educational entrepreneurs with motives that are, at best, only partially educational. (Hordern 2018a: 489)

One way of thinking about teachers' professional knowledge, which captures Furlong's and Whitty's, but perhaps above all Hordern's, ambition, is to establish a field of knowledge within teacher education in which academic and practice-based knowledge perspectives are addressed with scientific rigour. For Hordern, the educational tradition (we may read the didactics tradition) in Germany is such a field.

In a Nordic context, subject didactics has been described as a bridge of which the parent disciplines of the school subjects are represented by the abutment on one side and pedagogy by that on the other (Sjøberg 2010). One way to develop this bridge metaphor and discuss subject didactics as a field of knowledge in teacher education is to relate to Bernstein's concepts of singulars and regions (Bernstein 2000). According to Bernstein, a region is a knowledge field oriented to practice and application. Examples of regions are medicine, engineering, but also education which includes teacher education. Singulars represent here specific and delimited scientific disciplines like an academic subject (i.e. physics, chemistry, economics). The parent disciplines of the various school subjects and the discipline of pedagogy are singulars in this case. Singulars are thus clearly classified and framed, and knowledge is hierarchically organized, in contrast to knowledge in a region which is not so clearly classified and framed (also see Hordern 2016; 2018a).

The development of the didactic tradition in Sweden differs somewhat from that in Germany, where didactics as a knowledge tradition has held a strong position for a longer time (cf. Vollmer 2014; Schneuwly and Vollmer 2018; Schriewer 2017, Furlong and Whitty 2017; Hordern 2018b). When the modern version of didactics was established in Sweden in the 1980s, it was a field of knowledge within teacher education (see Figure 1.2). A battle with respect to the right to rule over the field then arose. Was didactics to be regarded as a subdivision of pedagogy? (Marton 1986; Brante 2016). Representatives of the school subjects' and their academic parent disciplines answered 'no' to that question. Thus, by framing the field of knowledge as subject didactics rather than (general) didactics, the importance of the content-specific aspects of teaching and learning was emphasized.

What has happened in Sweden, a development that has accelerated over the past ten years, is that subject didactics has moved its position in relation to, for example, pedagogy. Pedagogy, the broad discipline that historically governed the educational region in Sweden, has lost some of its hegemonic power to frame the focus of ITE. At the same time, subject didactics has become more cohesive, with more explicit external boundaries (see Figure 1.3). This development is evident

Powerful Professional Knowledge and Innovation 13

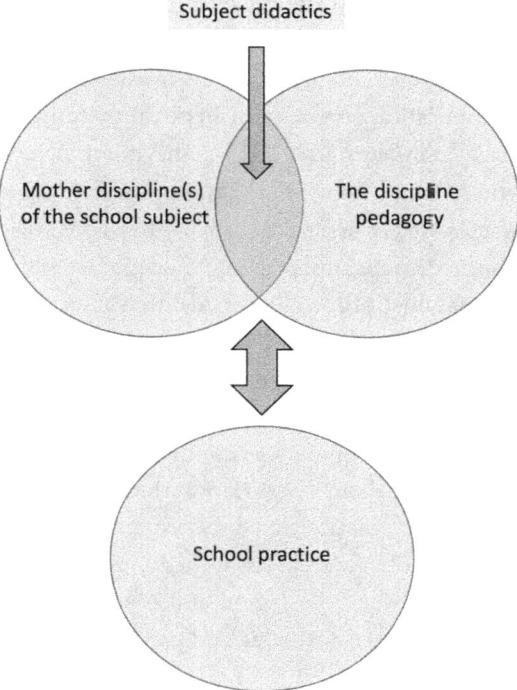

Figure 1.2 Subject didactics in Sweden pre-2010: A vaguely delimited field of knowledge in teacher education.

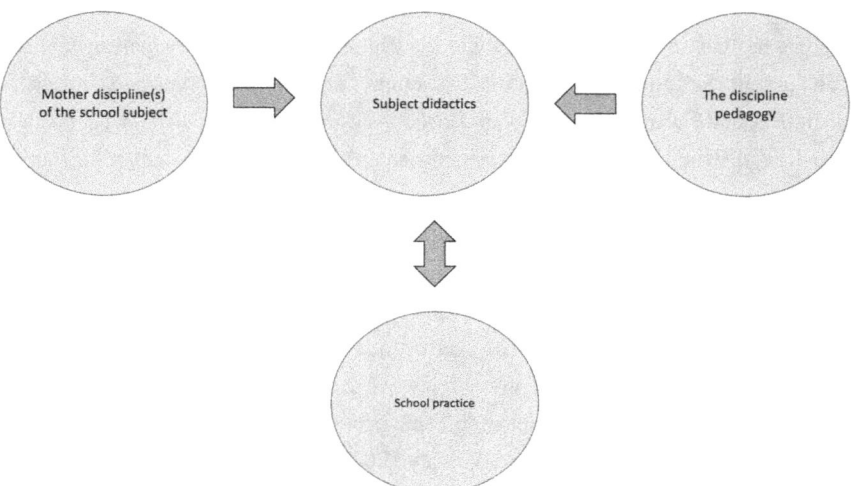

Figure 1.3 Subject didactics in Sweden post-2010: A field of knowledge in teacher education with boundaries.

in the more coherent framing of research problems and unifying theoretical and methodological perspectives. There has been an institutionalization of subject didactics in Sweden, professorships have been established and the national research councils' application processes are better at reflecting a growing subject didactical interest (Vetenskapsrådet 2015). The question is whether subject didactics has begun to have some of the features found in singulars.

By stressing practice-based perspectives, it has been possible to make a strong argument for subject didactic research in Sweden. In light of the declining results in the international student assessments, subject didactics has been pinpointed as a tool for supporting teachers' competence and thereby, in the long run, students' goal fulfilment. In this way, Swedish subject didactic research has benefitted from the international educational trend to support research that focuses on 'what works', a development Furlong and Whitty (2017) are critical of, and there is undeniably a challenge here (Hordern et al. 2021). Subject didactics must not let the logic of practice and too strong a focus on accountability determine the direction of research, as argued similarly by Hordern (2016) about the relationship between the region and the connected practice. There needs to be reciprocity between academia and practice which complies with the minimum scientific requirements.

However, subject didactics can also be a way of meeting the threat Furlong and Whitty (2017) see in a greater focus on generics in school and teacher education. The very core idea of subject didactics is that teaching and learning are linked to content representing a certain knowledge (Kansanen 2009). The unique nature of this content knowledge makes teaching and learning specific. The subject didactic knowledge that teachers cultivate then expresses a specific – theoretically and practically anchored – knowledge to teach this content knowledge. This means there are reasons to emphasize the role subject didactics can play in teacher education. Subject didactics may be understood as a field of knowledge in the region of education and teacher education where different singulars can meet. But, at the same time, it is a field for which it is evident that the external boundaries have become more distinct and have therefore begun to reflect features of singulars. The continuous development of subject didactics could thus be a vital part of a strategy to create the conditions for student teachers and in-service teachers to strengthen their professional knowledge.

In summarizing: Furlong and Whitty (2017) note that Young and Muller's reassertion of the importance of disciplinary knowledge in professional contexts does not exclude the importance of other kinds of knowledge. They stress there is a crucial pedagogical element in teacher education. Yet, we go further by arguing there is an essential didactic dimension to teachers' professional knowledge. This means there is a need to recognize the significance of subject didactics as a discipline in its own right, as is the trend in the Scandinavian countries. A key challenge is then to establish precisely how disciplinary knowledge, which is epistemologically strong, connects to other forms of knowledge and thereby influences practice. We therefore believe Furlong and Whitty are highlighting something important while asking:

> How can disciplinary knowledge and other external knowledges be brought together with professionals' reflective practice and practical theorising in professional arenas to produce really powerful professional knowledge and learning?
>
> Furlong and Whitty (2017: 49)

As we argued earlier, we think the role of subject didactics as a field of knowledge with distinct boundaries is crucial for tackling the question of framing and supporting the development of teachers' professional knowledge, knowledge that might be characterized as powerful from the social realism perspective.

Overview of Contributions

A broad range of subjects is covered in the chapters while the perspectives of primary as well as secondary school are addressed. The various chapters in this book are briefly presented here. Chapters 2 to 5 deal with Initial Teacher Training (ITE), while Chapters 6 to 11 focus on teachers' professional development (CPD).

In Chapter 2, "Reinventing Subject Teaching in Integrated Teacher Education Programmes for Primary School in Norway," Lise Iversen Kulbrandstad and Lars Anders Kulbrandstad discuss epistemic quality in relation to the reinvention of subject teaching in the subject Norwegian. Using the concept of powerful knowledge, the authors highlight how teacher education can give students intellectual power and powerful ways to analyse, explain and understand the world. Chapter 3, "Teacher Education and History Teachers' Powerful Professional Knowledge," by Mikko Puustinen, addresses Finnish history teacher education and teachers' powerful professional knowledge of how to teach history in a disciplinary way. Disciplinary school history is regularly questioned while teaching practice at training schools, in particular, is crucial. The chapter points to connections between the theoretical and practical aspects of education. In Chapter 4, "Embedding Epistemic Quality in the Pedagogy of

Student Geography Teachers," Alex Standish and David Mitchell focus on the relationship between the notion of epistemic quality and the discipline itself. The authors stress that student teachers must integrate conceptual, contextual and procedural knowledge into their curriculum such that their pupils learn to think like a geographer. In Chapter 5, "Epistemic Literacy as an Aim for Religious Education and Implications for Teacher Education," by Alexis Stones and Jo Fraser-Pearce, religious education is stressed. The authors discuss the ways in which the subject has its roots in various academic disciplines. Using the concept of epistemic literacy, they describe it as a means by which teachers might gain the powerful professional knowledge to support students' navigation while contemplating the epistemic complexities of the nature and meaning of existence presented through the religious education curriculum. Chapter 6, "Investigating Literature as Knowledge in School English," by Larissa McLean Davies, Lyn Yates and Wayne Sawyer, draws on a longitudinal project looking at early-career teachers of English. The authors consider a distinct and dynamic sense of what is powerful in literary studies and discuss why frameworks of the subject English are almost inevitably unsatisfactory on the policy level. They argue this fact makes teacher education face distinct challenges unlike those in other subjects. In Chapter 7, "Transforming Circular Economy Principles into Teachers' Powerful Professional Knowledge," Kalle Juuti and Niklas Gericke address the Finnish national core curriculum for basic education and the complexity of sustainability problems. The authors argue that powerful knowledge from several disciplines is required to understand the mechanism of the possible solutions and describes the teacher education course 'Circular economy inventions' as a tool for this. In Chapter 8, "Teachers as Curriculum Makers for School Mathematics of High Epistemic Quality," Brian Hudson draws on outcomes from the project supported by the Scottish Government (2010–12), *Developing Mathematical Thinking in the Primary Classroom*. The analysis of the data is informed by a theoretical framework that combines the ideas of epistemic quality, teachers as curriculum makers of teachers' powerful professional knowledge. Ann-Christin Randahl and Martin Kristiansson present in Chapter 9, "Establishing Links to Specialized Knowledge in Social Studies Teaching," a knowledge-building cycle on the concept of migration, and describe transformation processes related to teachers' development of knowledge. By using the legitimation code theory (LCT) framework, the findings underscore two critical relations for student teacher learning: the need for connecting theory to practice and to the teaching of specialized knowledge. In Chapter 10, "Supporting Teachers' Professional Development in Social Studies Education,"

Martin Stolare, Gabriel Bladh and Martin Kristiansson address aspects of subject matter selection and transformation from the perspective of Swedish teachers' professional development and knowledge practices in upper primary education. The focus is the societal issue of migration. The authors show that community-rooted views as well as the teachers' introduction to specialized knowledge provided a framework for the processes of subject matter selection and transformation. The focus of Chapter 11, "From a Personal to a Pedagogically Powerful Understanding of School Mathematics," by Cosette Crisan, is on the specialized content knowledge (SCK) in mathematics needed by teachers. The chapter considers how teacher education in England can empower teachers to develop a personal understanding of mathematics that is pedagogically powerful and argues that knowledge of more advanced mathematics could serve as a pedagogically powerful basis for understanding school mathematics.

In the last and concluding Chapter 12, "Implications of Powerful Professional Knowledge for Innovation in Teacher Education Policy and Practice," we return to the question that has been central through the book's different chapters: *How can the nature of teachers' powerful professional knowledge be characterized, and what are the implications for teacher education policy and practice?* An analysis is carried out of the various empirical studies described in Chapters 2 to 11. In this analysis, common themes and features are crystallized. It is evident that the PCK (pedagogical content knowledge) approach is a reference point when teachers' knowledge base is addressed. It is against the background of PCK, explicitly or implicitly, that the importance of teachers having deep content knowledge and the ability to combine theory and practice is discussed. The result of the analysis has inspired the launch of the concept subject-specific educational content knowledge (SSECK) as a 'didacticization' of the PCK approach. With the concept SSECK, we recognize that teachers' subject knowledge needs to be of a special nature and that there is an inherent didactic understanding in this knowledge. The development of SSECK is identified as essential for teachers and a dimension of powerful professional knowledge. This didactic view of teachers' knowledge base that SSECK represents, where questions regarding content selection are intimately related to transformation processes and the broader educational goal, supports the argument that subject-specific perspectives should be the central building block for teacher education in the future. This innovation would make it possible to establish a teacher education anchored in educational research without weakening the bond to practice. The latter is a prerequisite for the construction of a teacher education that is characterized by powerful professional knowledge

References

Alderson, P. (2020), 'Powerful Knowledge and the Curriculum: Contradictions and Dichotomies', *British Educational Research Journal*, 46 (1): ISSN: 0141-1926 Online ISSN: 1469-3518.

Bayrhuber, H. et al. (2017), *Auf dem weg zu einer Allgemeinen Fachdidaktik: Allgemeine fachdidadaktik, Band 1*, Münster: Waxman.

Bernstein, B. (1971), *Class, Codes and Control. Vol. 1, Theoretical Studies towards a Sociology of Language*, London: Routledge.

Bernstein, B. (2000[1996]), *Pedagogy, Symbolic Control and Identity: Theory, Research, Critique* (Rev. edn), Lanham, MD: Rowman and Littlefield Publishers.

Bladh, G., Stolare, M. and Kristiansson, M. (2018), 'Curriculum Principles, Didactic Practice and Social Issues: Thinking Through Teachers' Knowledge Practices in Collaborative Work', *London Review of Education*, 16 (3): 398–413. DOI: 10.18546/LRE.16.3.04

Brandom, R. (2000), *Articulating Reasons: An Introduction to Inferentialism*, Cambridge, MA: Harvard University Press.

Brante, G. (2016), 'Allmän didaktik och ämnesdidaktik – en inledande diskussion kring gränser och anspråk', *Nordisk Tidskrift för Allmän Didaktik*, 2 (1): 52–68.

Catling, S. and Martin, F. (2011), 'Contesting Powerful Knowledge: The Primary Geography Curriculum as an Articulation Between Academic and Children's (Ethno-) Geographies', *The Curriculum Journal*, 22 (3): 317–35. DOI: 10.1080/09585176.2011.601624

Chevallard, Y. (2007), 'Readjusting Didactics to a Changing Epistemology'. *European Educational Research Journal*, 6 (2): 131–4.

Cochran-Smith, M. (2016), 'Foreword', in G. Beauchamp, L. Clarke, M. Hulme, M. Jephcote, A. Kennedy, G. Magennis, et al. (eds), *Teacher Education in Times of Change*, X–Xvi, Bristol: Bristol University Press. DOI: 10.2307/j.ctt1t89fvx.5

Deng, Z. (2015), 'Content, Joseph Schwab and German Didaktik', *Journal of Curriculum Studies*, 47: 773–86. doi:10.1080/00220272.2015.1090628

Deng, Z. (2018), 'Bringing Knowledge Back In: Perspectives from Liberal Education', *Cambridge Journal of Education*, 48 (3): 335–51.

Duit, R., Gropengießer, H., Kattmann, U., Komorek, M. and Parchmann, I. (2012), 'The Model of Educational Reconstruction – a Framework for Improving Teaching and Learning Science', in D. Jorde and J. Dillon (eds), *Science Education Research and Practice in Europe: Cultural Perspectives in Science Education*, vol. 5, 13–37, Rotterdam: SensePublishers.

European Commission (2010), *Improving Teacher Quality: The EU Agenda* (Brussels, Directorate-General for Education and Culture, EAC.B.2 D (2010) PSH).

Furlong, J. and Whitty, G. (2017), 'Knowledge Traditions in the Study of Education', in G. Whitty and J. Furlong (eds), *Knowledge and the Study of Education: An International Exploration*, 13–57, Oxford: Symposium Books.

Gericke, N., Hudson, B., Olin-Scheller, C. and Stolare, M. (2018), 'Powerful Knowledge, Transformations and the Need for Empirical Studies Across School Subjects', *London Review of Education*, 16 (3): 428–44. DOI: 10.18546/LRE.16.3.06

Gericke, N., Hudson, B., Olin-Scheller, C. and Stolare, M. (2022), 'Researching Powerful Knowledge and Epistemic Quality across School Subjects', in B. Hudson, N. Gericke, C. Olin-Scheller and M. Stolare (eds), *International Perspectives on Knowledge and Curriculum: Epistemic Quality across School Subjects*, London: Bloomsbury Publishing plc.

Goodson, I. F. and Marsh, C. J. (1996), *Studying School Subjects: A Guide*. London: Falmer Press.

Hopmann, S. (2007), 'Restrained Teaching: The Common Core of Didaktik', *European Educational Research Journal*, 6 (2): 109–24.

Hordern, J. (2016), 'Regions and Their Relations: Sustaining Authoritative Professional Knowledge', *Journal of Education and Work*, 29 (4): 427–49. DOI: 10.1080/13639080.2014.958653

Hordern, J. (2018a), 'Is Powerful Educational Knowledge Possible?' *Cambridge Journal of Education*, 48 (6): 787–802. DOI: 10.1080/0305764X.2018.142721

Hordern, J. (2018b), 'Educational Knowledge: Traditions of Inquiry, Specialization and Practice', *Pedagogy, Culture and Society*, 26 (4): 577–91. DOI: 10.1080/14681366.2018.1428221

Hordern, J. (2019), 'Unpacking the Dynamics of Partnership and Pedagogic Relations', in N. Sorensen (ed.), *Diversity in Teacher Education*, 112–29, London: UCL IOE Press.

Hordern, J., Muller, J. and Deng, Z. (2021), 'Towards Powerful Educational Knowledge? Addressing the Challenges Facing Educational Foundations, Curriculum Theory and Didaktik', *Journal of Curriculum Studies*, 53 (2): 143–52.

Hudson, B. (2022), 'Evaluating Epistemic Quality in Primary School Mathematics', in B. Hudson, N. Gericke, C. Olin-Scheller and M. Stolare (eds) *International Perspectives on Knowledge and Curriculum: Epistemic Quality across School Subjects*, London: Bloomsbury Publishing plc.

Hudson, B., Henderson, S. and Hudson, A. (2015), 'Developing Mathematical Thinking in the Primary Classroom: Liberating Teachers and Students as Learners of Mathematics', *Journal of Curriculum Studies*, 47 (3): 374–98. DOI: 10.1080/00220272.2014.979233

Hulme, M., Rauschenberger, E. and Meanwell, K. (2021), 'Initial Teacher Education: What Matters Most and Has Worked Well', in B. Hudson, M. Leask, and S. Younie (eds), *Education System Design: Foundations, Policy Options and Consequences*, 141–53, Abingdon: Routledge/Taylor and Francis Group.

Jank, W. and Meyer, H. (2018), *Didaktische Modelle* (12. Aufl.) Frankfurt am Main: Cornelsen Scriptor.

Kansanen, P. (2009), 'Subject-Matter Didactics as a Central Knowledge Base for Teachers, Or Should It Be Called Pedagogical Content Knowledge?', *Pedagogy, Culture and Society*, 17 (1): 29–39. DOI: 10.1080/14681360902742845

Klafki, W. (1985/2001), *Dannelseteori och Didaktik – Nye studier*, Aarhus: Klim.

Marton, F. (red.) (1986), *Fackdidaktik Vol. 1 Principiella överväganden, yrkesförberedande ämnen*, Lund: Studentlitteratur.

Menter, I., Beauchamp, G., Clarke, L., Hulme, M., Jephcote, M., Kennedy, A., Cochran-Smith, M. (2016), 'Introduction', in *Teacher Education in Times of Change*, 3–18, Bristol: Bristol University Press. DOI: 10.2307/j.ctt1t89fvx.6

Morgan, J., Hordern, J. and Hoadley, U. (2019), 'On the Politics and Ambition of the "Turn": Unpacking the Relations between Future 1 and Future 3"', *The Curriculum Journal*, 30 (2): 105–24. DOI: 10.1080/09585176.2019.1575254

Ongstad, S. (ed.) (2006), *Fag og didaktikk i lærutdanning: Kunnskap i grenseland*, Oslo: Universitetsforlaget.

Qvortrup, A., Krogh, E. and Ting Graf, S. (2021), *Didaktik and Curriculum in Ongoing Dialogue*, London: Routledge.

Roberts, M. (2014), 'Policy and Practice: Powerful Knowledge and Geographical Education', *The Curriculum Journal*, 25 (2): 187–209. DOI: 10.1080/09585176.2014.894481

Schneuwly, B. and Vollmer, H. J. (2018), 'Bildung and Subject Didactics: Exploring a Classical Concept for Building New Insights', *European Educational Research Journal*, 17 (1): 37–50.

Schriewer, J. (2017), 'Between the Philosophy of Self-cultivation and Empirical Research: Educational Research in Germany', in G. Whitty and J. Furlong (eds), *Knowledge and the Study of Education: An International Exploration*, Oxford: Symposium Books.

Shulman, L. S. (2004), *The Wisdom of Practice: Essays on Teaching, Learning, and Learning to Teach*, San Francisco: Jossey-Bass.

Sjøberg, S. (2010), *Naturvetenskap som allmänbildning: En kritisk ämnesdidaktik* (3rd, rev. uppl.), Lund: Studentlitteratur.

Vollmer, H. (2021), 'Powerful Educational Knowledge through Subject Didactics and General Subject Didactics: Recent Developments in German-speaking Countries', *Journal of Curriculum Studies*, 53 (2): 229–46. DOI: 10.1080/00220272.2021.1887363

Winch, C. (2013), 'Curriculum Design and Epistemic Ascent', *Journal of Philosophy of Education*, 47 (1): 128–46.

Young, M. (2009), 'Education, Globalisation and the "Voice of Knowledge"', *Journal of Education and Work*, 22 (3): 193–204.

Young, M. (2013), 'Overcoming the Crisis in Curriculum Theory: A Knowledge-based Approach', *Journal of Curriculum Studies*, 45 (2), 101–18.

Young, M. (2015a), 'Powerful Knowledge as a Curriculum Principle', in M. Young, D. Lambert, C. Roberts and M. Roberts (eds), *Knowledge and the Future School: Curriculum and Social Justice*, 2nd edn, 65–88, London: Bloomsbury Academic.

Young, M. (2015b), 'The Progressive Case for a Subject-Based Curriculum', in M. Young, D. Lambert, C. Roberts and M. Roberts (eds), *Knowledge and the Future School: Curriculum and Social Justice*, 2nd edn, 89–109, London: Bloomsbury Academic.

Young, M. and Muller, J. (2010), 'Three Educational Scenarios for the Future: Lessons from the Sociology of Knowledge', *European Journal of Education*, 45 (1): 11–27.

Young, M. F. D. (2008), *Bringing Knowledge Back in: From Social Constructivism to Social Realism in the Sociology of Education*, Abingdon, Oxon: Routledge.

Uljens, M., (1997), 'Grunddrag till en reflektiv skoldidaktisk teori' in M. Uljens (ed) *Didaktik: teori, reflektion och praktik*, Lund: Studentlitteratur.

Vetenskapsrådet (2015), *Forskningens framtid! Ämnesöversikt 2014: utbildningsvetenskap*, Stockholm: Vetenskapsrådet.

Vollmer, H. (2014), 'Fachdidaktik and the Development of a Generalized Subject Didactics in Germany', *Education and Didactique*, 8 (1): 23–34. DOI: 10.4000/educationdidactique.1861

Wheelahan, L. (2015), 'Not Just Skills: What a Focus on Knowledge Means for Vocational Education', *Journal of Curriculum Studies*, 47 (6): 750–62. DOI: 10.1080/00220272.2015.1089942

White, J. (2012), 'Powerful Knowledge: Too Weak a Prop for the Traditional Curriculum', https://newvisionsforeducation.org.uk/2012/05/14/powerful-knowledge-too-weak-a-prop-for-the-traditional-curriculum

2

Reinventing Subject Teaching in Integrated Teacher Education Programmes for Primary School in Norway

Lise Iversen Kulbrandstad and Lars Anders Kulbrandstad

Introduction

Norwegian teacher education for compulsory school[1] was turned into a five-year integrated master's programme in 2017. This reform puts greater emphasis on subject teaching, profession orientation of all subjects and strengthening of the research base – for both teacher education programmes and teachers' professional practices (KD 2014, 2016a). In this chapter, we study this reinvention of subject teaching by tracing changes in the teacher education subject of Norwegian over the past forty years. We discuss ways in which this remaking helps ensure that teachers are equipped with powerful professional knowledge. The discussion draws on theories of professions, subject didactics, powerful knowledge and epistemic quality.

A few decades ago, subject teaching as part of Norwegian teacher education was based solely on transforming content from corresponding academic discipline studies. For example, the subject Norwegian relied on knowledge stemming from Nordic linguistics and Nordic literature studies. The teaching content primarily represented an extension of what was being taught in the subject Norwegian in upper secondary school, while, for instance, theories of literacy, which are very relevant for teachers of Norwegian in primary school, were not part of the curriculum. Subsequent reforms, both general reforms restructuring Norwegian higher education and reforms of teacher education per se, gradually changed the scope of subject teaching. The inclusion of teacher education in the University Act in the mid-1990s was groundbreaking because the act states that all study programmes must be research-based. This helped strengthen subject didactics as a research-based discipline, for example, by funding large research programmes through the Research Council of Norway, and by the Ministry of Education offering PhD grants to teacher education institutions. Another significant change was the growing acknowledgement of teaching as a profession that needs to build on both specialized theoretical knowledge and practical knowledge, and as such is trusted to build practice on professional judgements (Molander and Terum 2008; Utdanningsforbundet 2009).

Multidisciplinarity and content relevant to professional practices are known as the hallmarks of study programmes which are characterized as professional studies (Smeby 2008: 88). Following the master's reform in 2017, teacher education subjects in Norway may be characterized as having been reinvented as professional studies since they are based on specialized knowledge from subject-didactics research as well as from the traditional academic disciplines and include teaching practice. This reinvention of teacher education subjects is shown in the fact that students can no longer have exams in academic discipline studies approved as part of their integrated teacher education, which had been possible up until quite recently. This is because these studies include neither subject didactics nor supervised teaching practice (KD 2016a: 7).

In this discussion, we describe the reinvention of subject teaching as part of integrated teacher education that is the outcome of reforms over the past forty years. We use teacher education for grades 1–7 and the subject Norwegian as our example. We outline its development in the light of theoretical perspectives able to contribute to the understanding of student teachers' professional development, and in terms of theoretical perspectives that further understanding of how content in school subjects is handled as part of teachers' professional practices. We rely on the concepts of theoretical and practical syntheses (Grimen), powerful knowledge (Young) and epistemic quality (Hudson). The overarching question we consider is in which ways can the reinvention of subject teaching in Norwegian teacher education contribute to ensuring that graduate teachers are equipped with powerful professional knowledge.

In the following, we first outline the theoretical perspectives of the study and describe the motivation for the selection of materials and choice of methods. We then present results of the analysis of developments in Norwegian teacher education with a focus on the reinvention of the subject Norwegian chiefly by strengthening of the subject didactics. Finally, we discuss the research question with respect to these results, earlier research and the theoretical perspectives.

Theoretical Perspectives

Grimen (2008) explores the knowledge base for practising a profession. He distinguishes between *theoretical* and *practical syntheses*. In each case, knowledge elements are joined together to create a larger whole. In theoretical syntheses, concepts are explicitly defined and form part of structures that satisfy requirements for rigor and consistency. Professional practices are characterized by the other way of using knowledge – practical syntheses – where the elements of knowledge are combined based on what is required in specific situations during professional practice. The knowledge base from which the elements are taken is mixed and partly consists of theories from various relevant academic disciplines and partly of knowledge which stems from the professionals' own experiences or from other practitioners of the profession. Teacher education programmes with their balance between theories and practice, but with an emphasis on theories, are a necessary qualification for making practical syntheses in teaching. Student teachers are supposed to both acquire knowledge from the different subjects they are studying and learn how to handle knowledge as part of their future professional teaching practices, which, for example, means how to choose content and how to ensure that all school students acquire relevant and significant knowledge. The subjects build on knowledge from both subject didactics and the subject's traditional corresponding academic disciplines. By studying these, the students should obtain a theoretical foundation for making practical syntheses while working professionally.

Subject didactics in teacher education in Norway builds on the German tradition of Didaktik (Gundem et al. 2003; Klafki 2000). A widely used definition in the Norwegian context is the following:

> Subject didactics are all the reflections one can attach to a subject and to teaching this subject, which can provide increased knowledge about the subject's character, about the subject's legitimacy and increased knowledge about how the subject can be learned, taught, and developed. (Lorentzen et al. 1998: 8, our translation)

The didactical triangle focusing on the learner, the content, the teacher and the different relationships among them is a much-used model in subject didactics (e.g. Gericke et al. 2018: 437). In a report on teacher education in the United States, Bransford, Darling-Hammond and LePage (2005: 11) use a similar model to show how teachers' professional practice is developed. Their model is a Venn diagram with three circles representing knowledge about the learners and their development, subject and curricular knowledge, and knowledge about teaching and assessment. The intersection of the three circles represents *teachers' professional knowledge* and a vision of professional practice. To denote the unification of all these knowledge sources to form subject teaching as part of teacher education, the expression *to didactify* a subject (Madssen 1998; Hertzberg 1999) or *to didactify* knowledge (Ongstad 2006) has been introduced[2].

In his article 'What Are schools For?' Young (2009/2016: 113, 110) discusses what kind of knowledge is important in schools and introduces the term *powerful knowledge* for specialized knowledge, knowledge that can provide the 'basis for generalizable principles', and 'reliable explanations or new ways of thinking about the world'. Later, he specified that this knowledge is not to be understood as canonical: '[s]ocieties change, so every generation has to ask those questions again' (Young 2013: 101). Thus, the question of what students are entitled to learn is central to Young when he elaborates on powerful knowledge as a curriculum principle (Young 2013: 107). Schools should both transmit past knowledge and make the next generation capable of using that knowledge to build new knowledge. Teachers on their side should ask, 'What are the meanings that this curriculum gives my students access to or does this curriculum take my students beyond their experience and enable to envisage alternatives that have some basis in the real world?' (Young 2013: 106). Discussing the meaning of 'power' in powerful knowledge, Muller and Young (2019: 210) stress the importance of power as 'generative capacity' and describe teachers as 'crucial mediators of the transformative capacity of PK [powerful knowledge] in their subjects'.

While Young's concept is widely debated (e.g. Beck 2013; Young 2015; Nordgren 2017; Hoadley et al. 2019), it has clearly led to a renewed focus on the rationale for choosing content for teaching. Gericke et al. (2018) discuss Young's theory in light of didactical research. They criticize a suggestion he made that curriculum can be separated from pedagogy; instead, they see the questions of what and how to teach as being integrated parts of didactical research. Thus, they propose an expansion of the theory, namely, that *transformation* should be a key concept when describing powerful knowledge in relation to, for example, school subjects. Gericke et al. (2018: 429) define transformation as 'an integrative process in which content knowledge is changed into knowledge that is taught and learned through various processes that take place outside and within the educational system at the individual, institutional and societal levels'. Bladh, Stolare and Kristiansson (2018: 399) argue that Young's concept of powerful knowledge can be 'clarified and deepened by linking it to [. . .] Wolfgang Klafki's critical-constructive didactics' in which a theory of knowledge (categorical Bildung) and a theory of didactics (didactic analysis) are combined.

The discussion on powerful knowledge not only concerns the kind of content to be chosen or how it is transformed but also touches on the quality of the content school children are supposed to learn. Hudson (2018, 2019) discusses quality in light of the question of equity and access to knowledge. He introduces the concept of *epistemic quality* to address differences between two knowledge traditions in the teaching of mathematics, which offer students different opportunities to attain knowledge. One is characterized as having high epistemic quality. Here procedural knowledge of mathematical thinking and creative reasoning are fostered. The other approach is characterized as being of low epistemic quality because there is an overemphasis on propositional knowledge and rule following. These two quality characterizations are based on findings in didactical research projects in the field of mathematics (Hudson 2018: 394, 2019: 6). The concept of epistemic quality can thus be understood as an argument for bringing in different theoretical perspectives in subject teaching as part of teacher education – to broaden student teachers' knowledge base as well as develop their critical analytical competence to reflect on how theories meet practice.

Summing up, a combination of the theoretical perspectives can help us understand the concept of *powerful professional knowledge*: Teacher education subjects might contribute to student teachers' development of powerful professional knowledge by presenting a knowledge base built on different theories, making the students reflect on practice with the help of theories, and by focusing on the importance of the choice of content for quality teaching.

Materials and Choice of Methods

This chapter is part of a project on subject teaching in Norwegian teacher education in which we have conducted a qualitative content analysis of official documents from 1869 to 2017 (see Kulbrandstad and Kulbrandstad 2017). In the next section, we present the results of this study as a basis for describing the developments from 1980 to 2017. The documents analysed in this last period are primarily regulations issued by the Ministry, including curriculum guidelines. In addition, other texts like white papers, official reports and evaluations are brought in to contextualize the regulations. To use Goodlad's (1979) description of the curriculum's many forms of appearance, it is the overall levels we are concerned with: the curriculum of ideas and the formally adopted curriculum texts. The curriculum texts analysed are listed in the appendix.

To describe the gradual profession orientation of subject teaching in Norwegian teacher education, we focus on how the content of the subject Norwegian in teacher education for primary school has developed. Our emphasis is on the changing framing of the subject, the successive integration of subject didactics and the different ways in which school practice is linked to the subject. A subsequent close-up elaborates on how reading and writing have been themed in changing programmes, and how the subject didactics of Norwegian emerged.

In addition to the official documents just mentioned, we base the discussion on earlier research and debate in the field and on our own personal experiences as teacher educators and researchers. We have work experience in teacher education since the 1980s and were active participants in the government-appointed committees for preparing the four most recent reforms of teacher education in 1998, 2003, 2010 and 2017.

Norwegian Teacher Education Reforms between 1980 and 2017

Teacher education programmes for grades 1–7 in primary school have always been integrated (concurrent) programmes – that is, parallel studies of pedagogy, subjects and subject didactics combined with practice. For secondary school teachers, the education was traditionally 'consecutive' (sequential), meaning that students finish academic studies in their subjects before they enter teacher education (Eurydice 2015: 32). Today, integrated programmes might also be chosen for lower and upper secondary schools. The strong national regulation of all teacher education programmes is typical for Norway (Hammerness 2013). Acts are voted by Parliament and regulations issued by the government. The regulations include curricula (e.g. KD 2016b), while on top of these are national guidelines for developing programme descriptions for the various subjects at the local institutions (NRLU 2016).

Norwegian teacher education for compulsory school has been reformed five times since 1992. The reforms have been typical examples of professionalism from above (Evetts 2003), where the government initiates the reforms and appoints expert committees of teacher educators, teachers and student teachers to develop drafts. The work in the committees opens up for professionalism from inside, to use Evetts's concept. However, the Ministry itself sends the drafts on broad hearings and finally establishes the curriculum as regulations to the law. While dissatisfaction with the quality of teacher education has been one reason for the frequent reforms, another is the need for change caused by school reforms and school results being below the expectations of politicians (Ekspertgruppa 2016). For subject teacher educators, strengthening subject didactics has been an important driving force in the changing reforms.

Table 2.1 shows the overall framework and main changes brought by the latest reforms, taking the 1980 reform as the starting point. During this period, the education was extended from three to five years. Before the 2010 reform, Norway had a unified teacher education for grades 1–10 which actually qualified for teaching all subjects in all grades of compulsory school, even subjects that were not part of a student's study programme. In 2010, two different programmes – one aimed at grades 1–7 and the other at grades 5–10 – replaced the general teacher education. The 2010 reform is characterized as a reform with an 'enhanced focus on subjects' (KD 2009: 16). This is partly because the programmes are aligned to grades and partly because students study fewer subjects and are given the opportunity to take more credits in each of them. Since then, graduated students only have qualifications to teach the subjects they have studied. The professionalization of the education is first and foremost strengthened by the definition of all teaching subjects as 'profession-oriented teacher education subjects' (KD 2010a: 4). The subjects should correspond to the subjects in basic school and include subject didactics. In addition, so-called basic skills should be integrated and the teaching practice should be 'rooted' in the subjects (KD 2010b: 3). Teaching practice as part of the subject studies is traced back to 1992, but not realized in the curriculum before 1999. Before then, practice was part of pedagogy, which was actually named 'Pedagogy – theory and practice'. Since 2010, the regulation requires practice to be supervised, varied, assessed and adapted to student teachers' chosen subjects. Earlier, teaching practice could have been in any subject. The regulation of the 2010 reform also explicitly stipulates that teacher education subjects have to be research-based and that the subjects must be 'rooted in a research-active academic environment' (KD 2010a: 4). By making the master's level compulsory in 2017, the research base has been taken one step further since the students are expected to write a master's thesis. At the same time, the master's extension also strengthens the professional orientation of the subjects, partly by the fact that the master's thesis is to be 'profession-oriented and practice-based' (KD 2016a: 5). When the thesis is written within a teaching subject, it must be firmly rooted in the subject and subject didactics:

Table 2.1 Norwegian Teacher Education Programmes for Compulsory School 1980–2017

	1980	1992/94	1999	2003	2010	2017
Name of programme		General teacher education (Allmennlærerutdanning)			Primary teacher education 1–7 or 5–10 (Grunnskolelærerutdanning 1–7 or 5–10)	
Years of study	3	4	4	4	4	5 (master)
Qualifies for the grades	1–9	1–9	1–10	1–10	1–7 or 5–10	1–7 or 5–10
Compulsory subjects	Pedagogy: theory and practice Christianity Norwegian Arts and practical studies	Pedagogy: theory and practice Norwegian Mathematics Arts and practical studies Christianity Natural and Social sciences	Pedagogy Norwegian Mathematics Arts Christianity Natural and Social sciences Practical studies	Pedagogy Norwegian Mathematics Religion Reading, writing and mathematics for beginners	1–7: Pedagogy and pupil-related skills Norwegian Mathematics 5–10: Pedagogy and pupil-related skills	1–7: Pedagogy and pupil-related skills Norwegian Mathematics 5–10: Pedagogy and pupil-related skills
Practice in schools	Not decided in the curricula	80–90 days	100–120 days	100–110 days	At least 100 days	At least 115 days

> Emphasis on didactics and professional orientation is an expression of the fact that the master's specialization is to be in a teacher education subject, and not purely disciplinary. In the concept of professional orientation, there is a close connection between subjects, subject didactics, pedagogy and practice. (KD 2016a: 6, our translation)

As shown in Table 2.1, Norwegian has remained a compulsory subject in all of the different reforms of teacher education for grades 1–7. Table 2.2 shows the quantitative growth from 15 to 30 ECTS. For the whole time, it has been possible to opt for Norwegian studies beyond the mandatory level, since 2017 all the way up to master's level, which means 120 ECTS.

When it comes to the main components of the study of Norwegian, we first note the change that came about in 2010. From then on, the content of the subject is no longer described. Instead, the learning outcomes the students should have accomplished after completing the study are stated. However, the subject's reinvention is already evident in the changes in content descriptions from 1980 to 2003. In 1980, we can clearly see traces of two traditional strands of the academic subjects, linguistics and literature, in the teacher education subject, namely 'knowledge about language' and 'literature reading'. In addition, the curriculum emphasizes 'oral and written language use', which partly refers to the students' own language mastery and partly to the analysis of language use. A restructuring takes place already in the first reform (1992–4). Neither the students' own language skills nor the academic disciplines appear as elements of the main content. These are expressed in very general terms such as 'text base', 'theory base' and 'approaches'. The theory base included perspectives from linguistics and literary theory as well as literacy studies and subject didactics. In the 1999 reform, language and text are highlighted through three different perspectives: a use perspective (work with), a theoretical perspective (knowledge about) and a subject didactics perspective (reflections on content in a teaching perspective). Literary texts are included in the text concept, but so too are non-fiction texts and student texts written in different grades at school. In the 2003 reform, the Ministry's detailed management was evident even in the design of the curriculum for each subject since it was decided that all curricula should have the same structure: 'Academic and subject didactic knowledge', 'Being a teacher of X-subject' and 'Collaboration and reflection'. For Norwegian, the last one of these areas was partly about the ability to reflect on the subject Norwegian and partly the ability to collaborate with colleagues on assessment and in interdisciplinary projects. With this topic, one might say that the

Table 2.2 The Teacher Education Subject of Norwegian 1980–2017

	1980	1992/1994	1999	2003	2010	2017
Volume of compulsory Norwegian	15 ECTS	30 ECTS	30 ECTS	30 ECTS	30 ECTS	30 ECTS
Main components of the study of Norwegian	- Knowledge of language - Literature reading - Oral and written language use	- Text base - Theory base - Approaches	- Work with language and text - Knowledge about language and text - Language and text in a teaching perspective	- Academic and subject didactic knowledge - Being a teacher of Norwegian - Collaboration and reflection	Learning outcomes in knowledge, skills and general competencies	Learning outcomes in knowledge, skills and general competencies

student's competence is extended from what belongs to the individual subjects to the more general didactic perspectives. Academic and didactic knowledge are juxtaposed, and the profession orientation is apparent in the curriculum area 'Being a teacher of X-subject'.

As may be seen from the overview in Table 2.2, the foundations for reinventing subject teaching gradually strengthened during the period analysed. The fact that Norwegian as part of the current master's programme is studied as a profession-oriented teacher education subject entails that disciplinary knowledge and professional subject didactic knowledge are integrated, that the study subject is tuned to the school subject and its development, and that school practice is an important part of building up the students' knowledge base. Throughout, Norwegian is described as a subject concerned with language and texts. The master students are, for example, supposed to be able to reflect on the choice of texts adapted to children's age and background, texts that provide an entry point for Norwegian literature, and texts that open up for better understanding of oneself and others by developing imagination and empathy. At the same time, studies of language are supposed to build knowledge of one's own and others' language practices, as well as identity and insight into both critical reflection and an understanding of the ways languages and texts shape and are shaped by cultural communities. A democratic purpose is highlighted: The subject should qualify to work on language and texts in ways that develop confident and active participants who take part in democratic processes (NRLU 2016).

In the next section, we present a close-up on the reinvention by looking into two aspects of Norwegian subject didactics. The first concerns the teaching of reading and writing, which is an important part of the content that qualifies for teaching Norwegian in primary school. We illustrate how this topic has been dealt with through different eras of teacher education. Following up on this example, we look at the transition from methodology to subject didactics in the teacher education subject of Norwegian.

A Close-up on the Reinvention

As we have seen, subject didactics is an essential part of the professional orientation of subject teaching developed through reforms from 1980 to 2017. In the same period, subject didactics of Norwegian was established as a field of research (e.g. Smidt 1989; Hertzberg 1996; Dysthe ed. 2001; Madssen

1999; Kulbrandstad 2003; Ongstad 2004; Kulbrandstad 2009; Skjelbred 2010; Hvistendahl and Roe eds. 2014). This is a prerequisite for reinventing the teacher education subject as a multidisciplinary subject based on specialized knowledge from both subject didactic research and the traditional academic disciplines.

The essence of subject didactics is paying attention to the school subject and to teaching and learning. Throughout history, Norwegian teacher education programmes have had a concern for school practice. Yet, a crucial difference from the current situation is that for a long time the practical orientation existed without any specialized knowledge base. For example, the first national plan for teacher education in Norway from 1869 described a mother-tongue subject aimed at preparing the students for their work as teachers by including the reading book for elementary school as an important teaching material. Teaching methodology had a place in the subject since the student teachers were to be guided in how the reading book should be used in school. They also learned to practise one method of teaching beginning reading and writing (Kulbrandstad and Kulbrandstad 2017). In 1938, pedagogy became a central teacher education subject after having been established as an academic discipline. As part of teacher education, it took on a role as the subject in charge of the profession orientation by assuming the responsibility for the teaching methodology and the study of the school's curricula, among other things (Kvalbein 2002). Subject didactics gained a foothold in the subjects from the reform in 1980, but until the following reform this was primarily through collaboration with pedagogy and with an emphasis on how to teach. For example, reading and writing were to be taught as a methodology course in a partnership between Norwegian and pedagogy, yet without a foundation in theories and research. In 1992, methodology courses were replaced by theories of reading and writing and didactical perspectives as part of the subject Norwegian. In today's curriculum, literacy is an essential part of the subject in teacher education for grades 1–7. Attention is paid to different theories, research results, multimodality, reading and writing development, diversity of methods, assessment and adaptation to the school's increasing linguistic and cultural student diversity.

The changes in the content of the study of Norwegian obviously reflect changes in society, the school and the students' prerequisites, but not least changes in the view of what teacher education is. A significant transition was from understanding teaching as something for which one is principally trained by learning teaching methods to conceiving teaching as a profession resting on 'a particular theoretical and methodological knowledge base acquired through higher education' and which has 'room for the exercise of professional judgement' (Ekspertgruppa 2016: 31, our translation).

Supplanting methodology courses with research-based subject didactics also marks the transition from a situation where the profession orientation in teacher education was all about pedagogy to a situation where *all* subjects are to contribute to this orientation. For the teacher education subject Norwegian in particular, the interest in subject didactics can be traced back to the 1970s when an important initiative was the setting up of the national association for the teaching of Norwegian (Landslaget for norskundervisning, in short: LNU). In 1981, the association published a volume entitled *Norskdidaktikk* [Norwegian subject didactics]. The introductory article states:

> Subject didactics is the putty that ties theory to practice, the airy world of discipline studies to the massive reality of school life. The students will have a more reflected relationship with their subject; learn to see their subject knowledge in relation to the tasks that await them in school. (Madssen 1981: 9, our translation)

Madssen draws a clear distinction between subject methodology and subject didactics and describes the emergence of subject didactics as a reaction to an overly strong methodology orientation in teacher education. A report from LNU on the Norwegian subject in school and teacher education argued for this change by focusing on the need for students to develop their understanding of the subject: 'A student who has a conception of the subject[3] does not only have knowledge, he/she can also see the subject as a whole. And, above all, he/she has a perspective on the subject, i.e. he/she can see it from outside, in broader contexts' (LNU 1984: 158, our translation). The report also states that because the teaching profession as such requires constant action, teacher education must assist students in developing an ability to act based on theory. In order for teacher education to develop such readiness for action, changes in both theory and practice were later put on the agenda. The teaching of theory should be close to practice and the teaching of practices should be close to theory, to borrow an expression from Solstad (2010). Graduating from the master's programme introduced in 2017 with Norwegian as their master subject, student teachers are supposed to be able to provide teaching rooted in research and experience-based knowledge as well as having specialized knowledge in their subject (KD 2016b: 2). In Norwegian, knowledge from both Nordic linguistics and literature is part of this specialized knowledge. The choices of content from the academic disciplines are, however, different than before since content reflects to a greater extent what is needed to teach the school subject. Thus, more emphasis is put on children's literature as part of the literature studies, and on language development and multilingualism as part of the study of linguistics.

This close-up reveals the reinvention of Norwegian as a teacher education subject. As mentioned, the expression 'to didactify a subject' is used in Norway to describe such a process. For example, Ongstad (2004: 25, our translation) describes 'a well-developed, didactified profession-oriented subject' as a subject that has come far in integrating 'the subject didactic element in *the* subject so that the concept of "subject" (understood as the academic subject) is changed and the study content is in reality redefined. It has become the combination of subject and didactics'. Another way of putting this is that the professional practice of teachers of Norwegian should be built on a combination of knowledge of the subject, of the learners and of teaching (cf. Bransford et al. 2005).

Discussion

The research question framing this chapter is in which ways can the recent developments of subject teaching in Norwegian teacher education contribute to graduating teachers being equipped with *powerful professional knowledge*. With the subject Norwegian as our example, we described increased profession orientation as a *reinvention* of the subject and, in our view, the reinvention means a considerable step in the direction of preparing for powerful professional practices. Admittedly, concepts like Young's powerful knowledge or Hudson's epistemic quality were not on the agenda at the time the change took place. However, we see a concern for building an understanding of the purpose of teaching Norwegian and how it can contribute to the purpose of schooling, for providing students with meaningful ways of teaching, and for developing their critical analytical competence to reflect on how theories meet practice. This should be done not only by transmitting knowledge about past and present but also by envisaging alternatives, working on communication and choosing content that contributes to developing school children's identity, imagination, empathy and critical thinking.

Further, the quest for a specialized knowledge base is evident along with an awareness that development of this base requires extensive research efforts.

When teacher education passed from a three-year to a four-year programme, the Norwegian subject was expanded from 15 to 30 ECTS. These two changes reflect the realization that being a qualified teacher today demands a solid foundation in relevant knowledge. This was taken even further when teacher education became a five-year master's programme, including an independent research project leading to a 30 ECTS master's thesis. The rationale behind this important decision was that teaching entails the exercising of a profession that must be built on knowledge and insights from different epistemic traditions, the ability to perform critical reflection, a constant readiness to acquire new knowledge and a capacity to apply knowledge appropriately in complex practical situations (cf. Grimen's concept of practical syntheses).

The first cohort of students in the new teacher education programme have not yet completed their studies and thus we do not know how future Norwegian teachers will benefit from the reform. However, findings from research on teachers in Finland, where teacher education has been on the master's level since 1979 (Tirri 2014), indicate that going through an extended research-oriented academic education has considerably strengthened their professional competence. For instance, Afdal and Nerland (2014) interviewed newly graduated Norwegian and Finnish primary and lower secondary school teachers about how they thought they had developed through the teacher education and how they had experienced work as a teacher. The Finnish teachers held a master's degree, while the Norwegian teachers graduated from the unified, general Norwegian programme (the 2003 reform). The researchers found both common features and differences between the teachers from the two countries. As for the differences, the analysis showed that Finnish teachers tended to use a more academic vocabulary and more often referred to theory while describing their experiences. Overall, their knowledge base appeared to be more systematized and better structured than that of their Norwegian colleagues. Afdal and Nerland connect this dissimilarity to differences in the kind of teacher education the two groups of teachers had been given.

In summarizing the theoretical perspectives, we pointed to three essential criteria to enhance understanding of powerful professional knowledge: a firm foundation in relevant disciplinary theories and subject didactics, an ability to reflect on practice with help of this theoretical pool and a capacity to select and transform content and to choose methods for teaching given students in given contexts. We find that the analysis of how the teacher education subject Norwegian for grades 1–7 has developed over the past forty years reveals a move towards graduating teachers equipped with qualifications to realize such powerful professional practices. Still, several caveats should be issued. First, even if all students who go through teacher education for grades 1–7 will be qualified to teach Norwegian, not all of them will have chosen Norwegian as their subject for an in-depth study on the master's level. Although statistics are not yet available, it is clear that relatively few students are opting for Norwegian as the subject for their master's project. Of course, master's projects in other disciplinary subjects or in pedagogy would give students experiences also of use for the role as teachers of Norwegian, but they will not have acquired the amount of specific powerful knowledge one might wish that all teachers of this particular subject possess.

Another caveat is the need that was observed to develop research-based teaching. An interview study by Munthe and Rogne (2015) of teacher educators and student teachers from the 2010 reform concluded that research was emphasized in programmes across the country. At the same time, the research base was characterized as more teacher-focused with students as audience than student-focused where students were involved in research. It is likely that this will change with the master's reform. However, another finding of Munthe and Rogne represents yet another possible caveat. They found that faculty with research experience was not available to all students, and fewer taught in the programme for grades 1–7 than the programme for grades 5–10. Another aspect of this challenge is that there are still more teachers being recruited to teacher education who hold a PhD in the traditional academic disciplines than in subject didactics.

Conclusion

In this chapter, we described and discussed the development of the teacher education subject Norwegian for primary school. We characterized this development as a reinvention of the subject. The analysis illustrates how the nature of the Norwegian subject has altered over the past five decades such that the subject has become increasingly more oriented to the profession. We see this both in the emphasis on research-based subject didactics as part of the subject's knowledge base and in the latest reform that turned teacher education for compulsory school into a master's programme with the possibility of in-depth subject studies and own research experience writing professionally oriented master's theses. This development is an important step in the direction of educating teachers who can perform powerful professional practices.

Appendix: Curriculum Documents Analysed

Year	Curriculum document
1980	KUD (1980), *Allmennlærarutdanning. Studieplan*. [General teacher education. Study plan], Oslo: Universitetsforlaget.
1992/ 1994	KUF (1994), *Rammeplan for 4-årig allmennlærerutdanning. Justert utgave, juni 1994* [General plan for four year general teacher education. Adjusted edition, June 1994], Oslo: KUF/Lærerutdanningsrådet.
1999	KUF (1999), *Rammeplan og forskrift. Allmennlærerutdanning* [General plan and regulations for general teacher education], Oslo: KUF.
2003	UF (2003), *Rammeplan for allmennlærerutdanningen* [General teacher education. National Curriculum Regulations], Oslo: UF.
2010	KD (2010), *Forskrift om rammeplan for grunnskolelærerutdanningene for 1.–7. trinn og 5.–10. trinn,* [Regulations relating to the framework plan for primary and lower secondary teacher education for years 1–7 and 5–10].
	KD (2010), *Nasjonale retningslinjer for grunnskolelærerutdanningen 1. – 7. trinn* [National guidelines for primary and lower secondary teacher education for years 1–7].
2017	KD (2016), *Forskrift om rammeplan for grunnskolelærerutdanning for trinn 1–7* [Regulations relating to the framework plan for primary and lower secondary teacher education for years 1–7].
	KD (2016), *Forskrift om rammeplan for grunnskolelærerutdanning for trinn 5–10* [Regulations relating to the framework plan for primary and lower secondary teacher education for years 1–7].
	NRLU (2016), *Nasjonale retningslinjer for grunnskolelærerutdanning trinn 1-7* [National guidelines for primary and lower secondary teacher education for years 1–7].

Comments

The 2017 documents and several of the older ones are available in Norwegian and English at https://www.regjeringen.no/no/tema/utdanning/hoyere-utdanning/rammeplaner/id435163/ (accessed 7 August 2020).

During the period 1980–2017, the responsible ministry has been known under different names and abbreviations:

- KUF [Kyrkje- og undervisningsdeparementet]: The Ministry of Church and Education
- KUF [Kirke-, utdannings- og forskningsdepartementet]: The Ministry of Church, Education and Research
- UF [Utdannings- og forskningsdepartementet]: The Ministry of Education and Research
- KD [Kunnskapsdepartementet]: The Ministry of Education and Research

In 2017, the Ministry of Education delegated to Universities Norway and its national group of teacher education (NRLU) to develop national guidelines for the different teacher education subjects. See: https://www.uhr.no/temasider/nasjonale-retningslinjer/nasjonale-retningslinjer-for-larerutdanningene/.

Notes

1 Compulsory school in Norway consists of a compulsory ten-year module divided into primary (grades 1–7) and lower secondary (grades 8–10) education. All students also have the right to a three-year continuation in upper secondary education.
2 Norwegian: å *didaktifisere* et fag or å *didaktifisere* kunnskap
3 Norwegian: fagsyn

References

Afdal, H. W. and Nerland, M. (2014), 'Does Teacher Education Matter? An Analysis of Relations to Knowledge among Norwegian and Finnish Novice Teachers', *Scandinavian Journal of Educational Research*, 58 (3): 281–99. DOI: 10.1080/00313831.2012.726274.
Beck, J. (2013), 'Powerful Knowledge, Esoteric Knowledge, Curriculum Knowledge', *Cambridge Journal of Education*, 43 (2): 177–93. DOI: 10.1080/0305764X.2013.767880.
Bladh, G., Stolare, M. and Kristiansson, M. (2018), 'Curriculum Principles, Didactic Practice and Social Issues: Thinking Through Teachers' Knowledge Practices in Collaborative Work', *London Review of Education*, 16 (3): 398–413. DOI: 10.18546/LRE.16.3.04.
Bransford, J., Darling-Hammond, L. and LePage, P. (2005), 'Introduction', in L. Darling-Hammond and J. Bransford (eds), *Preparing Teachers for a Changing World*, 1–39, San Francisco: Jossey-Bass.
Dysthe, O. (ed) (2001), *Dialog, samspel og læring*, Oslo: Abstrakt forlag.
Ekspertgruppa (2016), *Om lærerrollen: Et kunnskapsgrunnlag*, Bergen: Fagbokforlaget.
Eurydice (2015), *The Teaching Profession in Europe: Practices, Perceptions, Policies*, Luxembourg: EU.
Evetts, J. (2003), 'The Sociological Analysis of Professionalism: Occupational Change in the Modern World', *International Sociology*, 18 (2): 395–415. DOI: 10.1177/0268580903018002005.
Gericke, N., Hudson, B., Olin-Scheller, C. and Stolare, M. (2018), 'Powerful Knowledge, Transformations and the Need for Empirical Studies across School Subjects', *London Review of Education*, 16 (3): 428–44. DOI: 10.18546/LRE.16.3.06.

Goodlad, J. I. (1979), *Curriculum Inquiry: The Study of Curriculum Practice*, New York: McGraw-Hill.
Grimen, H. (2008), 'Profesjon og kunnskap', in A. Molander and L. I. Terum (eds), *Profesjonsstudier*, 71–86, Oslo: Universitetsforlaget.
Gundem, B. B., Karseth, B. and Sivesind, K. (2003), 'Curriculum Theory and Research in Norway: Traditions, Trends and Challenges', in W. F. Pinar (ed), *International Handbook of Curriculum Research*, 517–34, Mahwah, NJ: Lawrence Erlbaum.
Hammerness, K. (2013), 'Examining Features of Teacher Education in Norway', *Scandinavian Journal of Educational Research*, 57 (4): 400–19. DOI: 10.1080/00313831.2012.656285.
Hertzberg, F. (1996), *Norsk grammatikkdebatt i historisk lys*, Oslo: Novus.
Hertzberg, F. (1999), 'Å didaktisere et fag – hva er det?', in C. Nyström and M. Ohlsson (eds), *Svenska i utveckling Nr. 13. Svenska på prov. Arton artiklar om språk, litteratur, didaktik och prov*, FUMS.Rapport nr. 196, 31–40, Uppsala: Uppsala universitet.
Hoadley, U., Sehgal-Cuthbert, A., Barrett, B. and Morgan, J. (2019), 'After the Knowledge Turn? Politics and Pedagogy', *The Curriculum Journal*, 30 (2): 99–104. DOI: 10.1080/09585176.2019.1601844.
Hudson, B. (2018), 'Powerful Knowledge and Epistemic Quality in School Mathematics', *London Review of Education*, 16 (3): 384–97. DOI: 10.18546/LRE.16.3.03.
Hudson, B. (2019), 'Epistemic Quality for Equitable Access to Quality Education in School Mathematics', *Journal of Curriculum Studies*, 51 (4): 437–56. DOI: 10.1080/00220272.2019.1618917.
Hvistendahl, R. and Roe, A. (eds) (2014), *Alle tiders norskdidaktiker: Festskrift til Frøydis Hertzberg på 70-åsdagen*, Oslo: Novus forlag.
KD (2009), *St.meld. nr. 11. (2008–2009). Læreren. Rollen og utdanningen*, Oslo: Ministry of Education and Research.
KD (2010a), *Forskrift om rammeplan for grunnskolelærerutdanningene for 1.–7. trinn og 5.–10. trinn*, Oslo: Ministry of Education and Research.
KD (2010b), *Rundskriv F-05-10: Forskrift om rammeplan for grunnskolelærerutdanningene for 1.–7. trinn og 5.–10. trinn og forskrift om rammeplan for de samiske grunnskolelærer-utdanningene for 1.–7. trinn og 5.–10. trinn*, Oslo: Ministry of Education and Research.
KD (2014), *Lærerløftet: På lag for kunnskapsskolen*, Oslo: Ministry of Education and Research.
KD (2016a), *Rundskriv F-06-16: Forskrifter om rammeplaner for femårige grunnskolelærerutdanninger for trinn 1–7 og trinn 5–10 – rundskriv med merknader, og engelsk oversettelse*, Oslo: Ministry of Education and Research.
KD (2016b), *Regulations Relating to the Framework Plan for Primary and Lower Secondary Teacher Education for Years 1–7*, Oslo: Ministry of Education and Research.
Klafki, W. (2000), 'The Significance of Classical Theories of Bildung for a Contemporary Concept of Allgemeinbildung', in I. Westbury, S. Hopmann and K. Riquarts (eds),

Teaching as Reflective Practice: The German Didaktik Tradition, 85–108, Mahwah, NJ: Lawrence Erlbaum.

Kulbrandstad, L. I. (2003), Lesing i utvikling: Teoretiske og didaktiske perspektiver, Bergen: LNU/Fagbokforlaget.

Kulbrandstad, L. A. (2009), '"Det finnes det vel ikke noe forskning på?" Et eksempel på studentinvolvering i forskning', Acta Didactica Norge, 3 (1): 1–21.

Kulbrandstad, L. I. and Kulbrandstad, L. A. (2017), 'Framveksten av et profesjonsrettet lærerutdanningsfag i norsk – nasjonale linjer og bidrag fra Hedmark', in Morten Løtveit (ed), Tidssignaler. Lærerutdanningsfag i utvikling. Utdanning av lærere på Hamar – 150 år, 137–66, Vallset: Oplandske Bokforlag.

Kvalbein, Inger Anne (2002), 'Pedagogikkfaget i norsk allmennlærerutdanning – en historie om vekst og fall', Norsk pedagogisk tidsskrift, 2–3: 111–22.

LNU [Landslaget for norskundervisning] (1984), Norskfaget i skole og lærerutdanning, Lillehammer: LNU.

Lorentsen, S., Streitlien, Å., Høstmark Tarrou, A.-L. and Aase, L. (1998), Fagdidaktikk: Innføring i fagdidaktikkens forutsetninger og utvikling, Oslo: Universitetsforlaget.

Madssen, K.-A. (1981), 'Fagdidaktikk: hva og hvorfor?', in K.-A. Madssen (ed), Norskdidaktikk, 9–27, Oslo: LNU/Cappelen.

Madssen, K.-A. (1998), 'Oppsummerende rapport', in KUF: Kvalitativ evaluering av norskfaget i allmennlærerutdanninga, Norsk 1, 4–40, Oslo: Ministry of Education.

Madssen, K.-A. (1999), Morsmålsfagets normtekster: Et skolefag blir til – norskfaget mellom tradisjon og politikk, avhandling for graden dr. polit, Trondheim: NTNU.

Molander, A. and Terum, L. I. (2008), 'Profesjonsstudier. En introduksjon', in A. Molander and L. I. Terum (eds), Profesjonsstudier, 13–27, Oslo: Universitetsforlaget.

Muller, J. and Young, M. (2019), 'Knowledge, Power and Powerful Knowledge Re-visited', The Curriculum Journal, 30 (2): 196–214. DOI: 10.1080/09585176.2019.1570292.

Munthe, E. and Rogne, M. (2015), 'Research Based Teacher Education', Teaching and Teacher Education, 46: 17–24. DOI:10.1016/j.tate.2014.10.006.

Nordgren, K. (2017), 'Powerful Knowledge, Intercultural Learning and History Education', Journal of Curriculum Studies, 49 (5): 663–82. DOI: 10.1080/00220272.2017.1320430.

NRLU [Nasjonalt råd for lærerutdanning] (2016), Nasjonale retningslinjer for grunnskolelærerutdanning trinn 1–7, Oslo: Universitets- og høgskolerådet.

Ongstad, S. (2004), Språk, kommunikasjon og didaktikk: Norsk som flerfaglig og fagdidaktisk ressurs, Bergen: Fagbokforlaget/LNU.

Ongstad, S. (2006), 'Fag i endring. Om didaktisering av kunnskap', in S. Ongstad (ed), Fag og didaktikk i lærerutdanning. Kunnskap i grenseland, 19–57, Oslo: Universitetsforlaget.

Skjelbred, D. (2010), Fra Fadervår til Facebook: Skolens lese- og skriveopplæring i et historisk perspektiv, Bergen: Fagbokforlaget/LNU.

Smeby, J.-C. (2008), 'Profesjon og utdanning', in A. Molander and L. I. Terum (eds), *Profesjonsstudier*, 87–102, Oslo: Universitetsforlaget.

Smidt, J. (1989), *Seks lesere på skolen. Hva de søkte, hva de fant*, Oslo: Universitetsforlaget.

Solstad, A. G. (2010), 'Praksisnær teori og teorinær praksis - den nødvendige relasjonen', *Norsk pedagogisk tidsskrift*, 94 (3): 203–18.

Tirri, Kirsi (2014), 'The Last 40 years in Finnish Teacher Education', *Journal of Education for Teaching*, 40 (5): 600–09. DOI: 10.1080/00313831.2012.726274.

Utdanningsforbundet (2009), 'Landsmøtet 2009. Vedtak, sak 3.2. Morgendagens barnehage og skole', www.utdanningsforbundet.no (accessed 6 August 2020).

Young, M. (2009/2016), 'What are Schools For?', in M. Young and J. Muller (eds), *Curriculum and the Specialization of Knowledge. Studies in the Sociology of Education*, 105–114, New York: Routledge.

Young, M. (2013), 'Overcoming the Crisis in Curriculum Theory: A Knowledge-based Approach', *Journal of Curriculum Studies*, 45 (2): 101–18. DOI: 10.1080/00220272.2013.764505.

Young, M. (2015), 'Curriculum Theory and the Question of Knowledge: A Response to the Six Papers', *Journal of Curriculum Studies*, 47 (6): 820–37. DOI: 10.1080/00220272.2015.1101493.

3

Teacher Education and History Teachers' Powerful Professional Knowledge

Mikko Puustinen

In order to stimulate powerful knowledge in history classrooms, teachers need to construct learning situations in which students learn the discipline, not just substantive knowledge or general competencies (Puustinen and Khawaja 2021). However, a common result of observation studies and a concern of teacher educators is that history teaching often focuses on transmitting a selected collection of factual knowledge (e.g. Cuban 2016; Nokes 2010; Saye et al. 2018). Teacher-centred methods and the memorization of a given narrative have dominated instruction.

Canadian historian Chad Gaffield (2001: 12–14) summarized the paradox of history education by comparing it to basketball. Gaffield describes how he and his classmates read about history at school, talked about history and wrote history, but never did history. This, he adds, would be akin to learning basketball after years of reading the interpretations and viewpoints of great players and watching them play, but never actually playing. Gaffield goes on to describe how university courses focused on various viewpoints of historians rather than getting to grips with the past. In sports terms, he began to play the game only at the doctoral-thesis level.

Before moving on to questions of the teaching discipline history, a few clarifications may be helpful. In the school context, 'learning the discipline' or 'historical thinking' does not refer, for example, to a deep understanding of research methodology. The aim is to widen students' understanding, not produce new knowledge like historians do (Husbands 1996: 26). The wide variety of academic historiography and paradigms may make it difficult to construct a universally shared model of 'historical thinking' used by historians (e.g. Thorp and Persson 2020). Moreover, history education research has several traditions that stress different aspects of historical expertise (e.g. Seixas 2017). Still, these reservations do not make pedagogized disciplinary models like historical thinking meaningless. On the contrary, even though the 'historical thinking' in history instruction models may not capture academic history per se, it, like analogous models in other school subjects, can be seen as important epistemic tools needed to grasp the disciplinary ways of thinking.

In this chapter, I examine the challenges teacher education faces in promoting history teachers' powerful professional knowledge. Although I draw my data and examples from history education, many of the challenges are common to other school subjects. Based on recent studies I have conducted with members of the Research Group for Social Studies Education at the University of Helsinki, I discuss the implications for teacher education policy and practice that could support the strengthening of subject teachers' powerful professional knowledge. By subject teachers, I refer to teachers who study their teaching subject as their major and are oriented to teaching in secondary education.

In order to generate meaningful professional knowledge, a subject teacher needs knowledge about teaching subjects and their background disciplines, knowledge about education and school systems in general, and the ability to master different pedagogical situations (*knowledge about education* and *knowledge for educational practice*, Hordern 2018). Promoting powerful professional knowledge requires bringing these different types of knowledge together (Furlong and Whitty 2017: 49; Maton 2014: 181). As a consequence, the teacher should be able to theorize and reflect on schooling and learning situations with disciplinary concepts that are drawn from both educational science and the background discipline(s) of the teaching subject. This is not an easy task for student teachers, working teachers or teacher education systems.

Two reasons explain why teacher education in Finland offers an interesting case study. First, from an international perspective, Finnish teacher education has adopted a particularly strong theoretical emphasis in recent decades (Säntti et al. 2018). Second, the Finnish teacher education system has a distinctive feature in that the teacher training schools are affiliated to universities. Ideally, university-based training schools can offer a first-class platform for merging teachers' academic knowledge with day-to-day schooling.

The starting point for my analysis is the observed imbalance between Finnish history teachers' understanding of their subject and their pedagogy (Puustinen and Khawaja, forthcoming). In interviews, teachers acknowledged that history was an interpretative subject and favoured pedagogical methods that would promote disciplinary history. However, during observed lessons, their pedagogy seemed to be reduced to transmitting facts without a disciplinary approach. I interpret these results by analysing the historical development and structure of teacher education. As a theoretical framework, I apply Erich Weniger's (1957) idea of two opposite, yet still similar, pitfalls in teachers' work: the tyranny of theory and the tyranny of experience. My main argument is that there is a need to re-innovate teaching practice periods as the connective glue between theory and practice in teacher education.

Theoretical Framework

While schooling has arguably changed over the last century, the changes are often other than intended (Tyack and Cuban 1995). Terms like 'habitual blindness' (Cassirer 1944, cited in Ertsas and Irgens 2017) and 'persistent tradition' (Cuban 2016) conceptualize how the structures of schooling and teachers' daily routines include different historical sediments descended from earlier times. If these habitual practices are not questioned, teachers may merely be repeating the routines adopted from previous generations.

German scholar Erich Weniger (1957: 18) used the concept of the tyranny of experience to criticize views that mere experience would be enough to justify practical actions. If a teacher's understanding is solely grounded in experience, it leads to prejudiced and fortuitous actions, namely, poor practice. Like many later scholars, Weniger emphasized the interaction between educational theory and practice. According to Weniger, we should avoid dichotomist thinking because both theory and practice will always exist per se and mutually depend on each other. There is no theory without educational practice, and practice always includes some kind of theoretical elements.

Weniger's analytical model (1957: 10–11) is based on three grades of theory. The theory of the first degree is hidden and non-articulated. It can be identified through action, not through arguments (Argyris and Schön 1978). The theory of the second degree can be expressed as arguments which are based on experience or theorems. Detecting the theory of the second degree requires reflecting on the premises of actions. A teacher who recognizes this can formulate her own theoretical basis.

The theory of the third degree refers to reflective and generic meta-theoretical thinking that is based on context-independent knowledge (Weniger 1957: 19) and is a theory that can be used for analysing practice. However, this requires reflection that is thoroughly open towards one's own actions, as well as analytical distance. Such thinking makes it possible to generate practice that is more rational. In this regard, Weniger's thinking resonates with Young (e.g. Young and Muller 2014), who emphasizes the context-independent nature of powerful knowledge. I argue that for subject teachers Weniger's meta-theoretical thinking needs to combine the different types of knowledge that comprise powerful professional knowledge.

Ertsas and Irgens (2017) re-develop Weniger's ideas in the context of professional theorizing. They understand the theory of the third degree as a means for generating context-independent professional knowledge. In order to theorize professionally, a teacher must be able to develop her practice without being restricted to primary experiences only (Ertsas and Irgens 2017). By drawing on the theory of the third degree, a teacher can legitimize practice, make implicit theories explicit through the theory of the second degree and critically reflect on the theory of the first degree. This can help teachers theorize their own work in a way that questions the traditions and habitual blindness inherent in the theory of the first degree.

Connecting theories of the first and third degree highlights the importance of the second level of Weniger's model. In this sense, teacher education's aim would be to develop intentional theory and articulate it explicitly. As powerful professional knowledge would bring different types of knowledge together, successful teacher education would create connections between theoretical educational knowledge and everyday work in classrooms. This requires engaging practice, the experience of the practitioner and theory. If theory loses touch with practice, its impact declines or ceases (Weniger 1957: 22).

The Reduction of Disciplinary Thinking

As noted, an observation study carried out in Finnish history classrooms indicated a clear discontinuity between teachers' intentions and pedagogical choices (Puustinen and Khawaja, forthcoming). The results revealed a somewhat traditional approach to history teaching with teachers on average lecturing for 40 per cent of the time. While lecturing, they used PowerPoint slides and occasionally asked some questions. These were usually closed questions in the sense the teacher had a specific correct answer in mind. Most classroom activities did not encourage open-ended enquiry or challenge conventional narratives. The nature or use of historical knowledge was rarely considered. Most observed lessons guided students to move information from one place to another in order to memorize it. Many student-centred activities appeared engaging at first sight, but eventually did not support disciplinary learning (Puustinen and Khawaja 2021; also see Fordham 2015). However, despite fact-based teaching, teachers acknowledged in the interviews that history was an interpretative subject and that they favoured pedagogical methods which would promote disciplinary history.

These results are consistent with other studies in which observed history instruction has often appeared to be merely emphasizing facts (Cuban 2016; Nokes 2010; Saye et al. 2018). At the same time, the results resonate with those studies in which teachers were interviewed or a discrepancy between interviews and classroom practices was observed (e.g. van Nieuwenhuyse and Wils 2019; Rosenlund 2016). While some teachers presumably say what they think the researcher wishes to hear, and some may be unfamiliar with disciplinary history, the educational background of Finnish history teachers suggests there is a need for a more coherent interpretation.

In Finland, student subject teachers study for five to six years before graduating and taking up a teaching position (Puustinen et al. 2018). Most of this time is spent in the subject department where students also complete their master's thesis. In an international comparison, the Finnish system resembles those found in many other countries, with 75 to 80 per cent of the emphasis on the teaching subject rather than general educational knowledge being comparable to the European average (Ecker 2018). Hence, the conclusion that teachers simply do not understand the discipline appears to fall short. Most history teachers should master their discipline, even though they may not necessarily participate in the production of new scientific knowledge (Fordham 2015). However, there is considerable variation among teacher education systems, universities and emphases across Europe, which makes more specific comparisons difficult.

In order to become certified teachers in Finland, students must complete pedagogical studies, which include two teaching practice periods (Puustinen et al. 2018). Teachers' pedagogical studies consist of about twenty separate courses, ranging from educational psychology to historical and philosophical aspects of education, amounting to a total of 60 ECTS credits. Generally, subject student teachers complete their pedagogical studies in one academic year and may complete these studies at any stage of their major studies. At the heart of history didactics are concepts like historical thinking and historical consciousness.

Considering the observation results and Finnish history teachers' education, it seems that teachers' disciplinary knowledge is connected neither to their educational knowledge nor to their pedagogy. In order to understand where and why disciplinary aims are lost, I now examine the historical development of Finnish teacher education in the light of Weniger's thinking.

The Changing Emphasis of Finnish Teacher Education

In recent decades, Finnish teacher education has developed from a prescriptive and practice-oriented model towards a research-based orientation (Säntti et al. 2018). The foundations of Finnish teacher education were laid in the nineteenth century. Class teachers, who taught at the primary level, were educated in teacher training colleges. Subject teachers, who worked on the secondary level, studied their major through their subject departments and participated in teaching practice periods at the university's training school. The whole teacher education system was reformed during the 1960s and 1970s. While the decision to educate primary school teachers to master's level marked a significant departure from the international trend (Simola and Rinne 2015: 262), the education of subject teachers continued to follow nineteenth-century structures. Yet, common to both education paths is an increased emphasis on educational research competencies (Puustinen 2018; Säntti et al. 2014; Sitomaniemi-San 2015).

During the first phase of the development, teaching was seen as a craft. Drilling ready-made teaching methods offered a fixed version of knowledge and practical tools that a teacher would need. Against this background, the message of reformers during the 1960s was quite clear. The theoretical basis of teacher education and a teacher's work were unequivocally inadequate (Committee Report [CR] 1967, 1968, 1969). However, at the same time, teacher educators were warned against providing an overly theoretical education for prospective teachers (CR 1969: 36). The connection between theory and practice was fragile.

During the 1970s, plans to reform Finnish universities ignited debate. Intentions to create a polytechnic model that would combine theoretical and practical knowledge in the spirit of multidisciplinary and critical thinking (CR 1972) were rejected by more conservative academic staff (Kivinen and Rinne 1996). As a result, teacher education was eventually organized according to more traditional academic guidelines. The emphasis on theory continued (Säntti et al. 2018) and the ability to think scientifically was presented as being characteristic of a teacher, as encapsulated in the suggestion that 'practical decisions should derive from research-based facts, not beliefs' (CR 1975: 41). Nevertheless, the committees of the time admitted that teachers were not supposed to be 'real researchers' and that there was not (as yet) a generally accepted theory of education or instruction (CR 1975).

The decision to educate all teachers to master's level was mainly driven by political decision-making and the general degree reforms pertaining to Finnish higher education (Simola and Rinne 2015). Consequently, on the practical level, teacher education was not ready to engage theory-based learning. The academization process of Finnish teacher education took several decades. For example, during the 1990s questions arose as to whether class teachers needed studies at master's level. The defensive reaction was to stress the theoretical aspects of teacher education more strongly. One implication of the new status was the rhetorical choice to present teachers' tasks more broadly than earlier: teachers were to be 'educational experts', not only schoolteachers (Säntti et al. 2018). This brought about a significant change in teacher education in the mid-1990s. Simply put, more theory and research methodology were added and teaching practice periods became shorter (Puustinen 2018; Säntti et al. 2014).

Unlike in earlier decades when the relationship between theory and practice was seen as problematic in one way or another, teacher education reports from the 2000s and 2010s do not recognize ambivalence (Säntti et al. 2018). On the contrary, a report from 2007 declares that 'a research orientation and teachers' day-to-day work are inseparable' (CR 2007: 37). The proposed solution to the decades-long challenge to combine theory and practice was personal practical theory (PPT), which every student teacher was encouraged to develop. The concept of PPT, as well as some analogous labels, refers to the interaction between the knowledge, beliefs and practices in the minds of teachers (Puustinen et al. 2018). The Finnish system shares these definitions, but places more emphasis on academic studies and scientific elements. The stated aim of PPT is to combine different elements experienced by students during their education. Yet, for some – possibly rhetorical – reason, the degree requirements of the teacher education programmes at the University of Helsinki do not define PPT.

While it is clear that the idea of PPT resonates with Weniger's aim to avoid the tyrannies of theory and experience, the vagueness of PPT raises questions. For example, if these personal and practical theories comprehend everything that a pre-service teacher (or qualified teacher) has met in pedagogy during their lives, do they actually say anything specific? Are there any criteria for PPT? Finally, if PPT is generated by experience and has no criteria, how does it differ from the everyday knowledge that represents the tyranny of experience?

These uncertainties relate to the educational knowledge of teachers. As noted, teachers are probably unable to generate powerful professional knowledge if the disciplinary knowledge of their teaching subject, knowledge about education and knowledge about educational practice are not connected. A somewhat open question relates to whether teaching practice periods have followed the theorization process of Finnish teacher education and, respectively, whether the theoretical aspects of pedagogical studies have a solid connection to teachers' everyday work (Puustinen et al. 2018). In an effort to understand this uncertainty, I next examine the history of Finnish teacher education from a different angle.

Decontextualized Educational Knowledge

Before the 1970s, teacher training colleges promoted a prescriptive and conservative orientation to teaching (Säntti et al. 2018). An uncontentious interpretation of this is that strict ideas of good instruction led to an understanding of the theorizing of everyday work as superfluous. Non-academic teacher education could be characterized as the tyranny of experience. Subsequently, the intensified emphasis on a research orientation presented a different scenario. In their analysis of the academization of Finnish teacher education, Simola and colleagues (Simola et al. 2015: 122) argue that the theoretical emphasis created a decontextualized and 'school-free' approach, namely, the 'science of how the teacher should teach and how the pupil should learn in school – as if it were not in school'.

The balance between theory and practice in Finnish teacher education has been turned upside down since the 1960s and 1970s (Säntti et al. 2018). The fixed views and drilling of ready-made teaching methods have been replaced by undefined personal practical theories. This development resembles the shift from curriculum Future 1 to Future 2, as described by Young and Muller (2010). Pedagogical knowledge that is based on undefined PPT seems to depend on the knower. Further, school-free pedagogy, namely, theorizing teaching without any connection to actual school, appears to be an illustrative example of the tyranny of theory.

Regarding teachers' powerful professional knowledge, the alienation of practical and theoretical educational knowledge makes it more difficult to bring different knowledge bases together. However, it is important to note that the tyranny of theory in teacher education does not automatically lead to the tyranny of theory at the practical level. On the contrary, I suggest that it leads back to the tyranny of experience in classrooms.

As mentioned, teacher training schools are a distinctive feature of Finnish teacher education in that they are administratively connected to the faculties of education. Ideally, this connection would prove highly valuable. Yet research suggests that the academization of Finnish teacher education has thrown these connections off track. As a consequence of the scientification process, the guidance during teaching practice periods was left to lower-level staff, namely, to teachers in university training schools (Simola 1997), while stronger pressure to produce publications persuaded teacher educators to focus on research, loosening connections to daily work in schools (Säntti et al. 2014). Today, professors are seldom involved in day-to-day classroom practice and most lecturers do not have the possibility to take part in teaching practice guidance. In this sense, the message from surveys completed by subject teacher students is clear: the theoretical and practical aspects of teacher education are not related (Puustinen 2018).

There is no all-inclusive research data to reject or confirm the discontinuity between pedagogical studies and teaching practice periods. However, some case studies focusing on history imply that teachers who mentor student teachers seem to be somewhat critical of the ideal of historical thinking (Norppa 2019; Veijola 2013). For example, didactical efforts to implement more evidence-based learning have been criticized for usurping the time that could be spent teaching substantive knowledge. Yet promoting students' powerful knowledge would require them to grasp the way in which historical knowledge is produced, and thus to understand how historical narratives are always created by someone (Puustinen and Khawaja 2021).

As noted, many or most history teachers seem to understand this at a theoretical level, but are unable or unwilling to implement disciplinary aims. Based on the historical development of Finnish teacher education, I suggest that the decontextualization of educational knowledge makes it hard for an individual teacher to combine disciplinary and educational knowledge and hence to critically reflect on the traditions of schooling. In the section that follows, I concretize how decontextualized educational knowledge can hinder history teachers' ability to break the tyranny of experience, and unpack the external influences that push teachers towards memorizing.

The Tyranny of Experience Dominates History Instruction

The nineteenth-century origins of school history as a national narrative transmitter are still deeply rooted in many school systems and public opinions.

Thus, curricula and assessment practices may at least to some extent reflect an emphasis on the substantial aspects of historical knowledge. This was also noticeable in the actions of the teachers who participated in our observation study. Even though the national core curriculum of that time (2016–21) obliged teachers to promote historical thinking, it also defined thirty-six substantive items that students are expected to learn (Finnish National Agency for Education 2015). The observed teachers duly had to juggle the content demands as well as disciplinary practices.

A particular challenge with respect to disciplinary intentions seems to arise if a large quantity of substantive knowledge is tested by multiple-choice questions (e.g. Smith et al. 2018). Still, essay-based tests can also be problematic. For example, although the matriculation examination that Finnish students must pass at the end of upper secondary school includes only essay-based questions, history tests have barely supported disciplinary aims (Puustinen et al. 2020). Only a minority of assignments have been document-based, and most of these have required analysing only one document. Sourcing and contextualization (Wineburg 1991) have been inconsistently required. Finally, the essential historical literacy skills have not been a requirement in the grading rubrics.

At the classroom level, curricula and testing requirements merge with the teacher's professional knowledge. A long tradition of research suggests that many teachers tend to teach in the same way that they were taught in school, even though their experiences may be at odds with their pedagogical education. In the case of history teaching, teachers and student teachers may have never experienced disciplinary pedagogy as students. Teaching at university level has traditionally involved lecturing. VanSledright (2010: 188) argues that students absorb what it means to learn and teach history during their time at university: 'Historians talk, students listen and take notes on the usually accurate assumption that they will soon be tested on their capacity to make sense and recall the scholarship [. . .] to which they were exposed.'

In a recent study (Puustinen and Vesterinen, forthcoming), we observed the teaching in two Finnish history departments. While the general approach was multidimensional, on many occasions the stress was on transmitting substantive knowledge. In another study (Veijola and Mikkonen 2016), approximately half of novice history students saw history as a collection of facts and fascinating stories. An equally sized group perceived history as a tool for understanding the world. These students emphasized causal relations and stressed the importance of sharing knowledge about history with other people in order to educate them. Very few students saw historical knowledge as the result of interpreting evidence.

An indirect sign of the continuous tradition of fact-based history instruction in schools is that the last perspective represents the orientation that national core curricula have emphasized since the 1990s.

Hence, it seems that many Finnish history teachers may only have learning experiences that focus on substantive knowledge and no concrete idea of how disciplinary pedagogy could be implemented. In their pedagogical practices, they follow what they know, namely, the fact-based tradition. Similarly, in a study conducted by Rosenlund (2016: 119) the Swedish teachers who were interviewed made references to their own time as students, as well as the advice given to them by more experienced colleagues. Rosenlund (2016: 177) argues that they were guided by a strong tradition based on teachers' and their colleagues' experiences.

Overall, while many history teachers and student teachers seem to hold an understanding of history as an interpretative discipline, they still have a strong perception that teaching history means passing on substantive knowledge about history (also see Sears 2014). This tradition is absorbed, not articulated, making it problematic to discuss and criticize. In Weniger's terms, history teachers seem to have difficulties in making non-articulated actions visible and thus transferable. To create a more disciplinary pedagogy, teachers should be able to understand how the National Core Curriculum and learning materials (e.g. textbooks) relate to each other and further the didactical ideals (i.e. supporting disciplinary history). Finally, all of these should be compared to school traditions and the teacher's own pedagogical thinking.

To conclude the Finnish case, the historical development of teacher education has not supported merging history teachers' educational and subject-specific knowledge with daily pedagogy. The fragmentary structure of subject teachers' education and the alignment of the theoretical and practical parts of the education may even have reinforced the status of the tradition that predominated in the classrooms in our observation study. In the final part of this chapter, I discuss how re-innovating the nineteenth-century idea of university-based teaching practice schools could go some way towards overcoming this persistent tradition.

Discussion: Re-innovating Teaching Practice Periods as Interaction between Theory and Practice

I have sought to understand how the development of Finnish teacher education can explain why history teachers are unable to implement disciplinary teaching despite their intentions to do so. One would presume that Finland's teacher education system, which emphasizes theoretical knowledge about education, and where all teachers are educated to master's level and teacher training schools are part of university organizations, would have overcome persistent traditions. Nonetheless, at least in the case of history teaching, traditional teacher-centred and fact-based pedagogy seems to play the dominant role. Why is the tradition so powerful and how can teachers' powerful professional knowledge be strengthened in order to aim for a more disciplinary pedagogy?

History teachers and student teachers face conflicting messages. On one hand, teacher educators and parts of the national curricula for both basic education and general upper secondary education emphasize the disciplinary aspect of history. On the other hand, the dominant teaching tradition, assessment practices and many learning materials emphasize the substantive knowledge that is expected to be memorized. In many ways, the controversy culminates during teaching practice periods. I argue that if the actual learning and teaching situations are not theorized with educational and subject-specific knowledge the tradition continues to supersede disciplinary views. The interpretative aims of teachers are reduced by decontextualized educational knowledge, which opens classroom doors to the tyranny of experience.

Weniger's theorization offers an analytical framework for examining these challenges. Regardless of the differences between national contexts, teachers are the bosses of their classrooms. They are gatekeepers who have enough freedom to make instructional decisions irrespective of curricular or administrative regulation (Tyack and Cuban 1995: 135). If teachers as gatekeepers lack the capability of meta-theoretical and context-independent thinking, they are more likely to be subject to the tyranny of experience, namely, to follow tradition.

Weniger's framework emphasizes the non-dichotomous understanding of theory and practice. While, according to Weniger, neglecting new ideas by stating that 'experience shows that . . .' usually means legitimizing lacklustre or poor practice (Ertsas and Irgens 2017), on the other hand theory is meaningless without a connection to practice. Hence, the aim is the ability to theorize, not merely accumulate knowledge about theories (Ertsas and Irgens 2017). The ability to think reflectively is also a publicly stated goal in the Finnish teacher education system. The notion of the reflective teacher is closely connected to the agenda of research-based teacher education, which aims to educate teachers not simply as the recipients of professional knowledge but as autonomous actors who also participate in knowledge production (Puustinen et al. 2018).

However, as I have argued, the development of Finnish teacher education in recent decades raises the question of whether the heavy emphasis on research abilities (Sitomaniemi-San 2015), and the loosening ties to classrooms, will support theorizing classroom experiences. While there would be little point criticizing the Finnish aim to support making theorizing and reflection visible by emphasizing PPT, it would be a mistake to think that merely vocalizing one's own theories would create a better practice. Theory in the form of 'school-free pedagogy' may not offer meaningful tools for a practitioner. As Rosenlund (2016: 183) notes in the context of history teaching, if teachers are supposed to re-design their instruction on their own or in discussion with colleagues, there is a risk that it will further strengthen the already dominant tradition. Similarly, Ertsas and Irgens (2017) refer to Ryle (1949), who pointed out that theorizing is something that everyone does, and that it can be done both intelligently and stupidly.

Translating the aforementioned considerations into powerful knowledge discourse means that there is no point in reflecting on everyday knowledge about teaching without disciplinary concepts and understanding. Given the tradition and non-articulated theory of first degree parallels to everyday knowledge as defined by Young and Muller (2014), in order to make theorizing meaningful and to duly extend and transform everyday understanding, subject teachers should be able to use theoretical concepts and other thinking tools drawn from both educational science and the background discipline(s) of their teaching subject.

Even classic sociological studies about schooling paid attention to the primitiveness of teachers' professional language (e.g. Lortie 2002). Teachers seem to lack the analytical tools to conceptualize the complexity of education amidst societal and institutional purposes, obligations and expectations. Concepts like the grammar of schooling (e.g. Cuban 2016) may enhance understanding about the stability of rituals, procedures and structures that are reflected in the teaching of particular subjects, and define the possibilities of an individual teacher. At the same time, an understanding of the structures and societal expectations could support the context-independent reflection and transformation processes of disciplinary knowledge.

From the perspective of subject teachers' professional knowledge, the theorization of pedagogical situations should not be separated from broader knowledge about education and teaching subjects. Regardless of theoretical expertise, every teacher needs some practical tools to implement pedagogical ideas. If a novice teacher cannot construct connections between education and the acute challenges she faces in the classroom, usable solutions have to be found somewhere. A likely, and safe, source for these solutions is the tradition that is familiar from one's own time as a student, or that is passed down from more experienced colleagues (Rosenlund 2016). As Dan Lortie (2002) noted in the 1970s, teachers spend most of their professional career alone in classrooms full of students. There is no one at hand to help in questioning the tradition and to support the development of professional knowledge. Without a strong epistemological foundation and professional knowledge, a novice teacher can easily lapse into traditional pedagogical methods. This requires training which draws together knowledge about education, subject-specific knowledge and knowledge about pedagogical situations.

Here, teaching practice periods are crucial. Mentor teachers who coach student teachers should be able to justify their own actions as well as give feedback on student teachers' work based on relevant theories and scientific knowledge, not on experience (Ertsas and Irgens 2017). In order to overcome the tyranny of experience, an unbeatable innovation would be re-innovating the initial idea of Finnish university-based teacher training schools. During the 1970s, when the existing teacher education system was established, and even in the mid-nineteenth century, when systematic teacher education began, developers emphasized the interaction between academic studies and practical training. University-based teacher educators, including professors, were assumed and recommended to participate in the guidance of teaching practice periods. These aims have gradually diminished in view of advances in the identification process of Finnish teacher education.

In this chapter, I have used history education and Finnish teacher education as an example to analyse the challenges associated with promoting subject teachers' powerful professional knowledge. In Finland, the theorization of teacher education and emphasis on research methods during education have been salient. The message of this chapter is that adding more theory will probably not break persistent traditions if the connections to schooling and teaching practice periods decline. On the policy level, this would call for careful consideration of the way in which academic meriting through publications and actual teaching work with student teachers could be meaningfully balanced in the teacher education context.

The discontinuities in history teaching may well resonate with other school subjects. For example, working with primary sources would ideally strengthen students' historical thinking, but can likewise be used as another means for memorizing historical details or as a trivial group activity that does not support learning the discipline. Similarly, in physics, lab activities can be used merely to reproduce known results or just as a fun activity, instead of subject-specific sense-making (e.g. Sickel et al. 2015). In both cases, without sufficient professional knowledge, teachers are unable to design activities that would demonstrate knowledge production in their respective disciplines.

It is noteworthy, however, that the situation may be more complex in those school subjects that do not have a clear background discipline. Social studies, for example, which draws its content from several academic fields, typically lacks a coherent knowledge structure, conceptual network and disciplinary basis that would define rules for knowledge production (Hansen and Puustinen 2021). Considering the aim of combining subject teachers' educational and subject-specific knowledge, social studies and other multidisciplinary subjects may pose a greater challenge for teacher education and curriculum development than those subjects which rely more heavily on particular disciplines.

I began this chapter by comparing learning history without engagement in doing history to learning basketball without actually playing the game. To conclude, I would like to apply Gaffield's example to teacher education: On one hand, learning to teach without actually doing any teaching in a real classroom will separate theory from practice and strengthen the tyranny of experience. On the other hand, learning to teach only by imitating others will do the same. The re-innovating of teaching practice periods would mean bringing theory into classrooms in a way that leads to theorizing practice and justifies actions based on theory, not on habit.

References

Argyris, C. and Schön, D. (1978), *Organizational Learning: A Theory of Action Perspective*, Reading, MA: Addison-Wesley.
Cassirer, E. (1944), *An Essay on Man*, New Haven, CT: Yale University Press.
Committee Report (1967), *Opettajanvalmistustoimikunnan mietintö* [Report of the Committee for the Planning of Teacher Training], Helsinki: Valtion painatuskeskus.
Committee Report (1968), *Opettajanvalmistuksen opetussuunnitelmatoimikunnan mietintö* [Report of the Curriculum Planning Commission for General Teacher Training], Helsinki: Valtion painatuskeskus.
Committee Report (1969), *Peruskoulunopettajakomitean mietintö* [Report of the Comprehensive School Teacher Committee], Helsinki: Valtion painatuskeskus.

Committee Report (1972), *Filosofisten ja yhteiskuntatieteellisten tutkintojen toimikunnan mietintö* [The Committee Report of the Degrees in Philosophy and Social Sciences], Helsinki: Valtion painatuskeskus.

Committee Report (1975), *Vuoden 1973 opettajankoulutustoimikunnan mietintö* [Report of the Teacher Education Committee of 1973], Helsinki: Valtion painatuskeskus.

Committee Report (2007), *Opettajankoulutus 2020* [Teacher Education 2020], Helsinki: Yliopistopaino.

Cuban, L. (2016), *Teaching History Then and Now: A Story of Stability and Change in Schools*, Cambridge, MA: Harvard Education Press.

Ecker, A. (2018), 'The Education of History Teachers in Europe – A Comparative Study: First Results of the "Civic and History Education Study"', *Creative Education*, 9: 1565–610.

Ertsas, T. I. and Irgens, E. J. (2017), 'Professional Theorizing', *Teachers and Teaching*, 23 (3): 332–51.

Finnish National Agency for Education (2015), *National Core Curriculum for General Upper Secondary Education*, Helsinki: Author.

Fordham, M. (2015), 'Teachers and the Academic Disciplines', *Journal of Philosophy of Education*, 50 (3): 419–31.

Gaffield, C. (2001), 'Towards the Coach in the History Classroom', *Canadian Issues – Thémes Canadiens*, October 2001, 12–14.

Hansen, P. and Puustinen, M. (2021), 'Rethinking Society and Knowledge in Finnish Social Studies Textbooks', *Journal of Curriculum Studies*. DOI: 10.1080/00220272.2021.1881169

Hordern, J. (2018), 'Is Powerful Educational Knowledge Possible?', *Cambridge Journal of Education*, 48 (6): 787–802.

Husbands, C. (1996), *What Is History Teaching?*, Buckingham: Open University Press.

Kivinen, R. and Rinne, R. (1996), 'Teacher Training and Higher Education Policies in Finland Since World War II', in H. Simola and T. Popkewits (eds), *Professionalization and Education*, 76–96, Helsinki: University of Helsinki.

Lortie, D. (2002), *Schoolteacher: A Sociological Study* (2nd ed.), Chicago: University of Chicago Press.

Maton, K. (2014), 'Building Powerful Knowledge: The Significance of Semantic Waves', in E. Rata and B. Barrett (eds), *Knowledge and the Future of the Curriculum: International Studies in Social Realism*, 181–97, London: Palgrave Macmillan.

Van Nieuwenhuyse, K. and Wils, K. (2019), 'History Education Research into Historical Consciousness in Flanders', in A. Clark and C. Peck (eds), *Contemplating Historical Consciousness: Notes from the Field*, 49–59, New York: Berghahn.

Nokes, J. (2010), 'Observing Literacy Practices in History Classrooms', *Theory & Research in Social Education*, 38 (4): 515–44.

Norppa, J. (2019), 'At the Riptide of Theory and Practice', Paper presented at doctoral candidates' research seminar 4.12.2019, Helsinki, Finland.

Puustinen, M. (2018), *Puhumalla teoretisoitu? Aineenopettajakoulutuksen kasvatustieteellistyminen ja asiantuntijapuhe 1970-luvulta 2010-luvulle* [Theorized by Speaking? Disciplinization of Subject Teacher Education and the Rhetoric of Policy Texts from the 1970s to 2010s], Helsinki: University of Helsinki.

Puustinen, M. and Khawaja, A. (2021), 'Envisaging the Alternatives: From Knowledge of the Powerful to Powerful Knowledge in History Classrooms', *Journal of Curriculum Studies*. 53 (1), 16–31. DOI: 10.1080/00220272.2019.1703273

Puustinen, M. and Khawaja, A. (forthcoming), 'Observing the forms of knowledge and the use of historical sources in Finnish upper secondary schools'.

Puustinen, M., Paldanius, H. and Luukka, M-R. (2020), 'Sisältötiedon toistamista vai aineiston analyysia? Tiedonalakohtaiset tekstitaidot historian ylioppilaskokeen tehtävänannoissa ja pisteytysohjeissa [Repeating Substantive Knowledge or Analysing Historical Evidence? Disciplinary Literacy Skills in the History Test in the Matriculation Examination]', *Kasvatus & Aika*, 14 (2): 9–34.

Puustinen, M. and Vesterinen, I. (forthcoming), 'Historian osaaminen ja asiantuntijuus yliopisto-opintojen perusteella [The Expertise of History Based on University Studies]'.

Puustinen, M., Säntti, J., Koski, A. and Tammi, T. (2018), 'Teaching: A Practical or Research-based Profession? Teacher Candidates' Approaches to Research-based Teacher Education', *Teaching and Teacher Education*, 74: 170–79.

Rosenlund, D. (2016), *History Education as Content, Methods or Orientation?*, Frankfurt am Main: Peter Lang.

Ryle, G. (1949), *The Concept of Mind*, London: Hutchinson.

Säntti, J., Rantala, J., Salminen, J. and Hansen, P. (2014), 'Bowing to Science, Finnish Teacher Education Turns its Back on Practical Schoolwork', *Educational Practice and Theory*, 36 (1): 21–41.

Säntti, J., Puustinen, M. and Salminen, J. (2018), 'Theory and Practice in Finnish Teacher Education: A Rhetorical Analysis of Changing Values from the 1960s to the Present Day', *Teachers and Teaching*, 24 (1): 5–21.

Saye, J. W., Stoddard, J., Gerwin, D. M., Libresco, A. S. and Maddox, L. E. (2018), 'Authentic Pedagogy: Examining Intellectual Challenge in Social Studies Classrooms', *Journal of Curriculum Studies*, 50 (6): 865–84.

Sears, A. (2014), 'Moving from the Periphery to the Core: The Possibilities for Professional Learning Communities in History Teacher Education', in R. Samwell and A. von Heyking (eds), *Becoming a History Teacher: Sustaining Practices in Historical Thinking and Knowing*, 11–29, Toronto: University of Toronto Press.

Seixas, P. (2017), 'A Model of Historical Thinking', *Educational Philosophy and Theory*, 49 (6): 593–605.

Sickel, A., Banilower, E. R., Carlson, J. and Van Driel, J. H. (2015), 'Examining PCK Research in the Context of Current Policy Initiatives', in A. Berry, P. Friedrichsen and J. Loughran (eds), *Re-examining Pedagogical Content Knowledge in Science Education*, 199–213, New York: Routledge.

Simola, H. (1997), 'Kouluhallituksen varjosta tieteen valoon [From the Shadow of the Board of Education to the Light of Science]', in J. Kivirauma and R. Rinne (eds), *Suomalaisen kasvatustieteen historia – lyhyt oppimäärä* [The History of Finnish Education Science – Short Course], 215–56, Turku: University of Turku.

Simola, H., Kivinen, O. and Rinne, R. (2015), 'Didactic Closure: Professionalization and Pedagogical Knowledge in Finnish Teacher Education', in H. Simola (ed), *The Finnish Education Mystery: Historical and Sociological Essays on Schooling in Finland*, 113–33, New York: Routledge.

Simola, H. and Rinne, R. (2015), 'Education Politics and Contingency: Belief, Status and Trust Behind the Finnish PISA Miracle', in H. Simola (ed), *The Finnish Education Mystery: Historical and Sociological Essays on Schooling in Finland*, 252–72, New York: Routledge.

Sitomaniemi-San, J. (2015), *Fabricating the Teacher as Researcher: A Genealogy of Academic Teacher Education in Finland*, Oulu: University of Oulu.

Smith, M., Breakstone, J. and Wineburg, S. (2018), 'History Assessments of Thinking: A Validity Study', *Cognition and Instruction*, 37 (1): 118–44.

Thorp, R. and Persson, A. (2020), 'On Historical Thinking and the History Educational Challenge', *Educational Philosophy and Theory*, 52 (8): 891–901.

Tyack, D. and Cuban, L. (1995), *Tinkering Toward Utopia: A Century of Public School Reform*, Cambridge, MA: Harvard University Press.

VanSledright, B. (2010), *The Challenge of Rethinking History Education*, New York: Routledge.

Veijola, A. (2013), *Pedagogisen ajattelun kehittyminen aineenopettajakoulutuksessa: Tutkimus suoravalituista historian opettajaopiskelijoista* [Development of Pedagogical Thinking in Subject Teachers' Education: The Study of Directly Selected History Teacher Students], Jyväskylä: University of Jyväskylä.

Veijola, A. and Mikkonen, S. (2016), 'Mitä historia on: aloittavien historianopiskelijoiden historiakäsitykset [What is History: Novice Students' Understandings of History]', *Kasvatus and Aika*, 10 (3): 6–21.

Weniger, E. (1957), 'Theorie und Praxis in der Erziehung [Theory and Practice in Education]', in E. Weniger (ed), *Die eigenständigkeit der erziehung in theorie und praxis* [The Independence of Education in Theory and Practice], 7–22, Weinheim: Beltz.

Whitty, G. and Furlong, J. (2017), *Knowledge and the Study of Education: An International Exploration*, Didcot, Oxford: Symposium Books.

Wineburg, S. (1991), 'Historical Problem Solving: A Study of the Cognitive Processes Used in the Evaluation of Documentary and Pictorial Evidence', *Journal of Educational Psychology*, 83 (1): 73–87.

Young, M. and Muller, J. (2010), 'Three Educational Scenarios for the Future: Lessons from the Sociology of Knowledge', *European Journal of Education*, 45 (1): 11–27.

Young, M. and Muller, J. (2014), 'On the Powers of Powerful Knowledge', in B. Barrett and E. Rata (eds), *Knowledge and the Future of the Curriculum: International Studies in Social Realism*, 41–64, New York: Palgrave Macmillan Limited.

4

Embedding Epistemic Quality in the Pedagogy of Student Geography Teachers

David Mitchell and Alex Standish

Introduction

This chapter focuses on research question 3 of the KOSS research network: How can the nature of teachers' powerful professional knowledge be characterized and what are the implications for teacher education policy and practice (although we also address the nature of powerful knowledge and epistemic quality in the subject of geography). Our specific aim here is to demonstrate how we embed theories of powerful knowledge and epistemic quality in our initial teacher education (ITE) curriculum and apply them to enhance novice geography teachers' professional knowledge and curriculum making. Our central argument is that the quality of the novice geography teacher's classroom practice (or curriculum enactment) cannot be separated from the depth of their theoretical and philosophical understanding of both geography (including an engagement with its epistemology) and education. Following the suggestion of Gericke et al. (2018), we illustrate this with examples from ITE secondary-level geography at the UCL Institute of Education.

We begin the chapter by explaining the need for deeper engagement with the subject discipline in teachers' curriculum planning and enactment by stimulating a culture of curriculum thinking in schools. We then draw on theories of powerful disciplinary knowledge (PDK) (Young 2008; Young and Muller 2010), epistemic quality (Hudson 2018) and teachers identifying as professional knowledge workers and curriculum makers, rather than as technically efficient content 'deliverers' (see Young and Lambert 2014; Mitchell and Lambert 2015; Mitchell 2020). These ideas support our reasoning that new teachers need to develop an understanding of *what* is PDK for teaching high-quality geography, *why* this is important and *how* they can use this understanding in practice. We propose that, by connecting practical aspects of initial teacher education (lesson and curriculum planning for instance) with philosophical and epistemological understanding, novice teachers can learn to plan curricula of good epistemic quality.

Why Do We Need Deeper Engagement with Curriculum Theory?

Teachers' thinking has tended to be drawn away from asking *what* to teach to asking *how* to teach effectively. Curriculum thinking has thus been displaced by a technical focus on teaching and an assumption that any learning is a good thing, in an uncritical 'learnification' of schooling (Biesta 2017). In some initial teacher education programmes, curriculum theory and epistemology have been underplayed in a trend towards 'training' in a more generic classroom technique. This relates to the weakness of curriculum making in schools (Deng 2018a; Mitchell and Lambert 2015). One way to explain this shift is the dialectical relationship of society and curriculum (see Huckle 1985; Hartley 1997) as we will briefly discuss in the context of changed times.

We are in the intensely competitive and consumerist world of late capitalism. Accountability has intensified, with schools and teachers increasingly driven by performance in examination results and inspection reports (Biesta 2010; Ward 2012; Pring 2013). Education is highly marketized and schools compete to grow and thrive. At the same time, young people are conceived by some people as consumers who demand to see the immediate relevance to their learning, or even to be entertained by their teachers, if they are to engage in lessons and be compliant (see Hartley 1997; Furedi 2009; Ecclestone and Hayes 2009; Morgan 2014 for different analyses of overemphasis on student opinion in curriculum planning). In this postmodern world, boundaries are weakened: between teacher and pupil; curriculum and pedagogy; disciplinary knowledge and the everyday (Standish 2012). Technology is changing everyone's relationship with information and how knowledge is constructed, to such an extent that Google and social media raises serious questions about the value and authority of teachers and curriculum, in the student's mind at least (Morgan 2014).

Teachers are under great pressure in such times and pulled in many directions. On one hand, they must achieve good exam results while, on the other, they try to design engaging, activity-based lessons. The cost of this tension is that careful, discipline-based curriculum thinking is replaced by 'late capitalism thinking' (Mitchell 2020: 172). To cope with the pressure, teachers must become ever more efficient in their use of time, often outsourcing curriculum thinking to Google, ready-made lessons and intense sharing sometimes uncritically within the department. This has been described as 'hyper-socialised' curriculum enactment (Mitchell 2016/2020).

Many geography teachers *do* want to engage with their subject in deep curriculum thinking and have succeeded. These teachers are resisting the pressures by navigating through late capitalism and hyper-socialization (Mitchell 2016/2020). They do so by not succumbing to 'deliverology' (Pring 2013) which is too often taken as a common-sense notion of teacher professionalism (see Mitchell and Lambert 2015) but turning to their professional knowledge identity as a *geography* teacher. Such engagement in deep and critical curriculum thinking cannot be taken for granted and is hard-won. The battle begins in the future geography teacher's own schooling and university study and continues in their initial teacher education, where theory is first applied to the classroom.

Powerful Knowledge and Epistemic Quality in the ITE Curriculum

In their early days of school practice, it is vital that beginning teachers have a conception of what a 'good geography' education for children looks like (Mitchell and Lambert 2015). From this foundation, theories of curriculum, pedagogy and assessment can be built, all embedding a notion of the 'epistemic quality' of geography (Standish, under review). Here, we outline our ITE curriculum framework that builds the student teacher's professional knowledge, competence and identity as a geography 'curriculum maker' (Young and Lambert 2014). We see the professional knowledge of the teacher as a type of practical wisdom, what the Ancient Greeks termed *phronesis*. The teacher has to develop good judgement with respect to planning, teaching and assessing learning, and they need to embody and model the academic values inherent to the profession. Hence, we believe in the *practical competence* and wisdom of teachers being connected to a theoretical body of knowledge about education and geography education specifically: the secondary geography ITE curriculum (Table 4.1).

This curriculum framework draws upon a tradition of geography education at the IOE that stretches back through the work of Norman Graves, Frances Slater, Michael Naish, David Balderstone and David Lambert. More recently, we have

Table 4.1 Secondary Geography Initial Teacher Education Curriculum, UCL IOE

Aims (Why?)	Curriculum (What and when?)	Teaching Methods (How?)	Pupils' Learning	Assessment
Philosophies of education; Exploring the purposes and meaning of education and schooling (citizenship, democracy, vocation, character); History of education and geography education; School as a professional community; Exploring the aims and value of geography	Sociological approaches to knowledge: e.g. constructivist, social realist and cultural restoration; Powerful disciplinary knowledge and epistemic quality in geography; Curriculum levels: national, school and classroom; Knowledge types: conceptual, contextual, procedural and moral; Curriculum making, subject didactics and pedagogical content knowledge; Professional associations and the curriculum; Curriculum design: selection and sequencing of knowledge and skills; Curriculum change over time; Progression and thinking geographically; Geographical skills, including maps and GIS; Literacy and numeracy in geography	Linking theory and practice; Teaching methods: enquiry, direct instruction, dialogic teaching, questioning, modelling and collaborative learning; Lesson planning; geography education resources, including textbooks; Fieldwork; Homework	Educational psychology; Childhood development; Learning theories and learning cycles; Adolescent behaviour/classroom management; Differentiated learning/SEN/EAL; Socio-economic background, cultural differences and learning; Research on learning geographical knowledge and skills	Assessment types and purposes: formative, summative, diagnostic and evaluative; Linking assessment to curriculum and progression in geography; Exploring what to assess in geography, when and why; Planning for assessment opportunities; Consequential validity: assessment outcomes and how to use them; Giving feedback to pupils; School assessment policies and practices; External assessment: GCSE and A Level

incorporated ideas from Biesta (2010/17), Derry (2020), Hudson (2016/18), Orchard and Winch (2012), Willingham (2009), Young and Muller (2010/16), as well as geographers such as Bennetts (2005), Jackson (2006), Roberts (2013) and Gardner et al. (2015).

This curriculum framework stretches across the professional teacher training course and should therefore not be viewed as a linear programme of teaching. While we initially start with aims and move on to curriculum, teaching methods, learning and assessment, as the course progresses we move back and forth to revisit each area. What matters for student teachers is learning to see the connections and to move between them. As we do so, student teachers are encouraged to study and make use of chapters from *Learning to Teach Geography in the Secondary School* (Biddulph, Lambert and Balderstone 2015). In the following sections we outline the initial stages of this journey, looking at educational aims and how we approach knowledge in curriculum making.

Educational Aims

In preparation for the course, student teachers are tasked to read some authors who take contrasting philosophical approaches to the meaning and purpose of education and then provide a written response addressing some of the ideas raised. Although by no means a definitive list, suggested authors include John Dewey, Michael Oakeshott, John White, Michael Reiss, Michael Young and Ken Robinson, giving a range of approaches while combining older and newer thinking. What is the purpose of education? What does it mean to be educated? These questions are an ideal place to start a course of teacher education since this is the primary purpose of schooling and student teachers need to understand the range of approaches and ways of answering these questions. They are also 'living philosophical questions', by which we mean that how they are answered changes over time and place, and is linked to societal, and individual, beliefs and values.

The students' written and verbal responses are drawn upon in seminars discussing the purpose of education. Here, students explore how and why schools pursue multiple objectives, and they learn to distinguish and to see connections between intrinsic aims (educational) and extrinsic aims, such as employment, preparation for citizenship, health and well-being and tolerance for other beliefs and value systems. At the end of the course, one student commented how she still dwells on this discussion and 'thinks about it all the time' (the purpose of education). This is how it should be since most of what a teacher does will relate to some broader notion of educational or social purpose.

Introducing Young's notion of powerful knowledge early in the course enables student teachers to gain some perspective on the subject they are teaching and how it is of value to the children. Young (2011) seeks to explain that which distinguishes schools as an institution in the modern era. He makes the case that 'the primary purpose of education is for students to gain access to different specialist fields of knowledge' (Young 2011: 149). In contrast to knowledge of the powerful (who controls the knowledge), Young sought a better understanding of the knowledge *itself*. Hence, he counterpoised that powerful knowledge 'refers to what the knowledge can do – for example, whether it provides reliable explanations or new ways of thinking about the world' (Young 2011: 150). In doing so, Young, drawing on Durkheim, differentiates between different knowledge types: between everyday and disciplinary knowledge, between different domains of knowledge, and between specialist disciplinary knowledge and the school curriculum. For Young (2011: 151), powerful knowledge is context-independent knowledge, meaning 'knowledge that is developed to provide generalizations and makes claims to universality; it provides a basis for making judgements'.

How pupils might use the transformative potential of PDK in their lives is an important area worthy of further research, but beyond the scope of this chapter. However, we do help novice teachers to explore how PDK is interpreted by different geography educators, such as Huckle (2017) and Morgan (2019) who emphasize critical thinking and see the power of disciplinary knowledge in revealing hidden structures which might lead to action, changing human–nature relationships, for example. We view the power of disciplinary knowledge as opening new ways of seeing, which help the novice teacher to explore different curriculum and educational philosophies and so develop their personal philosophy. We explore how geographic education contributes to free thinking and full participation in society, enhancing human 'capability' to open choices in life (see Lambert, Solem and Tani 2015; www.geocapabilities.org). We also refer to the work of Leesa Wheelahan, who explains how access to the generative concepts and objectivity taught through PDK enable young people to 'transcend the particular context' in which they live (Wheelahan 2010: 107), and thereby contribute to the functioning of liberal democracy and national economy as educated citizens (Rata 2012).

Curriculum Planning and Epistemology

A strong theoretical understanding of curriculum and epistemology allows students to recognize and plan for epistemic quality, therefore taking responsibility for making the curriculum. As we explore herein, epistemic quality means drawing the pupil into disciplined and systematized ways of thinking, reflecting educational aims of enquiry into how the world is organized, the nature of geographical knowledge and thinking geographically.

The conversation about curriculum proceeds from the discussion about educational purpose. As Young notes, questions about what schools should teach are 'philosophical and political questions about who we are and what we value' (Young 2008: xvi). Curriculum is a course of study for achieving educational and social purposes, and hence must be considered in relation to these. As Erich Weniger surmises, 'it is probable that school subject and discipline must first conjoin in relation to a third entity that instils meaning into both the purpose of the discipline and the goals of instruction' (Weniger 2000: 116). Weniger's 'third entity' is what we commonly refer to as *school subjects*, which provide an introduction to disciplinary and cultural knowledge, but *re-contextualized* in an institution with a particular mission (Bernstein 2000). While PDK tells us about the specialized nature of disciplinary knowledge, school subjects will be pulled in different directions according to societal aims for education as well as the mission of the school and its cultural context (national, regional and local). For instance, Marsden (1997) noted how geography as a school subject has historically been influenced by a combination of 'good causes', pedagogy and subject content, which lead to different emphases in the curriculum. While early in the twentieth-century nationalism and empire framed the geography curriculum, towards the end of the century environmentalism and development had become significant frames of reference. Marsden stresses the importance of maintaining a balance between subject, pedagogy and social causes such that the curriculum does not to drift into indoctrination, undermining its epistemic quality. One way to accomplish this is to keep PDK at the centre of curriculum thinking, such that social causes and questions of values are explored within a disciplined, academic frame of reference.

Next, we need to say more about what it means to introduce a pupil to PDK in the school context. Each discipline explores an aspect of truth about the world and our humanity, which can be scientific, moral or aesthetic (Standish and Sehgal Cuthbert 2017). In doing so, each discipline has, over generations, established systems of thought comprising networks of specialist concepts, ways of thinking and methods of enquiry. Drawing on the work of Lev Vygotsky, Jan Derry (2020) calls this 'systematicity'. Hence, learning a subject means gaining access to a system of concepts (or schemata):

> Only within a system can the concept acquire conscious awareness and a voluntary nature. Conscious awareness and the presence of a system are synonymous when we are speaking of concepts, just as spontaneity, lack of conscious awareness, and the absence of system are three different words for designating the nature of the child's concept. (Vygotsky, cited in Derry 2020: 10)

In essence, teachers seek to enable children to develop more sophisticated, objective and scientific schemata. This does not equate to knowledge transfer; far from it. Children must use the conceptual tools and methods provided by the subject to interpret and interact with the world as they see fit. Jennifer Nagel (2014: 8) proposes that 'Knowledge links a subject to a truth.' The knowledge provides a means of comprehending some aspect of the real world, and enhances the individuals' agency or capabilities for interacting. Derry (2020) suggests that 'systematicity' relates to what is distinctive about human engagement because the concepts (matter) enable the pupil to 'constitute meaning', which in turn may govern their interactions with the world (see Figure 4.2). The pedagogical implications are that education involves bringing pupils into different systems of knowledge, which means understanding and utilizing the concepts, theories, norms and ways of thinking that constitute each of them. A novice teacher will need to have a thorough understanding of this systematicity and the ways of thinking that are particular to the subject and will need to develop ways of packing subject knowledge for learning (Pedagogical Content Knowledge – see Deng 2018b).

In order to achieve epistemic quality in pupils' learning, curriculum making must bring the three elements introduced above (teacher, pupil and subject knowledge) into a relationship with each other. This approach is captured by the Curriculum Making Model (Geographical Association 2020) – see Figure 4.1. The model visually illustrates how these three elements must combine and be kept 'in balance' by the teacher in their planning. However, it does not explain the nature of the relationships between them, nor does it provide guidance on how to combine them.

Recently, we have been drawing on the European continental tradition of subject didactics (linked to *Bildung*), which 'places the teacher at the heart of the teaching-studying-learning process' (Hudson 2016: 9), the outcome of which is pupils' engagement with the subject knowledge (see Figure 4.2). As Hudson (2018) proposes in the context of mathematics instruction, epistemic quality depends on having a dynamic and fallible view of knowledge and sees learning as the construction of meaning in the classroom. Thus, while the quality of

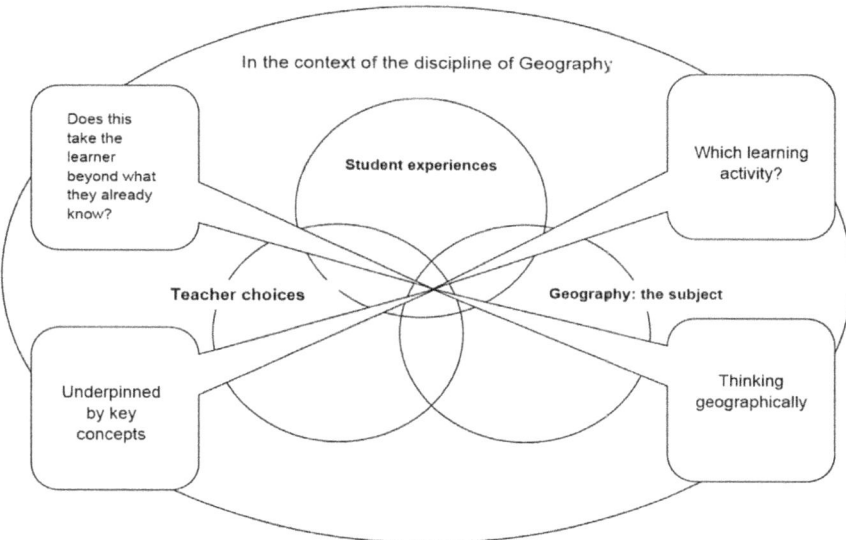

Figure 4.1 Curriculum making model (Geographical Association 2020).

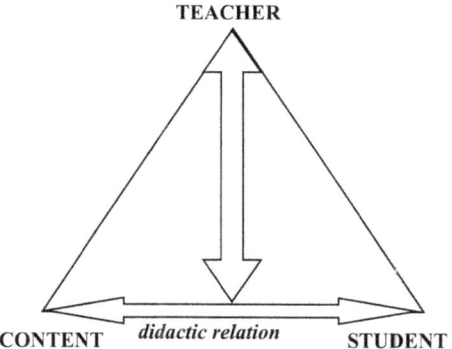

Figure 4.2 The didactic triangle (Hudson 2022, this volume).

the knowledge itself is important (in disciplinary terms), so too is the didactic approach in which the teacher seeks to nurture habits of enquiry and criticality in their students.

While the teacher brings their specialist disciplinary knowledge into the classroom, they must recontextualize this knowledge and break it down such that the pupil is able to comprehend it and work towards an epistemic ascent (Winch 2013). They do this by helping the pupil to move between matter (subject content) and meaning: 'The task of an educational system . . . is to ensure movement from everyday meanings to abstract and general concepts and then back again' (Hugo 2014: 2). Teachers will often refer to this as 'scaffolding' or 'relating to the pupils' experience'. This is because 'We understand new things in the context of things we already know' (Willingham 2009: 210), which many teachers instinctively learn through their practice.

Geography's Epistemology

What is geography as PDK? What is its 'system of meaning' and way of thinking and what do these look like in a school curriculum? These questions are key aspects of our curriculum framework (Table 4.1).

It is a significant challenge to encompass the vast array of intellectual thinking and research that takes place under the heading of geography. Part of geography's difficulty is that it straddles and unites the social and physical sciences and hence by its very nature gets pulled in different methodological and epistemological directions. Some of these originate from wider social theory rather than the discipline itself, such as structuration theory, post-structuralism, postcolonialism and feminism, and have led to questioning of universal and context-independent knowledge itself (Wheelahan 2010). Geography is also sometimes viewed as a humanities subject because geographers explore questions about how people live in and interact with their environment. At school and university, geography therefore introduces children to moral questions about welfare, spatial justice, quality of life, progress and the sustainability of economic and social systems.

Nevertheless, student teachers need to be able to communicate to pupils a coherent account of geography as PDK, although we recognize that students will do this differently depending upon where they sit within the discipline. It can be helpful to conceptualize PDK as a 'living tradition' (Livingstone 1992). By this, we mean that it provides an intellectual framework for understanding patterns and change on the Earth's surface at a given point in time. The questions we ask and seek answers to vary by generation, culture and location, and thus we would expect the nature of geography to change over time (see Hartshorne 1939; Peet 1998; Holt-Jensen 2009; Creswell 2013).

Geography's core concepts or ideas that frame our thinking include: space, place, region, scale, landscape, change, systems, human–environment interactions. Hanson (2004) suggests that the *geographic advantage* confers understanding of: relationships between people and the environment; the importance of spatial variability (the place-dependence of processes); processes operating at multiple and interlocking geographic scales; and the integration of spatial and temporal analysis. This view captures aspects of the geographer's perspective including spatial variability, bringing together the human with the environment, the integration and connectivity of phenomena, scales and processes (including time and space).

Geography is divided into a series of sub-disciplines such as geomorphology, climatology, biogeography, cultural geography, urban geography and political geography. Moreover, within sub-disciplines there is further specialism into glaciologists, hydrologists, political ecologists and so on. In each, the purpose is to develop abstract, *propositional knowledge* or a system of concepts, models, theories and principles that helps to explain one aspect or layer of the Earth's surface. The geographer's perspective is to synthesize knowledge between Earth's different layers in order to comprehend spatial patterns and differences. In essence, geography is a holistic or integrative pursuit and thus its overarching knowledge structure is horizontal (Matthews and Herbert 2008; Holt-Jensen 2009). This means that abstract, propositional knowledge must correspond to and seek to explain real-world objects, events and behaviour. The latter we can call *contextual knowledge* – which is concrete, factual and particular to a given location or distribution (Young and Muller 2016). As with most sciences, there is an integral relationship between the general, abstract theories and the particular, concrete patterns the theories are seeking to make sense of.

Procedural knowledge is a third category of knowledge referring to the procedures, skills and methods of enquiry that are unique to the particular discipline (Clifford et al. 2013). It is these that scientists use to guide their testing and refinement of hypotheses in the field. In geography, this can mean applying established quantitative and qualitative scientific methods and learning to conduct enquiries into geographical phenomena. Such methods are different for the physical geographer and the human geographer and the geography student must therefore be inducted into both. These include mapping, measurement, surveys, document analysis, field sketching, Geographical Information Systems, applying critical approaches like analysing and clarifying values positions and perspectives – on place-making processes, for instance.

Phil Gersmehl (2014) describes how geographers usually work in one of two (complementary) ways: *topically* or *thematically* – 'the study of patterns at a broad scale' usually focused on one geographical layer or sub-discipline at a time (e.g. climate, economy, culture), or regionally 'the study of many things in one area' (Gersmehl 2014: 28) (see Figure 4.3). With topical or thematic geography (also referred to as systematic geography), the aim is to understand the distribution

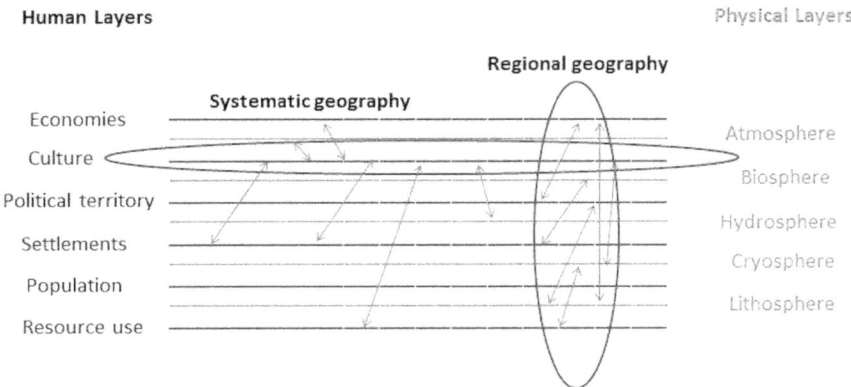

Figure 4.3 A visual representation of systematic and regional geography (Standish 2018).

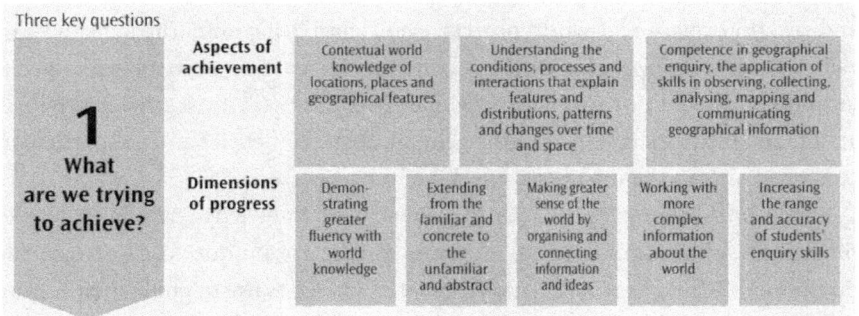

Figure 4.4 Planning for student progress – step 1 (QCA, cited in Gardner et al. 2015).

of one phenomenon or process and how this is pattern is influenced by other factors.

Despite growing specialization and fragmentation at university level, some common language and epistemological frameworks are evolving for geography as a school subject. The Geography National Curriculum distinguishes between locational knowledge, place knowledge, human and physical geography and skills. In addition, the Geographical Association has adopted terminology similar to the knowledge types introduced above for its curriculum and assessment framework (Figure 4.4) – (Gardner et al. 2015). Some of the key publications that have helped in this regard are Bennetts (2005) on the links between understanding, progression and assessment (as well as aims for geography education) and Jackson's 'Thinking Geographically' (2006).

Epistemic quality derives from curricula that develop knowledge and ways of thinking that are specific to the discipline, and pitched at the appropriate level for the pupils. The geography teacher must create opportunities for pupils to apply concepts and theories to real-world case studies; to draw comparisons between places and regions; to move between different scales to explore patterns and relationships; for synthesizing knowledge in order to identify inter-relationships; to appreciate diverse landscapes and peoples; and, to explore the challenges people face in particular environments (Standish, under review).

How Do Powerful Knowledge and Epistemic Quality Inform Curriculum Planning?

Curriculum planning is always a highly practical activity. It occurs at a range of scales, from whole stages of a child's education spanning years to short sequences of five or six lessons. Being highly practical combined with the pressures we described earlier can distract the teacher's focus. However, curriculum planning can be theoretically informed if the teacher has the necessary set of conceptual resources, as outlined in our curriculum framework. Acquiring these resources can help to embed epistemic quality in teachers' planning, in turn reproducing quality in the geography curriculum enacted in the classroom. Courses of teacher preparation are key to allowing teachers to develop the conceptual resources they need (Orchard and Winch 2012). In this section, we give an example of how curriculum theory was utilized by one student teacher in her curriculum planning.

Our example is a key course assignment to plan, teach and evaluate a sequence of lessons. This is the essence of the subject teacher's work and outwardly straightforward. Yet we require a careful and robust rationale for why and how the geography is to be taught, and then a critical analysis of the outcomes of that planning for classroom teaching and learning. The novice teacher must engage deeply with the discipline of geography and conceptions of education to show they are curriculum makers (not just delivers). Both the rationale and analysis reveal the extent to which student teachers have developed the conceptual tools they need to embed epistemic quality in their practice.

The first part of the module is taught in the university; then student teachers begin teaching practice in schools and apply their theory in practical planning and curriculum making. As discussed earlier, students learn about and reflect on their own perspective toward: philosophies of education; the discipline of geography and school geography, including the notion of 'thinking geographically' (see Jackson 2006; Creswell 2013); curriculum theory, including powerful knowledge and subject didactics; pedagogy and assessment. Student teachers learn that to be a fully 'professional' geography teacher they must recognize and take on a role and responsibility for geography curriculum leadership. The notion of curriculum planning (Graves 1979), is supplemented by the notion of 'curriculum making' (GA 2020) and subject didactics (Klafki 2000) to help the student teachers pay attention to how geography, the pupil and the teacher connect. Following the notion of the 'didactic relation' between the pupil and the subject (Klafki 2000) student teachers are encouraged to see their role as facilitating this relationship, through how they choose to select and present geography for the pupil and design ways to help the pupil develop the concepts, contexts and procedures of geography.

The essence of what we are trying to achieve in this module is critical and careful attention to geography as an educational resource by the student teachers. This develops their ability to:

understand different philosophies and traditions of education and explain their own vision for education in relation to these;

see 'the curriculum' is not just something 'delivered' – grasp their role as 'curriculum maker';

describe 'geographical knowledge' accurately in terms of conceptual, contextual and procedural knowledge and what it means to 'think geographically';

apply the discipline of geography, giving children access to 'powerful knowledge' (new ways of thinking);

plan learning and assessment activities with purpose (for progression in 'high quality' geographical knowledge);

evaluate geographical learning, to reflect and improve the quality of their curriculum planning and teaching.

(UCL IOE Student Teacher Module Guidance 2019)

The student teachers first produce a theorized rationale for what geography they will teach, why and how. They then design their sequence, often using a concept map to illustrate their thought process behind the content and linkages, a summary table to show the planned sequence and sometimes a shorter table to indicate how a particular geographical concept was being taught within the wider topic. The following example from a student's assignment work illustrates how the module develops teacher knowledge and application to curriculum planning and enactment.

Student teacher A planned, taught and evaluated a sequence of lessons about population issues, with an explicit aim of increasing pupils' critical consciousness. We suggest that this student's work demonstrates that they have developed conceptions of PDK and pedagogical content knowledge (PCK). Teacher A is aware and open about their personal philosophy of education – as education for societal change and social justice. As discussed earlier in this chapter, this is a justifiable approach to education. It is important that novice teachers consider their underpinning aims and purposes for education and recognize that other educational philosophies shape how a geography curriculum is 'made' by the teacher. Importantly for our argument in this chapter, student teacher A keeps returning to geography's disciplinary concepts and content (an epistemologically robust geographical content), even though she is also concerned with how she designs learning activities with critical consciousness and social justice in mind. The excerpts offer some evidence of this.

Student teacher A sees geography as having a distinctive epistemological structure (its conceptual structure), which contributes to (or is perhaps even essential to) a broader educational aim of equipping children to explore significant controversial and value-laden issues in wider society:

> The teaching of geography holds a unique opportunity for examining controversial issues, which are inherently geographical in their nature. Specifically, studying population on a range of scales allows for the exploration of controversial issues such as migration, urbanisation and overpopulation...
>
> ...developing critical consciousness is intrinsically linked to one's interpretations of the world and the values which form them (Roberts 2013; Biddulph et al. 2015).
>
> (Student teacher A assignment excerpt 2019)

Student teacher A applies a concept of 'powerful knowledge' and thinks about whose knowledge is represented, drawing on Freirean perspectives. She balances her attention to geography, the learner's needs and the teaching approach:

> Different pedagogies can be explored in empowering children in this way. 'Powerful knowledge', that which cannot be acquired through everyday experiences, has the ability to provide new ways of thinking about the world and provide reliable explanations (Young 2011). Young (2011) classifies it as 'specialist' knowledge and as such it must be taught by specialist teachers in an educational context. The acquisition of powerful knowledge could be particularly

empowering for those with little or no social capital at home . . . However, it is important to consider what constitutes 'powerful knowledge' and who decides what knowledge is important (Young 2011). If children take on a passive role in receiving knowledge through transmission, they risk simply 'adapting to the world as the fragmented view of reality deposited on them' (Freire 1970: 73).

(Student teacher A assignment excerpt 2019)

Student teacher A is forthright in embracing education for change and adopts a critical enquiry strategy. But she keeps returning to the centrality of the distinctive nature of the discipline of geography in the content of her teaching:

Using critical enquiry to awaken pupils to the fact that CO2 emissions are in fact linked to wealth and consumption patterns (UN 2015) and not population size is important in challenging rhetoric that chastises poorer countries and protects environmentally damaging systems of the wealthy. . .

. . . (Pupils develop) locational, procedural and contextual knowledge on a range of scales. Studying a range of case studies can help pupils gradually develop a more complex understanding of the concept of 'place' and aids their ability to think geographically (Biddulph et al. 2015).

Student teacher A plans learning and assessment activities purposefully, for progression, showing how her concept map supports her thinking about linkages. She has an appreciation of geographical concept development, while paying attention to significant, real-world contexts. She discusses and justifies the content of her sequence as geography knowledge. Importantly, her explanations of her planning and teaching show that she fits geographical content into networks of specialist concepts. There is a coherence to these networks relating to geography's (disciplinary) structure. Her concept map of planning a topic of population (Figure 4.4) is illustrative here, particularly when examined in light of her written explanations. She connects the key concepts of place and space to more fine-grained concepts such as 'urban sprawl', 'migration' and 'climate change' by using the notion of 'second-order concepts' in geography (Taylor 2009). These include 'change' and 'interaction' as significant for curriculum planning because they add a layer to the distinctive system of thought in the discipline of geography. By making these connections, student teacher A justifies her attention to changing urban landscapes, environments and sustainability. Figure 4.4 shows these flowing from key and second-order concepts of geography. Student teacher A thus illustrates the 'systematicity' in her thinking to which Derry (2020) refers. Therefore, in her planning, this novice teacher seeks to give children access to a more sophisticated and objective schemata of thinking about population and migration issues (refugee crises for example) which they will come across in everyday life in politically charged debates with real-world consequences. This is the epistemic quality of geography to which we refer, and why equipping novice teachers to plan lessons of high epistemic quality is important.

> Population studies develop geographical understanding as a result of the interconnectedness of a range of geographical concepts and topics (Figure 4.5). The breadth of topics that can be explored when studying population provides an opportunity to explore a range of scales . . . global population growth in lesson 9; regional migration in lesson 6; and local population growth in lessons 8 and 10.
>
> In addition to breadth, it is important to develop conceptual understandings, which enables students to go beyond their personal geographies by giving them access to different ways of seeing and interpreting the world (Roberts 2013). Carrying out independent research on refugees in Lesson 6, for example, develops conceptual understanding through a focus on . . . (core) locational knowledge of the place they are moving from, contextual knowledge (i.e. looking at the Mediterranean refugee crisis), abstract concepts (i.e. push and pull factors) and other concepts (i.e. migration itself or conflict). Furthermore, the sequence uses a range of case studies . . . to gradually develop a more complex understanding of the concept of 'place' (Biddulph et al. 2015). Second-order concepts are also embedded in the sequence, for example change (of urban landscapes) and interaction (between humans and physical landscapes), two second-order concepts identified by Taylor (2009).
>
> (Student teacher A SS1 assignment excerpt 2019)

This teacher includes a short table (Figure 4.5) in her assignment to show her planning for developing a concept of migration. She plans for pupils to understand migration as human movements interconnected with urbanization, natural environments and economic pressures. She also attends to different representations of migration, handling the construction of geographical knowledge of migration with care. She thus shows consideration of both the discipline and the child's experiences (their misconceptions or stereotypes) here.

Student teacher A relates progression to generic conceptions of cognition hierarchies, referencing Bloom (1956). But this does not dominate attention to progression in geographical conceptual depth and complexity:

learning objectives for each lesson firstly required pupils to 'understand' or 'describe' a concept, and secondly to 'evaluate' or 'argue', which requires pupils to apply newly acquired knowledge to issues with increasing complexity (Bennetts 2005).

(Student teacher A SS1 assignment excerpt 2019)

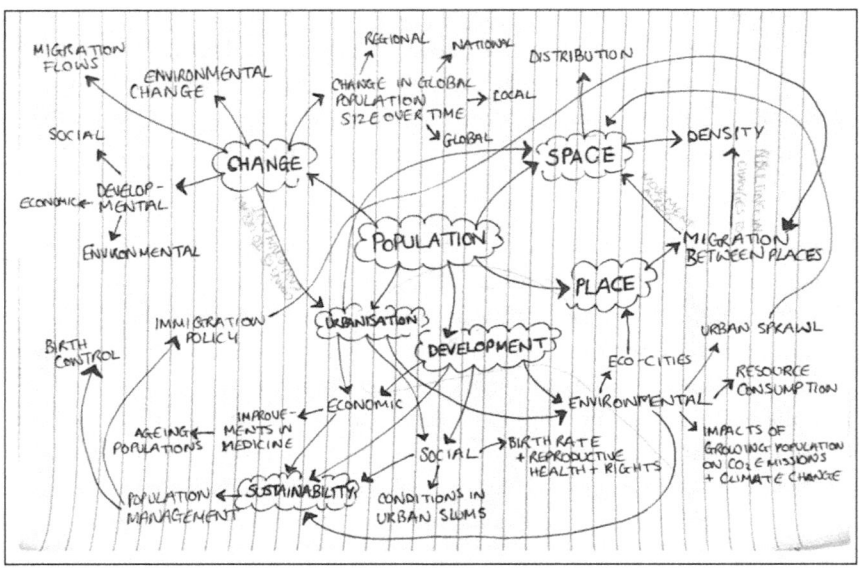

Figure 4.5 Concept map of population.

Lesson no.	Progression of 'migration' concept
5	Defining migration; identifying and explaining challenges and barriers to migration
6	Identifying and analysing representations of migration; evaluation of migration as experienced by refugees
7	Classification of 'push' and 'pull' factors leading to migration; analysis of the impacts of migration on urbanisation
8	Analysis of the environmental, economic and social impacts of urbanisation as a result of migration and population change
10	Analysis of the impacts of urbanisation on environmental protection

Figure 4.6 Student teacher A: Planning the progression of the concept 'migration'.

In summary, through the course and the assignment, student teacher A balanced her attention to the child (significance for them), the teaching approach and geography, thereby reflecting subject didactics theory (Klafki 2000). She also engaged with both geography's epistemology and a conception of education, without losing sight of either which, we suggest, goes some way to addressing the call made by Gericke et al. (2018).

Conclusion

In this chapter, we argued that novice teachers can develop a deep understanding of 'quality' in their subject teaching that connects right across from aims and planning to the assessment and evaluation of teaching. We offered a way to approach this as teacher educators – judging epistemic quality comes from combining a robust educational philosophy with epistemological principles, derived from the disciplinary thought and tradition.

In particular, we addressed the front end of course structure (aims and curriculum) as there is a logical chain of reasoning from aims through to the evaluation of teaching, although reflective thinking can start at any pedagogical stage and work along the continuum. For pupils to be inducted into PDK and have access to epistemic quality, effective teaching is necessary. Hence, we do not intend to diminish the significance of teaching, learning and assessment, which proceed from educational aims and curriculum making; but for the purposes of this chapter they were beyond our scope. As Gericke et al. (2018) suggest, there is a pressing need for further empirical work that follows subject-specific PDK and epistemic quality from curriculum planning into classroom teaching and pupils' work as evidence. While we illustrated PDK and epistemic quality in the curriculum making of a novice teacher, the success of any curriculum plan depends on the degree to which it achieves epistemic thinking for the pupils, and thus the assessment of learning is necessary for a fuller evaluation of curriculum planning. The visual models (didactic triangle and Curriculum Making model) help the novice teachers to hold these threads together right through from selecting what to teach to assessing learning and evaluating their teaching.

A strong notion of subject discipline and education as potentially transformative and how this can be applied in practical planning, teaching, assessment and evaluation is the way that powerful professional knowledge (PPK) can be characterized. Here, we have shown one way of acquiring this knowledge during a teacher preparation course. Novice teachers can then take this knowledge into schools, helping to rebalance school teaching cultures away from narrow performativity agendas towards purposeful curriculum thinking. There is scope for further research into the nature of PPK. In addition to research which follows PDK into the classroom, we suggest also asking: how does the PPK held by novice teachers' change as they become more experienced?

References

Bennetts, T. (2005), 'The Links between Understanding, Progression and Assessment in the Secondary Geography Curriculum', *Geography*, 90 (2): 152–70.

Bernstein, B. (2000), *Pedagogy, Symbolic Control and Identity: Theory, Research, Critique* (revised edn), Oxford: Rowman and Littlefield.

Biddulph, M., Lambert, D. and Balderstone, D. (2015), *Learning to Teach Geography in the Secondary School* (3rd edn), Abingdon: Routledge.

Biesta, G. (2010), *Good Education in an Age of Measurement*, Abingdon: Routledge.

Biesta, G. (2017), *The Rediscovery of Teaching*, Abingdon: Routledge.

Bloom, B. S., Engelhart, M. D., Furst, E. J., Hill, W. H. and Krathwohl, D. R. (1956), *Taxonomy of Educational Objectives: The Classification of Educational Goals: Handbook I: Cognitive Domain*, New York: David McKay Company.

Clifford, N., Cope, M., Gillespie, T. and French, S. (2013), *Key Methods in Geography* (3rd edn), London: Sage Publications.

Cresswell, T. (2013), *Geographic Thought: A Critical Introduction*, Chichester, West Sussex: Wiley-Blackwell.

Deng, Z. (2018a), 'Rethinking Teaching and Teachers: Bringing Content Back into Conversation', *London Review of Education*, 16 (3): 371–83.

Deng, Z. (2018b), 'Pedagogical Content Knowledge Reconceived: Bringing Curriculum Thinking into the Conversation on Teachers' Content Knowledge', *Teaching and Teacher Education*, 72: 155–64.

Derry, J. (2020), 'A Problem for Cognitive Load Theory – the Distictively Human Lifeform', *Journal of Philosophy of Education*, 54 (1): 5–22.

Ecclestone, K. and Hayes, D. (2009), *The Dangerous Rise of Therapeutic Education*, Abingdon: Routledge.

Freire, P. (1970), *Pedagogy of the Oppressed*, New York: Continuum.

Furedi, F. (2009), *Wasted: Why Education Isn't Educating*, London: Continuum Press.

Gardner, D., Weeden, P. and Butt, G. (eds) (2015), *Assessing Progress in Your Key Stage 3 Geography Curriculum*, Sheffield: Geographical Association.

Geographical Association (2020), 'Curriculum Making', https://www.geography.org.uk/Curriculum-Making-Explained last accessed 17 September 2020.

Gericke, N., Hudson, B., Olin-Scheller, C. and Stolare, M. (2018), 'Powerful Knowledge, Transformations and the Need for Empirical Studies across School Subjects', *London Review of Education*, 16 (3): 428–44. DOI: 10.18546/LRE.16.3.06

Gersmehl, P. (2014), *Teaching Geography* (3rd edn), New York: Guildford.

Graves, N. (1979), *Curriculum Planning in Geography*, London: Heinemann Educational.

Hanson, S. (2004), 'Who Are 'We'? An Important Question for Geography's Future', *Annals of the Association of American Geographers*, 94 (4): 715–22.

Hartley, D. (1997), *Re-Schooling Society*, London: Falmer.

Hartshorne, R. (1939), *The Nature of Geography: A Critical Survey of Current Thought in Light of the Past*, Lancaster, PA: Association of American Geographers.

Holt-Jensen, A. (2009), *Geography: History and Concepts – A Student's Guide* (4th edn), London: Sage.

Huckle, J. (1985), 'The Future of School Geography', in R. Johnston (ed.), *The Future of Geography*, London: Methuen.

Huckle, J. (2017), 'Powerful Geographical Knowledge is Critical Knowledge Underpinned by Critical Realism', *International Research in Geography and Environmental Education*, 28 (1): 70–84.

Hudson, B. (2016), 'Didactics', in D. Wyse, L. Hayward and J. Pandya (eds), *The SAGE Handbook of Curriculum, Pedagogy and Assessment: Two Volume Set*, 107–24, Los Angeles: Sage Publications.

Hudson, B. (2018), 'Powerful Knowledge and Epistemic Quality in School Mathematics', *London Review of Education*, 16 (3): 384–97.

Hugo, W. (2014), 'Semantic Density and Semantic Gravity' (editorial), *Journal of Education*, 59: 1–14.

Jackson, P. (2006), 'Thinking Geographically', *Geography*, 91 (3): 199–204.

Klafki, W. (2000), 'Didaktik Analysis as the Core of Preparation of Instruction', in Ian Westbury, Stefan Hopmann and Kurt Riquarts (eds), *Teaching as a Reflective Practice: The German Didaktik Tradition*, 139–59, Mahwah, NJ: Lawrence Erlbaum Associates Inc. Publishers.

Lambert, D. Solem, M. and Tani, S. (2015), 'Achieving Human Potential Through Geography Education: A Capabilities Approach to Curriculum-making in Schools', *Annals of the Association of American Geographers*, 105 (4): 723–35.

Livingstone, D. (1992), *The Geographical Tradition*, Oxford: Blackwell.

Marsden, W. (1997), 'On Taking the Geography out of Geographical Education – Some Historical Pointers in Geography', *Geography*, 82 (3): 241–52.

Matthews, J. and Herbert, D. (2008), *Geography: A Very Short Introduction*, Oxford: Oxford University Press.

Mitchell, D. (2016), 'Geography Teachers and Curriculum Making in Changing Times', *International Research in Geographical and Environmental Education*, 25: 121–33.

Mitchell, D. (2020), *Hyper-Socialised – Enacting the Geography Curriculum in Late Capitalism*, Abingdon: Routledge.

Mitchell, D. and Lambert, D. (2015), 'Subject Knowledge and Teacher Preparation in English Secondary Schools: The Case of Geography', *Teacher Development: An International Journal of Teachers' Professional Development*, 19 (3): 365–80.

Morgan, J. (2014), '21st Century Learning – Again', *Schooling Capitalism Wordpress Blog*, https://schoolingcapitalism.wordpress.com/2014/03/25/21st-century-learning-again/ last accessed 24 March 2016.

Morgan, J. (2019), *Culture and the Political Economy of Schooling: What's Left for Education?* Abingdon: Routledge.

Nagel, J. (2014), *Knowledge: A Very Short Introduction*, Oxford: Oxford University Press.

Orchard, J. and Winch, C. (2012), 'What Training Do Teachers Need? Why Theory is Necessary to Good Teaching', *IMPACT 22 Philosophical Perspectives on Education Policy*, Philosophy of Education Society of Great Britain: Wiley-Blackwell.

Peet, R. (1998), *Modern Geographical Thought*, Malden, MA: Wiley-Blackwell.

Pring, R. (2013), *The Life and Death of Secondary Education for All*, Abingdon: Routledge.

Rata, E. (2012), *The Politics of Knowledge in Education*, New York, Oxon: Routledge.

Roberts, M. (2013), *Geography Through Enquiry: Approaches to Teaching and Learning in the Secondary School*, Sheffield: Geographical Association.

Standish, A. (2012), *The False Promise of Global Learning*, London: Continuum.

Standish, A. (2018), 'The Place of Regional Geography', in M. Jones and D. Lambert (eds), *Debates in Geography Education*, 2nd edn, 65–74, London: Routledge.

Standish, A. (under review), 'Embedding Epistemic Quality in Trainees' Geography Curriculum Planning', *Teaching and Teacher Education* (submitted September 2020).

Standish, A. and Sehgal Cuthbert, A. (eds) (2017), *What Should Schools Teach? Disciplines, Subjects and the Pursuit of Truth?* London: UCL Institute of Education Press.

Taylor, E. (2009), 'Concepts in Geography', *GTIP Think Piece*, Geographical Association. https://www.geography.org.uk/write/mediauploads/research%20library/ga_tp_s_concepts.pdf last accessed 14 October 2020.

UCL IOE (2019), 'Student Teacher Module Guidance – Subject Studies 1', *Secondary Geography PGCE Course Handbook 2019*.

UN (2015), United Nations Sustainable Development Summit, New York, 25-27 September 2015.

Ward, S. (2012), *Neoliberalism and the Global Restructuring of Knowledge and Education*, New York: Routledge.

Weniger, E. (2000), 'Didaktik as a Theory of Education', in I. Westbury, S. Hopman and K. Riquarts (eds), *Teaching as a Reflective Practice: The German Didaktik Tradition*, London: Lawrence Erlbaum.

Wheelahan, L. (2010), *Why Knowledge Matters in Curriculum: A Social Realist Argument*, London: Routledge.

Willingham, D. (2009), *Why Don't Students Like School? A Cognitive Scientist Answers Questions and How the Mind Works and What It Means for the Classroom*, San Francisco: Jossey Bass.

Winch, C. (2013), 'Curriculum Design and Epistemic Ascent', *Journal of Philosophy of Education*, 47 (1): 128–46.

Young, M. (2008), *Bringing Knowledge Back In: From Social Constructivism to Social Realism in the Sociology of Education*, London: Routledge.

Young, M. (2011), 'What are Schools For?', *Educação, Sociedade and Cultures*, 32: 145–55. www.fpce.up.pt/ciie/revistaesc/ESC32/ESC32_Arquivo.pdf

Young, M. and Lambert, D. (2014), *Knowledge and the Future School: Curriculum and Social Justice*, London: Bloomsbury.

Young, M. and Muller, J. (2010), 'Three Educational Scenarios for the Future: Lessons from the Sociology of Knowledge', *European Journal of Education*, 45 (1): 11–26.

Young, M. and Muller, J. (2016), *Curriculum and the Specialization of Knowledge: Studies in the Sociology of Education*, London: Routledge.

5

Epistemic Literacy as an Aim for Religious Education and Implications for Teacher Education

Alexis Stones and Jo Fraser-Pearce

Introduction

Drawing on notions of powerful knowledge (Young and Muller 2010; Young 2014), German and Nordic traditions of *Bildung*-informed *didaktik* and Klafki's (1995) *categorial Bildung*, we present the case for epistemic literacy as a conceptual framework for teachers and students to develop a more nuanced understanding of the nature of knowledge than epistemology provides. Epistemic literacy describes the ability to use this knowledge to understand one's personal epistemology and communicate critically through appropriate disciplines. It also provides an approach to cultivate capabilities that extend beyond school.

We define epistemic literacy as the ability to appreciate and recognize the distinct forms, frameworks and systems of knowledge, method, language and data that pertain to particular disciplines and personal experience. If students and teachers are to avoid epistemological misconceptions and develop insights into the specific knowledge forms presented in Religious Education (RE) in England's secondary school curriculum, we argue that they should be given opportunities to develop epistemic literacy to help navigate the challenging and epistemologically complex questions that exist in the interfaces between subject disciplines. In this chapter, we pay particular attention to the RE curriculum area of religion and science as this is where the need for epistemic literacy manifests in sharp relief due to the ontological, epistemological and affective nature of the issues and questions raised. This conceptual framework is proposed as a tool for transformation from RE's parent disciplines of the academy to the school subject, as well as a principle or aim that one might develop through the subject.

The genesis of epistemic literacy is the result of an empirical study, while its rationale is theoretical. This chapter attempts to reconcile both of these aspects of the concept and explore the implications for teacher education. We consider epistemic literacy to be an aspect of powerful professional knowledge (Furlong and Whitty 2017) that is crucial for decision-making inside and outside the RE classroom. In doing so, we aim in particular to address KOSS research question 3, which focuses on how the nature of teachers' powerful professional knowledge should be characterized and the implications this holds for teacher education policy and practice. We argue that teacher education policy and practice need to recognize the significance of teachers' and students' subjective relationships to different types of knowledge in order to support the development of epistemic literacy.

The chapter begins with an overview of RE in England to familiarize the reader with the subject in question. We then introduce complementary notions of powerful knowledge and *Bildung*-informed *didaktik* to frame the relationships between everyday and expert knowledge in relation to school subject, student and teacher. The RE curriculum area of 'Big Questions' in religion and science is a case study to identify the need for a nuanced approach to knowledge that contextualizes a need for epistemic literacy. A discussion of the concept of epistemic literacy ensues before it is considered as a tool for transformation, an aim for the subject and, finally, a principle for teacher education.

Overview of Religious Education (RE) in England

History

The RE curriculum in England before the public examination stage is difficult to describe in universal terms as the subject holds a unique legal status that privileges some schools with the choice of curriculum content and design. This is not the case with schools of a religious character and while, for the purposes of this chapter, we are concerned with the 'common' school, our discussion applies to all schools.

RE's origins lie in the Sunday School Movement of the 1870s that taught Religious Instruction (RI) as a social and spiritual project to educate working children in literacy, numeracy and Christianity, as part of an effort to reduce delinquency. Over time, RI lost its explicit Christian confessional nature stemming from its affiliation with the Church. The 1944 Education Act established RI's role to boost moral fabric and national identity towards the end of the Second World War. This changed, however, when the 1988 Education Reform Act produced the reformulated subject: Religious Education, and included non-Christian and non-religious perspectives, indicating the perceived shedding of its confessional skin in a secular curriculum (Parker and Freathy 2011; Cox and Cairns 1989; Woodhead and Clarke 2015).

RE is currently a subject that teaches students about the beliefs and practices in the six religions most commonly practised in the United Kingdom (Buddhism, Christianity, Hinduism, Islam, Judaism and Sikhism) and non-religious positions, including Humanism. Philosophy and ethics are taught both discretely and as part of the study of religious and non-religious perspectives. The Commission on Religious Education (RE Council 2018) proposes a significant move away from the non-statutory status and a 'national entitlement for all' with a prioritization of the multidisciplinary possibilities of the subject. 'Religion and worldviews' is the recommended name for both the subject and a curriculum that reflects the current national and international religious and non-religious landscape (RE Council 2018). The RE Council's explicit introduction of worldviews into the subject's conceptualization also subsumes the intersectional nature of religion and non-religion. This denotes personal epistemologies and beliefs regarding ontology, purpose and teleology as multilayers of influences and combinations thereof which highlight the need for a multidisciplinary approach to the subject that is able to capture the sociocultural nature of personal and institutional worldviews (see RE Council 2018; Chater 2020; Cooling 2020).

Disciplines and Pedagogies

For purposes of this chapter, readers should bear in mind the pedagogies of RE, according to the literature, are considered to be

> expressions of certain assumptions about how education and religion can be brought into a relationship within the context of a secular education system; indeed they combine a particular view of religion(s) with a particular view of education. (Grimmitt 2000: 17)

Appreciation of the composite disciplinary nature of RE demands that we recognize the subject has changed through evolution and not revolution, that is, in response to the complexities of historical, social, political influences and teacher agency (Parker and Freathy 2011). There is an assumption in RE teacher education that a critical perspective towards its history and current discussions is nurtured to inform decision-making regarding pedagogy, aims and content selection (Barnes et al. 2008). This critical perspective gives teachers insight into how knowledge functions in the subject. It also presents teachers with the possibility that the subject is open to change and transformation.

The academic parent disciplines in the university relating to RE today are, typically, theology, philosophy, religious studies, history, anthropology and sociology, although religion features in other disciplines including psychology, literature, politics and human geography. RE's ecclesiastic beginnings founded a pedagogical combination of Christian morality and Bible studies with parent disciplines of theology and philosophy. In the 1960s and 1970s, the influence of religious studies scholarship and subject networks brought the study of non-Christian religion and non-religious perspectives first to the academy and then to the RE curriculum. This shift introduced new parent disciplines from religious studies traditions: theology of Christian and non-Christian faiths, anthropology, sociology, aspects of psychology and conceptual themes such as ritual, sacred texts and art, which have since become established disciplinary aspects of RE (Cox and Cairns 1989; Chater 2019, 2020). The disciplines mentioned are scholarly traditions and approaches to knowledge that provide distinct ontological assumptions and epistemological structures for 'knowing' religion and non-religion. The pedagogical approaches to RE (see, for example, Grimmitt 2000) are the results of transformations of parent disciplines and aims of the subject that maintain assumptions about ways of 'knowing' and the purposes of the subject. The following is an illustration of this understanding of RE's pedagogies and related aims: the critical realist pedagogy associated with Wright (2007) combines one of RE's aims to promote the ability and entitlement to assess truth claims (Hand 2004) with a philosophical inquiry.

When content is interpreted through a pedagogical approach, certain lenses and purposes are used or prioritized by the teacher or curriculum author. Two examples to illustrate this are: (1) an enquiry into 'goodness' for the purposes of moral development and empathy for the other, draws on the epistemology of philosophy; and (2) an ethnographic study of pilgrimage to promote community cohesion draws on epistemologies of religious studies, theology, sociology, anthropology and psychology. An epistemic problem arises when curricula, textbooks or teachers present transformed material isolated from its epistemological source. We are concerned that this approach provides a 'relatively static' view of the knowledge found in the university disciplines that is accessible only to some, not all, young people (Young 2014). Indeed, a transformed curriculum is potentially experienced as facts if memorization is prioritized over a critical approach to epistemologies. When the transformation has taken place elsewhere there are implications for depriving students of epistemic access (Young 2014). Young's (2008, 2014) position that the disciplines are the best method we have to make sense of the world and seek truth, in its broadest sense, perhaps overlooks the selection of content and pedagogical transformations which do not include students and teachers. Without students' or teachers' access to this process, the pedagogies are prone to normative approaches to knowledge. We propose that epistemic literacy holds the potential to deconstruct pedagogical transformations and prevents normativity through more transparency and critical engagement with the knowledge frameworks, values and structures in play.

Knowledge: Everyday, Expert and Categorial *Bildung*

We propose that the notions of powerful knowledge (Young 2008, 2014) and *Bildung*-informed *didaktik* may be seen as two complementary theories to frame a form of literacy that supports the navigation of everyday and expert knowledge while considering the connections between the school subject, student and teacher. We begin with powerful knowledge because areas of RE scholarship and curriculum proposals have responded to this by prioritizing an explicitly disciplinary approach to the subject (RE Council 2018; Kueh 2020). Young's (2008) social theory of knowledge draws on and Vygotsky to elucidate how knowledge works structurally, that is, to distinguish between the profane and sacred (Durkheim) and the everyday and scientific (Vygotsky). A premise of Young's powerful knowledge depends on a distinction between knowledge forms and the claim that children have an entitlement to extend beyond their everyday knowledge and experience to acquire expert (or theoretical) knowledge to make sense of the world. He argues the best way to do this is through the disciplines and their structures defined by disciplinary conceptual boundaries, epistemic rules and related questions. Hence, schools exist to redress and implement social justice through epistemic access to powerful knowledge that provides induction to established methods to search for truth in its broadest sense (Young 2014).

The powerful knowledge project challenges the socially unjust monopoly of knowledge of the powerful, and yet there is irony in some recent iterations of a so-called 'knowledge-led' curriculum in England. This development is motivated by the English government's Department of Education's reforms in the early to mid-2010s driven by Hirschian interpretations of cultural literacy and 'gap-filling' to enact social justice (Hirsch 2016). This turn to a content- and fact-based (rather than conceptual and disciplinary) curriculum is amplified by the proliferation of assessment technologies, cognitive science and memorization techniques of a meritocratic and functionalist system that can operate in person and online. When one considers the RE curriculum and its proposed philosophical aims of moral and spiritual development as well as generic content pertaining to ethics and existential questions, one wonders how such a functionalist system can facilitate any meaning for students. However, we suggest that the framework of powerful knowledge, particularly as an alternative to a child-centred or content-led education (Young 2008; Young and Muller 2010), requires a complementary framework to bring the child's world, and the teacher's knowledge and understanding of the child's world, into play. For this reason, we turn to the German and Nordic tradition of *Bildung*.

Emerging from classical Greek and Roman education traditions, humanism, Enlightenment and modern liberal education, *Bildung* encapsulates a purpose-driven approach to education for the 'state of mind of a person that puts him in a position to impose order on himself, as well as on his relations to the world . . . the state of which one can assume responsibility' (Klafki 2007: 147). It is also conceived as relating both to the development and integrity of moral and intellectual dimensions and for which 'academic disciplines are an indispensable resource/vehicle' (Deng 2018: 160).

Despite the long-standing and generative nature of *Bildung*, Klafki's (2007) contributions brought constructive critique (Hopmann 2007; Bladh et al. 2018) with a framework he calls *categorial Bildung* that distinguishes the different categories of curriculum content (*material*) from the pedagogical processes of selecting the content and presenting it in ways that the student can relate to (*formal*). The *material Bildung* is conceived as objective in as much as the curriculum content is *provided* by the institution, with the *formal Bildung* perceived as subjective. The teacher's process demands the understanding of a specific relationship between the *material* and the individual along with the informed development of approaches, methods and examples in which the 'specific always represents something general' (Bladh et al. 2018: 402) or brings insight beyond the example. This process also requires an awareness of the temporal nature of the objective and subjective curriculum, or what Klafki calls 'epoch-typical key problems', such as war, famine, injustice or other contemporary issues, with the intention of developing 'abilities regarding self-determination, co-determination and solidarity in relation to the key issues' (Bladh et al. 2018: 402). There are similarities between the reinvigoration of the teacher's autonomy regarding the nature of knowledge in relation to the content and life of the child in both *categorial Bildung* and powerful knowledge (Willbergh 2016), and we will address this later on in the chapter.

Before concluding this section, we raise the pertinent issue of normativity in both frameworks of powerful knowledge and *categorial Bildung* with regard to a typical RE curriculum containing notions of religious knowledge and experience. Vernon (2020) highlights how powerful knowledge can be perceived through a Durkheimian lens as hierarchical if the teacher's role is to induct the student into constructs entailing a more sophisticated way of thinking, whereas a Vygostkian approach places more value in the child's experience. The dualist perspective of both theorists draws attention to the fact that everyday 'knowledge' and 'experience' are formulated in sociological terms in relation to the purpose of education. If we consider the experience and knowledge accounted for in the RE curriculum regarding the study of religion and non-religion, this includes gnosis, agnosis, mystery, revelation, the numinous, religious experience and knowledge, esoteric and spiritual knowledge. Personal and universal experiences such as suffering, family and community are also part of the RE curriculum in its attempt to include the life world of the student. The dualist perspective becomes problematic here, in the sense that the expert's role is to unlock children's everyday experiences and epistemic potential to move from the everyday to the expert (Young 2008). Even though a school is a secular setting, it is significant that it is made up of individuals who may experience aspects of this area of the RE curriculum. A dualist approach tacitly devalues their experience in epistemic terms and is therefore potentially negligent regarding epistemic access (Catling and Martin 2011). Klafki's *categorial* approach is grounded in a commitment to *Bildung* that facilitates a reciprocal relationship between the *material* and *formal Bildung*, not only for the teachers in their pedagogical processes, but also for the student. This can enable the teacher's *and* the student's self-knowledge (how one relates to objective *material*) and the moral dimension of *Bildung* that applies to living with others in the world, as a result of *Bildung* in relation to the sociocultural environment of the classroom.

'Big Questions' in Religion and Science – a Case for Epistemic Literacy

The conceptual framework for epistemic literacy developed as a result of our empirical study that considered pupils' perceptions of the relationship(s) between religion and science (Mujtaba, Reiss and Stones 2017; Pearce et al. 2019; Stones et al. 2020). This study consisted of an intervention of six science lessons with content pertaining to religion, ethics and philosophy and RE lessons concerned with debates surrounding religion, science and epistemology.[1] The lessons were taught over one term to students aged fourteen to sixteen years in ten schools, and focus groups were interviewed before and after the intervention. The central concern of the research was that school biology does not reflect the recent developments of a 'new biology' that challenges atomic understandings of cancer, for example, with proposals of complex, chaotic and holistic systems as more accurate and open to, but not coercive in, correlation with theological interpretations. We postulated that the current school biology paradigm contributes to the perceived conflict between religion and science. This perception limits students' understanding of the discrete knowledge forms found in RE and school science that relate to existential or 'big' questions (Billingsley 2013). The resulting study responded to this concern and sought to discover students' perceptions of the relationships between religion and science. Through the intervention lessons, an approach to science and RE was presented to promote less perceived conflict by making the different epistemological characters of religion and science explicit.

We drew on Billingsley et al.'s (2013) identification of 'epistemic insight' as recognition of the disciplinary distinctions required for correct understanding of the different epistemologies of religion and science. This lack of insight was apparent in the data we analysed. One student's response to a question about whether there is a connection between science and religion – 'Science is purely about the truth so I don't think you could compare it to non-truth versus the truth' (Pearce et al. 2019) – illustrates the confusion of language and ontology that has supported a polarization to inhibit the comparison of science and religion.

Students' perceptions of religion and science were also defined by conflict due to a reluctance to simultaneously accept a religious and scientific understanding of life; for example:

> I don't think you can [accept evolution and believe in God] because if there's two different things then I don't think you can believe in them both. (Pearce et al. 2019)

These binary perceptions are reflected in the literature with a range of empirical studies. For instance, Preston and Epley's (2005) study highlights that for most of their participants '[T]he ultimately valuable belief (a) explains everything and (b) is explained by nothing' (Preston and Epley 2005: 831). In other words, convincing explanations of ultimate reality are those that leave no room for complexity, doubt or the unknown, an insight that is supported by the notion of perceived 'competition for explanatory space' (Preston and Epley 2005).

Even when there was a change in perception, the following example indicates a common trend in the data. Students who could perceive a difference in the knowledge forms moved from a perception that science and religion were competing for 'explanatory space' (ibid.) to an awareness of the distinctness of the two fields; but they lacked the appropriate language to perceive the epistemological and ontological implications of these differences:

> I think that they don't really go well together because, for example, the theory of evolution right . . . They say that one animal evolved from another, but the thing is how did that animal get there in the first place? I think that religion made that. (Sarah, before the intervention)
>
> I think that they [religion and science] – yes, they have *opposed style but then they have different things about them and they have different beliefs about what the world is and what it's about.* [our italics] (Sarah, after the intervention)
>
> (Stones et al. 2020)

While the fields search for systemic and material mechanisms (science) and metaphysical meaning and purpose (religion), both fields are engaged in *a search for answers*. Some students' views changed and were able to see this shared territory:

> Yes, I think science and religion have quite a lot in common because there's a cross section between the belief and the evidence. (Ranvir, after the intervention)
>
> (Pearce et al. 2019)

In the example of Ranvir, 'a cross section between the belief and the evidence' indicates some understanding of the different explanatory criteria of the fields. These observations made us aware that RE needs a conceptual framework to build on the notion of epistemic insight (Billingsley et al. 2013) to support the navigation of RE's epistemic character. The data also indicated that use of language was linked directly to the ability to operationalize understanding of the discrete fields of religion and science and hence we adopted the idea of epistemic literacy as it encapsulates the act of using words with an understanding of the grammar of the related concepts and methods (Hannam et al. 2020).

The data also pointed to the role of identity in the tendency of some participants to clarify their positions, for example, as 'a Christian' or 'someone who believes in science' as a prefix to a response (Mujtaba, Reiss and Stones 2017). Similarly, in their empirical study, Gottlieb and Wineberg (2012) noted the ways in which a sample of a combination of religious, non-religious, historians, scientists and clergy responded to stimuli relating to the narratives of Thanksgiving and Exodus. The authors identified a code of 'membership' in the data to denote a sense of belonging to one or more groups: theologian, faith member, colonial American, historian, scientist. When participants experienced a sense of 'multiple membership', this led to the 'use of multiple frameworks of epistemological assumptions (e.g. historical, theological, scientific) for interpreting documentary evidence', which the authors describe as 'epistemic switching . . . because . . . they typically involved more than a shift from one self-description to another. They generally signalled a shift from one set of assumptions about the nature of knowledge to another' (Gottlieb and Wineberg 2012: 98).

Gottlieb and Wineberg's observations suggested that individuals' personal, religious, non-religious and academic backgrounds affect one's epistemic priorities. In their study, the authors identified that 'membership' dictated whether a source was largely viewed as historical or religious. In other words, a source or epistemology is never encountered neutrally.

This seems especially pertinent when the field of study is 'big questions' holding the potential for autonomous engagement (in the Deweyan sense) not dictated by unconscious inference or learned definitions according to assessment criteria. It might also be considered a question of epistemic justice if students are deprived of autonomous engagement with concepts that have a broader significance beyond their school life.[2] The authors draw our attention to the importance of considering access to the existential nature of curriculum content: 'People don't live and die as historians. They live and die as people' (Gottlieb and Wineberg 2012: 118).

A curriculum that anticipates the powerful knowledge or *Bildung* of the student's present *and* future recognizes their potential, not merely their student identity and stage in life. Following a *categorial Bildung* that builds a dialectic between objective and subjective curriculum, in the following sections we propose that epistemic literacy is needed to take account of the possibility that personal, emotional and identity-driven approaches to epistemologies have a significant impact on the individual's epistemic access to content that 'triggers' (Gottlieb and Wineberg 2012) various epistemic responses which students can learn to recognize for themselves.

Epistemic Literacy: Clarifying the Concept

We will explain how 'epistemic' and 'literacy' help to clarify the possibilities of what we propose. Here, 'epistemic' refers to knowledge associated with the discipline as well as ways of knowing. For us, this means academic and school subject disciplines, and everyday knowledge relating to the field of big questions concerning religion and science. We define literacy here as an ability that allows someone to do something with these different kinds of knowledge. An example of this is the ability to grasp the reasons for a range of responses to a biological description of evolution. Teachers' or students' responses might reflect an interest in science learned at school or elsewhere. A lack of interest, inability to understand, or even hostility are equally possible if the study of science is deemed to undermine a metaphysical understanding of reality that relates to a religious community and identity. The capabilities (Sen 1992, 1999) approach of this kind of literacy also refers to the ability to navigate knowledge and knowing that one is yet to encounter.

Epistemic literacy is a kind of meta-knowledge or knowledge about how knowledge works. The ability is thus understanding and being able to use one's own knowledge in reference to, and in relationship with, expert (*material*) knowledge forms and their grammar of method, evidence, criteria and language. The ability is informed by Klafki's (1995) *categorial Bildung* and demands a dialectical relationship between objective and subjective knowledge.

We do not refer to an imperialist understanding of literacy in which a powerful community decides what the dominant language is (Hannam et al. 2020); rather, we refer to Furlong and Whitty's (2017) recommendations to create 'integrated knowledge traditions' that draw on subject networks, scholars and teachers. Shaw (2019) and Hannam et al. (2020) are scholars from integrated traditions whose formulations of religious literacy, and religion and worldview (R&W) literacy, have helped us clarify the concept of epistemic literacy. Although we are concerned with knowledge and ways of knowing rather than solely or explicitly religion or worldviews, religious and R&W literacies are relevant to epistemic literacy since all three literacies relate to the navigation of personal and disciplinary knowledge. Epistemic literacy specifically applies to situations where different knowledge cultures (disciplinary and personal) come into contact. This is particularly evident in the RE field of religion and science. Here, one's experience, preferences and sociocultural associations with types of knowledge come into play when one encounters the curriculum. Notions of religious and R&W literacy have helped clarify the need for an appropriate attitude and the need for reflexivity while studying religion, worldviews *and* knowledge and knowing. We intend that epistemic literacy is seen as an aspect of religious and R&W literacy to help teachers and students deal explicitly with the role of (and relationships with) knowledge and knowing in the study of religion and worldviews.

Shaw's (2019) theory of R&W literacy draws on hermeneutics and *Bildung* to frame a nuanced approach to encounters with religion and worldviews. R&W literacy describes a critical awareness of the nature of worldview through knowledge of the complexities of the real religious and non-religious landscape. It includes recognition of the role of reflexivity in developing this knowledge, and the resulting dispositions of tact and sensitivity for the purposes of encounter with the phenomena and adherents.

Reflexivity, proposed by Hannam et al. (2020), as part of the authors' understanding of religious literacy, is a useful framework to help frame personal knowledge in epistemic terms. Reflexivity is a process through which one can become rational about irrational processes. The process of becoming epistemically literate is to develop awareness of one's own epistemic preferences, switching and blind spots and gain insight into one's relationship with different knowledges, sources and authorities. Our hope is that this will have a democratizing effect that challenges the epistemic devaluation of everyday knowledge in comparison to expert knowledge (Young 2008; Vernon 2020) and recognizes its worth in contributing to epistemic access leading to notions of human flourishing.

We consider that the experience of having one's personal knowledge as a validated and distinct form of knowledge is akin to unlocking freedoms and provides one with capabilities (Sen 1992, 1999). This can act as a template to unlock further freedoms that may manifest across other areas of the school curriculum and beyond school. This is not to say that 'anything goes' and opinion can now be considered knowledge. On the contrary, epistemic literacy is a tool for distinguishing *between* opinion and knowledge through a nuanced and reflexive understanding of how knowledge works. Thus, epistemic literacy facilitates an inclusive education with democratizing and emancipatory potential through a qualified approach to knowledge in the RE curriculum. We hope, therefore, that the ethical value of epistemic literacy is evident due to its relationship with access, inclusion and capabilities.

Epistemic Literacy in the RE Curriculum

The following example illustrates epistemic literacy in relation to understandings of creation in the RE curriculum field of religion and science.

Reductive accounts of religion and science perpetuate the enduring 'conflict model' that reflects perceived tensions between modernity and tradition, secularity and religion (Harrison 2015). The reification of 'religion' and 'science' is part of this conflict model. The nature of science has an underlying pluralism that is limited by an essentialist view (Reiss 2018). We add that 'religion' is an umbrella term which describes at the very least, but is not limited to, a range of beliefs, practices, arts, politics and histories that can be known as an insider or outsider (Panjwani and Revell 2018). These plural and interdisciplinary natures of religion and science are reflected in their various and related disciplines. The example of a sacred narrative of creation can be understood to contain religious truths, according to theology. It can also be considered a record of the concerns of the author's or authors' society according to history, sociology or anthropology. It would not be considered a current scientific document since it was not written according to current scientific theories; indeed, to consider it a scientific document would be to misconceive the epistemic character of the source. Yet, in the tradition of Durkheim (2001), further disciplinary lenses such as the history, sociology or anthropology of science *would* highlight a scientific perspective which was integral to the author's or authors' theology. Thus, one's appreciation of the source is enriched through understanding of this epistemic nuance.

Our understanding of epistemic literacy is key here, to attend to the transformation of the disciplinary lenses. The teacher is asked to deconstruct and be explicit about the disciplinary lenses applied to such sources, rather than presenting them as simply 'alternative approaches' to sacred texts. Attention should also be given to the distinctness and role of 'everyday knowledge' in relation to revealed and sacred texts, personal existential perspectives and concerns, as well as the role of disciplines. Our intention here is to avoid uncritical, normative or liberal interpretations of the curriculum. Inclusion is at stake if students are deprived of personal engagement when their own perspectives on authority, epistemology and ontology are not acknowledged appropriately.

Putting Epistemic Literacy to Use: A Tool for Transformation

We propose that the use of epistemic literacy has the potential to democratize knowledge beyond the orthodoxy of the academy by incorporating the broader aims of education and helping students and teachers navigate: (1) the disciplines associated with RE; and (2) the relationship(s) between the disciplines and the lifeworlds of the pupils, thereby bringing expert and everyday knowledge into relationship with each other. We also consider epistemic literacy as a principle to be used as a tool for transformation. Grounded in the tradition of *didaktik*, transformation and educational aims are reconciled in the relationship between teacher, content and student. Here, we briefly consider epistemic literacy as a principle or tool for transformation, in the tradition of 'recontextualization' (Bernstein 1999), to form the institutional subject (Deng 2018).

Gericke et al. (2018) build on the *didaktik* triangle in their approach to transformation to add the provocations that a socially engaged curriculum demands. These questions ask of the curriculum: Why, what and for whom? These criteria assert fundamental questions of the significance of curriculum and thus the triangle is amended by the authors (see Figure 5.1).

The transformation of the parent disciplines to the school subject of RE depends on the authors' adaptation of the didactic triangle (Fig 5.1). This framework facilitates response to societal and institutional changes through the disciplines, and is in line with Young's view of the lenses as the best method we have to understand the world (Young 2008). The authors' framework treats the extrinsic and intrinsic as interdependent through its connection 'to the life world of the students' (Gericke et al. 2018: 437).

Epistemic literacy provides a meta-approach and conceptual framework for this multifarious and nuanced transformation. Drawing on *categorial*

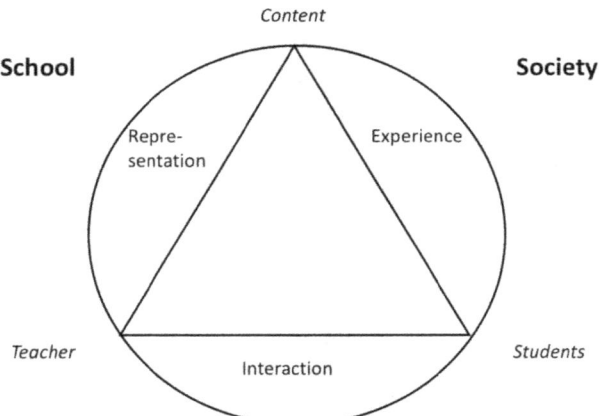

Figure 5.1 The didactic triangle (developed from Hopmann 1997) (Gericke et al. 2018: 437).

Bildung and the call for exemplary content and approaches to *formal Bildung* to illuminate *material Bildung* for the student, the teacher can draw on epistemic literacy to take seriously the knowledge and ways of knowing in the classroom. The teacher is thus able to make content and pedagogical selections that acknowledge the student's 'everyday knowledge'. The teacher can also include 'epoch-typical key problems' in an epistemically informed way that recognizes students' perspectives and relationship with knowledge presented in the curriculum. As with understandings of powerful knowledge that acknowledge the systematicity of knowledge, we conceive epistemic literacy as powerful professional knowledge that is specific to the role of the teacher and the subject (Furlong and Whitty 2017). The epistemically literate teacher's choices of content and pedagogy are informed by their knowledge of the everyday experience, knowledge and lifeworld of the student and the expertise provided by the discipline.

Epistemic Literacy as a Principle for Teacher Education

We hope we have made the case for epistemic literacy in relation to the teacher's *and* the students' relationships with knowledge. We consider epistemic literacy to be part of teachers' powerful professional knowledge which, therefore, should be included as part of teacher education policy and practice. The nature of the RE teacher's powerful professional knowledge includes awareness of the nature of knowledge and an ability to see the significance of the 'knower'. The teacher's powerful professional knowledge recognizes that the teacher is as prone to epistemic bias as the student. The teacher and teacher educator should be wary of this and commit to a teacher education that encompasses a process of developing epistemic literacy as powerful professional knowledge that continues throughout one's career. Teachers need to develop the ability to discern their own relationships with knowledge and encourage the same in students. Theory is not sufficient, however, and we propose that this process needs to be experiential for the student teacher and lead to learning and development beyond teacher formation.

Initial Teacher Education (ITE) in England is based around the requirements to meet a collection of Teachers' Standards[3] in order to reach Qualified Teacher Status. There is an enduring place and need for epistemic literacy as a professional tool for the critically reflective teacher to gain a nuanced understanding of knowledge. This requirement continues into one's career as reflection is always necessary if one is teaching or learning. The capabilities approach that has informed epistemic literacy relates to the futures of the student *and* teacher beyond ITE and can enable the teacher to deal with content and approaches they encounter *beyond* teacher formation.

Teacher education is usually in partnership with the school and university and priority is given to either a university-based or a school-based route. Both routes can benefit from the recognition that epistemic literacy is crucial for the development of powerful professional knowledge. The university-based route has a scholarly aspect which often requires master's-level engagement with philosophies of education and subject-specific scholarship. A critical understanding of theory surrounding the historical, global, national and local contexts of the nature and purpose of RE forms part of the development of the RE teacher in relation to their developing practice. Epistemic literacy is suited to this process since the teacher is tasked with developing their *own* critical relationship with knowledge. Meaningful and rigorous ITE demands this from the outset and should convince the reflective teacher of the need for appropriate guidance and mentoring in forming their own epistemic literacy for the RE curriculum and classroom.

School-based routes for ITE generally attach less focus on subject scholarship, which means knowledge is less likely to be deconstructed and recontextualized as a student teacher. The need for epistemic literacy is equally crucial in this process to support the development of powerful professional knowledge. Mentoring in these school-based routes demands an awareness of teachers' and students' epistemic biases and epistemic literacy provides a framework to address this. As RE teachers can be isolated in these professional routes, we suggest there is a need for the RE subject community to affirm the importance of epistemic literacy as integral to RE.

Teacher educators and mentors in schools also need to respond with commitment to their own powerful professional knowledge. Rather than a burden, this could be seen as a way to reinvigorate the subject, profession and RE networks. The earlier overview of the history of RE indicates the responsiveness of the subject in its nature and purposes. Today's climate of 'post truth' or 'fake news' (Blake -Turner 2020) strengthens the call for epistemic attention that RE should respond to, just as it has with the proposal for a religion and worldviews curriculum in light of the plural religious and non-religious landscape. The warning of unconscious epistemic switching, identified by Gottlieb and Wineberg, supports that urgency. Indeed, awareness of one's own bias is a protective 'tool' against the *influence* of bias.

We think that consideration of epistemic literacy should be integral to RE teacher education because it holds the potential to increase the power of the parent and school subject disciplines as well as the ethically informed aims of RE through a *Bildung*-informed *didaktik* approach. The development of teachers' own epistemic literacy during ITE supports the subject in an academic and personal way, adding to the epistemic potential and possibilities for the subject's identity and nature. Teachers' autonomy in their choices concerning content and pedagogical approaches requires an ability to be (as far as is possible) self-aware, knowingly objective and subjective, and have empathy with students. This is to avoid normative or uncritical actions and choices, unconscious prejudices or preferences, blind spots or misconceptions. The empathy required by a teacher to exemplify an epistemic literacy of appropriate tact, sensitivity and reflexivity demands an approach to ITE that is more than theoretical and involves the teacher on a personal level. This approach to ITE needs to be mindful of the teacher's own *Bildung* and involve an ethical commitment to understanding the nature of knowledge.

Such an approach to ITE based on the cultivation of *Bildung* should be introduced at a formative stage for teachers. This is to inform the values employed in transformation decision-making outside and inside the classroom, and the responsibility that comes with that. Epistemic literacy frames this responsibility as it takes one's relationship with knowledge seriously. There are implications here for the teacher's *and* the students' relationship with knowledge, and teacher education policy and practice need to recognize this as part of the teacher's powerful professional knowledge.

Teacher education should value the reflexive nature of teaching to highlight the teacher's and students' subjective relationships with knowledge. The student teacher can *experience* this as part of their professional education, by engaging with their peers' epistemic perspectives, according to the approaches we propose for epistemic literacy. The epistemic diversity of the RE classroom is therefore rehearsed in ITE, and this contributes to the development of this powerful professional knowledge. When this professional knowledge, or epistemic literacy, is taken into the 'real life' of teaching, it would ideally lead to an inclusive and flexible *Bildung* that accounts for epistemic differences among students, while recognizing and mitigating the teacher's own biases.

We have previously alluded to the importance of epistemic literacy as a transformational tool, and this also brings implications for policy and practice in teacher education. Teachers come from various undergraduate backgrounds, meaning that disciplinary blind spots and preferences are likely. Teachers are often faced with curriculum content such as an RE textbook or resource in which 'transformations' can be epistemically biased (prioritizing either everyday or expert knowledge) or favour particular disciplinary approaches. Without epistemic literacy, this could result in content being presented uncritically, prone to disciplinary blur and epistemic inaccessibility due to bias which a teacher and student may be unable to discern. We contend that teachers' powerful professional knowledge requires development of their own epistemic literacy through an initial teacher education that values experiences of 'aha' moments of 'seeing the strings' of knowledge construction. This will enable teachers to be empathetic and understanding of the epistemic challenges faced by students. Teachers will thereby cultivate an epistemically literate approach to *Bildung*, attuning them to the complexities and nuances required for classroom transformations.

Acknowledgements

The authors thank the Templeton World Charity Foundation for funding this research as part of the Big Questions in Classrooms initiative.

Disclosure Statement

There are no potential conflicts of interest. All participants' names are pseudonyms.

Notes

1. RE lessons for the intervention were designed and data from the participating students were analysed. Detailed accounts of the lessons, methods, results of the baseline and qualitative data and subsequent discussions can be found in articles published for the project (Mujtaba, Reiss and Stones 2017; Pearce et al. 2019; Stones 2020). Lesson plans and corresponding resources are available on the International Society for Science and Religion website: https://www.issr.org.uk/projects/the-new-biology/.
2. Gottlieb and Wineburg conclude that epistemology and identity can have an impact on each other in two ways: 'by providing cognitive conditions for holding particular beliefs and knowledge or the self' and 'by triggering different kinds of identification

and belonging' and, furthermore, that epistemology and identity are 'two seemingly distinct constructs [that] may be much closer than has previously been assumed' (2012: 117-118).
3 Teachers' Standards are based around the following categories: promoting high expectations, how students learn, subject knowledge, lesson planning, differentiation, assessment and wider professional responsibilities (Department of Education 2019).

References

Barnes, L. P., Brandom, A. M. and Wright, A. (2008), *Learning to Teach Religious Education in the Secondary School: A Companion to School Experience*, London: Routledge.

Bernstein, B. (1999), 'Vertical and Horizontal Discourse: An Essay', *British Journal of Sociology of Education*, 20 (2): 157–73.

Billingsley, B., Taber, K. S., Riga, F. and Newdick, H. (2013). Secondary School Students' Epistemic Insight into the Relationships between Science and Religion: A Preliminary Enquiry', *Research in Science Education,* 43 (4): 1715–32.

Bladh, G., Stolare, M. and Kristiansson, M. (2018), 'Curriculum Principles, Didactic Practice and Social Issues: Thinking Through Teachers' Knowledge Practices in Collaborative Work', *London Review of Education*, 16 (3): 398–413.

Blake-Turner, C. (2020), 'Fake News, Relevant Alternatives, and the Degradation of Our Epistemic Environment', *Inquiry: An Interdisciplinary Journal of Philosophy*. https://doi.org/10.1080/0020174X.2020.1725623.

Catling, S. and Martin, F. (2011), 'Contesting *Powerful Knowledge*: The Primary Geography Curriculum as an Articulation Between Academic and Children's (Ethno-) Geographies', *The Curriculum Journal*, 22 (3): 317–35.

Chater, M. (2019), *We Need to Talk About Religious Education*, London: Jessica Kingsley Publishers.

Chater, M. (2020), *Reforming RE: Power and Knowledge in a Worldviews Curriculum*, London: John Catt Publishing.

Cooling, T. (2020), 'Worldview in Religious Education: Autobiographical Reflections on the Commission on Religious Education in England Final Report', *British Journal of Religious Education*, 42 (4): 403–14.

Cox, E. and Cairns, J. M. (1989), *Reforming Religious Education: The Religious Clauses of the 1988 Education Reform Act*, London: Kogan Page.

Deng, Z. (2018), 'Pedagogical Content Knowledge Reconceived: Bringing Curriculum Thinking into the Conversation on Teachers' Content Knowledge', *Teaching and Teacher Education*, 72: 155–64.

Department of Education (2019), *ITT Core Content Framework*, London: Crown Copyright.

Durkheim, E. (2001), *The Elementary Forms of Religious Life*. Trans. C. Cosman. Oxford: Oxford University Press.

Furlong, J. and Whitty, G. (2017), 'Knowledge Traditions in the Study of Education?', in *Knowledge and the Study of Education: An International Exploration*, 13–57, Didcot: Symposium.

Gericke, N., Hudson, B., Olin-Scheller, C. and Stolare, M. (2018), 'Powerful Knowledge, Transformations and the Need for Empirical Studies Across School Subjects', *London Review of Education*, 16 (3): 428–44.

Gottlieb, E. and Wineburg, S. (2012), Between Veritas and Communitas: Epistemic Switching in the Reading of Academic and Sacred History, *Journal of the Learning Sciences*, 21 (1): 84–129.

Grimmitt, M. (2000), *Pedagogies of Religious Education: Case Studies in the Research and Development of Good Pedagogic Practice in RE*, Essex: McCrimmons.

Hand, M. (2004), 'Religious Education', in J. White (ed), *Rethinking the School Curriculum, London*, 152-164, London: Routledge/Falmer.

Hannam, P., Biesta, G., Whittle, S. and Aldridge, D. (2020), 'Religious Literacy: A Way Forward for Religious Education?', *Journal of Beliefs & Values*, 41 (2): 214–26.

Harrison, P. (2015), *The Territories of Science and Religion*, Chicago: University of Chicago Press.

Hirsch, E. D. (2016), *Why Knowledge Matters*, Boston: Harvard Education Press.

Hopmann, S. (2007), 'Restrained Teaching: The Common Core of Didaktik', *European Educational Research Journal*, 6 (2): 109–24.

Hopmann, S. (1997), 'Wolfgang Klafki och den tyska didaktiken', in M. Uljens (ed) *Didaktik: Teori, reflektion och praktik*, 215–28, Lund: Studentlitteratur.

Klafki, W. (1995), 'Didactic Analysis as the Core of Preparation of Instruction (Didaktische Analyse als Kern der Unterrichtsvorbereitung)', *Journal of Curriculum Studies*, 27 (1): 13–30.

Klafki, W. (2007), 'Didactic Analysis as the Core of Preparation of Instruction (Didaktische Analyse als Kern der Unterrichtsvorbereitung)', in Westbury and Millburn (eds), *Rethinking Schooling*, London, Routledge.

Kueh, R. (2020), 'Disciplinary Haring: Making the Case for the Disciplinary in Religion and Worldviews', in M. Chater (ed) *Reforming RE: Power and Knowledge in a Worldviews Curriculum*, 131–47, Woodbridge: John Catt Educational Ltd.

Mujtaba, T., M. Reiss, and A. Stones. (2017), 'Epistemic Insight: Teaching about Science and RE in Schools', *School Science Review* 99 (367): 67–75.

Panjwani, F. and Revell, L. (2018), 'Religious Education and Hermeneutics: The Case of Tteaching about Islam', *British Journal of Religious Education*, 40 (3): 268–76.

Parker, S. G. and Freathy, R. J. K. (2011), 'Context, Complexity and Contestation: Birmingham's Agreed Syllabuses for Religious Education Since the 1970s', *Journal of Beliefs & Values*, 32 (2): 247–63.

Pearce, J., Stones, A., Reiss, M. J. and Mujtaba, T. (2019), '"Science is Purely About the Truth So I Don't Think You Could Compare It to Non-Truth Versus the Truth",

Students' Perceptions of Religion and Science, and the Relationship(s) Between Them: Religious Education and the Need for Epistemic Literacy', *British Journal of Religious Education*, 1–16.

Preston, J. and N. Epley (2005). 'The Explanatory Value of Meaningful Beliefs', *Psychological Science* 16: 826–32.

Reiss, M. J. (2018), 'Worldviews in Biology Education', in K. Kampourakis and M. J. Reiss (eds), *Teaching Biology in Schools: Global Research, Issues, and Trends*, 263–74, New York: Routledge.

Religious Education Council (2018), *Commission on Religious Education Final Report -religion and Worldviews: The Way Forward*, London: Religious Education Council.

Sen, A. (1992), *Inequality Unexamined*, Oxford: Oxford University Press.

Sen, A. (1999), *Development as Freedom*, Oxford: Oxford University Press.

Shaw, M. (2019), 'Towards a Religiously Literate Curriculum – Religion and Worldview Literacy as an Educational Model', *Journal of Beliefs & Values*, 41 (2): 150–61.

Stones, A., Pearce, J., Reiss, J. and Mujtaba M. (2020), 'Students' Perceptions of Religion and Science, and How They Relate: The Effects of a Classroom Intervention', *Religious Education*, 115 (3): 349–63.

Vernon, E. (2020), 'Teaching to the Epistemic Self: Ascending and Descending the Ladder of Knowledge', *The Curriculum Journal*, 31 (1): 27–47.

Willbergh, I. (2016), *Bringing Teaching Back in: The Norwegian NOU The School of the Future in Light of the Allgemeine Didaktik Theory of Wolfgang Klafki*, Norway: Department of Education, University of Agder.

Woodhead, L. and Clarke, C. (2015), *A New Settlement: Religion and Belief in Schools*, London: Westminster Faith Debates.

Wright, A. (2007), *Critical Religious Education, Multiculturalism and the Pursuit of Truth*, Cardiff: University of Wales Press.

Yasri, P., Arthur, S., Smith, M. and Mancy, R. (2013), 'Relating Science and Religion: An Ontology of Taxonomies and Development of a Research Tool for Identifying Views', *Science & Education*, 22 (10): 2679–707.

Young, M. (2008), *Bringing Knowledge Back In*, London: Routledge.

Young, M. (2014), *Knowledge and the Future School*, London: Bloomsbury.

Young, M. and Muller, J. (2010), 'Three Educational Scenarios for the Future: Lessons from the Sociology of Knowledge', *European Journal of Education*, 45 (1): 2010, Part I.

6

Investigating Literature as Knowledge in School English

Larissa McLean Davies, Lyn Yates and Wayne Sawyer

Introduction

Since the turn of the century, discourses about knowledge in the curriculum have been mobilized to speak back to skills-based curriculum imperatives and redirect attention to the content and purposes of school subjects, and the epistemological purposes of schooling. These arguments (Moore and Muller 1999; Young and Muller 2010; Moore 2013) imply an important connection between tertiary academic disciplines and the school curriculum (Moore and Muller 1999; Young and Muller 2010; Muller and Young 2019; Moore 2013). Although the case made for powerful knowledge of this kind is said to support humanities disciplines such as history, others have convincingly argued that many of the characteristics said to distinguish powerful knowledge in fact presume a science-like disciplinary field (Barrett et al. 2018; Yates et al. 2017). Indeed, the sharp opposition between objective truths and social interests initially made by Young and others (Young and Muller 2013; Young 2013) is inappropriate for humanities and social science subjects. Questions about epistemic value, or which kinds of knowledge or knowing are being built in these subjects, have some usefulness but, as we will argue here, in the case of literary studies what happens in classrooms is not just a separate 'pedagogical' issue but is inherently related to the 'power' of this discipline.

While Muller and Young address some of these concerns and criticisms (Muller 2009; Muller and Young 2019), acknowledging a different, 'horizontal' rather than 'vertical' disciplinary organization and a different form of powerful knowledge for history, as opposed to physics, their exploration of powerful knowledge is yet to fully address the social origins and contexts of enquiry, as well as the questions and judgements that relate to disciplinary fields in the humanities. An investigation of knowledge in humanities subjects must take account of the 'ongoing, changing and disputed social nature of their questions and focus, and the creative constructive elements that are intrinsic to this form of disciplinary knowledge' (Yates 2017: 46) as well as the social and geographical contexts in which these questions of knowledge are being raised. The humanities have always been characterized by different perspectives or contending frameworks that change over time and place. This is particularly apparent in settler societies such as Australia, where postcolonial theories and, in more recent times, re-orientations towards the global south (West-Pavlov 2018; McLean Davies et al. 2017) are unsettling and contesting imperial understandings of what might constitute powerful and significant knowledge.

In this chapter, we focus on knowledge in the subject English, particularly a core element of this subject: literary studies. The teaching of the mother-tongue (here English) – and the teaching of literature specifically – is central and often mandated in the secondary years of schooling, yet is notoriously and paradoxically difficult to pin down in terms of epistemic quality (Hudson et al. 2015). While agreeing with other scholars (Doecke 2017; Doecke and Mead 2017; Yandell 2017) that the arguments of Young and others do not adequately capture or represent the ways knowledge is made in English classrooms, between students, and between teachers and students, we argue that it is possible, and politically desirable, to discern a perspective on the distinctive knowledge qualities of this field.

To ground this discussion empirically, we draw on a four-year Australian research project exploring stakeholders' understandings of knowledge in the school subject English and, more specifically, perceptions of the nature and purpose of literary knowledge. Central to this project is a longitudinal study of early-career English teachers and the ways in which their understandings of literary knowledge are voiced and further developed in the context of their new institutional settings. Note that this approach is not intended to say that whatever teachers do or say about their practice is equally 'good' (one of the legitimate starting points of the knowledge debates). Instead, we are trying to uncover *distinctive forms* of knowledge that are important in this subject. Answering this holds implications for good practice, for how students may benefit from their work in this area, and for teacher education. In this way, our project engages with concepts that are central to the Knowledge and Quality Across School Subjects and Teacher Education (KOSS) Network and, in particular, with two key questions of the KOSS research programme:

- How can the nature of powerful knowledge and epistemic quality in different school subjects be characterized?
- How can the nature of teachers' powerful professional knowledge be characterized, and what are the implications for teacher education policy and practice? (Hudson et al. 2019)

As we will explore in more detail below, in a subject like English where knowledge is not routinely part of the practical discourse, and where scholars sometimes dispute whether this curriculum area even has a 'knowledge-base', examining epistemic quality and powerful knowledge has particular impacts. In the first year of our project, we discovered that teachers often rejected or expressed discomfort with the concept of 'literary knowledge' as a way of articulating the important core of their subject. But later interviews showed that the teachers did articulate (and expand) important epistemological priorities as they had continued to reflect on their subject through these beginning years. These insights offer some new ways of thinking about the kinds of literary knowledges, and knowing, being developed in classrooms. Indeed, we contend that a distinctive form of knowledge or knowing *is* being developed in English and literary studies, one which although not propositional or science-like is enabling in the sense of taking students into a broader and more powerful way of knowing the world. In the final part of this chapter, we explore what this means for understandings of knowledge in English, and for some of the directions in pre-service teacher education programmes.

The Complexity of, and Case for, Exploring Literary Knowledge in Secondary School English

Much discourse around English teaching draws attention to its amorphous, changeable and indefinable nature (Locke 2007) as 'a problem' or even the 'deviant case' (Medway 1990: 1) in comparison with other school subjects. Memorably, those who gathered for the now famous Dartmouth Seminar in 1966, an event which strongly set the course for English teaching in areas of the Anglophone world for the next sixty years (Goodwyn et al. 2019; Doecke 2016; Sawyer et al. 2016), specifically addressed the question 'What is English?'. Attendees largely focused on teachers' practices, treating 'English' as 'whatever English teachers do' (Squire 1968; Britton 1970; Dixon 1967/1975).[1] Evans, like others, drew attention to the shaky linguistic grounds of the subject's very title:

> The point about 'English' as the name of a subject is that it is an adjective being made to serve as a noun. So 'English' is always pointing toward an absence – the noun. Is the subject English literature, language, society, culture, people? (1993: 184)

Durrant cautioned that 'English is not self-contained, one dimensional, fixed and immutable – as some traditionalists would have us believe – but rather it is ever in a state of flux' (2004: 6). Locke responded to the question of 'What is the subject English?' with:

> The simple answer is: many things - clusters of practices, not always particularly coherent, more or less related to curriculum and other documents, socially and historically situated, and riven with contestation from the start. (Locke 2007: 7)

This indeterminacy has significant impacts on the ways pre-service teachers experience teacher preparation courses. In a recent study of teachers and knowledge (Yates et al. 2017), one participant compared her experience of Learning Area or 'Method' classes in science and English, the two subjects she taught. She reflected that asking questions of the nature of the subject occupied significant time in English, as opposed to her science-focused Learning Area class:

> There is no debate about what constitutes school subject Physics compared with English where that discussion occupies quite a lot of the year, so in Physics you move straight on to talking about good pedagogy. (Yates et al. 2017: 112)

This seemingly universal agreement that English cannot be readily defined has clear effects on the ways questions of epistemology are perceived and approached in this subject. The influential *Bullock Report, A Language for Life*, which reviewed the role of subject English in England, went so far as to maintain that English 'does not hold together as a body of knowledge which can be identified, quantified, then transmitted' (DES 1975: 5). Medway later argued that the subject English offers 'nothing less than a different model of education . . . knowledge to be made, not given; knowledge comprising more than can be discursively stated' (Medway 1980: 10). Green argues that, in English, knowledge 'in itself and of itself is not enough' and must be considered alongside both identity and pedagogy (2018: 7).

Arguably, a core part of the challenge in understanding the nature and purpose of the subject English and its epistemological underpinnings also arises from the relative disconnection between the university/academic discipline of English, and English as a school subject. While some other school subjects like the sciences have obvious links with relevant university disciplines, as Green notes, school English has never enjoyed similar relationships (Green 2018). Indeed, the tertiary discipline of English, especially as literary studies, is itself in a state of flux (Yates et al. 2019; Mead 2011).

These indeterminacies in the history of the discipline and in subject English mean that recent debates about powerful knowledge in the curriculum do not capture the social and dynamic nature of English (Doecke and Mead 2017). We nonetheless argue, like Green (2018), that it is timely and essential to consider questions of knowledge, or 'ways of knowing' (Medway 2010) in this central curriculum area. Young's question, posed in 2013 – 'What is the important knowledge that pupils should be able to acquire at school?' – remains relevant, and his reminder that, '(i)f as curriculum theorists, we cannot answer this question, it is unclear who can, and it is more likely that it will be left to the pragmatic and ideological decisions of administrators and politicians' (Young 2013: 103) is particularly sobering. This is certainly the case for those of us working in the field of English education, where politicians and media pundits cross-fertilize to advocate that certain kinds of cultural knowledge are propositional and essential (McGowan 2019). The danger of rejecting Young's social justice-oriented argument for powerful knowledge for all (Young et al. 2014; Muller and Young 2019), or continuing to argue that questions of knowledge are too difficult or nebulous to approach in English, is that we risk implying that teachers do not have significant knowledge to bring into their practice, and that students do not leave secondary English with knowledge, or ways of knowing, that are significant for, and in, their lives.

As Glazener notes, literature, notwithstanding the complexities mentioned earlier, is:

> identified as a measure of excellence . . . made an index of the health and strength of a people; credited with fostering modes of public reflection crucial to civil society; entrusted with values and forms of experience believed to be at risk in modern life; and held to play a special role in readers' intellectual, moral, and emotional development. (2015: 4–5)

Despite the changeable nature of English, and indeed, the changing definition of 'Literature', which has expanded with the introduction of multimodal texts (Beavis 2013), studying literature – by which we mean here sustained engagement with 'aesthetic texts' (Misson and Morgan 2006) – remains a core driver of individuals becoming English teachers (Goodwyn 2012). Teacher registration authorities in both Australia and England continue to require a specified minimum amount of undergraduate literary studies as a prerequisite for teacher education studies in

English (AITSL 2011; DfE 2011). British Government Reports of the twentieth century, including Newbolt (1921), Newsom (1963) Bullock (1975) and Cox (1989), as well as Dixon's influential book *Growth Through English* (1967/1975)[2] – while presenting a range of paradigms of the subject English – all effectively confirm the significance of literary study and the importance of teachers' engagement with literary texts. Thus, amidst the shifting sands of the subject English, this commitment to the literary serves to reinforce its centrality to English.

Still, while literature is valued, a diversity of perspectives remains on the kinds of knowledge that encounters with literature represent. This is also seen in debates about text selection and censorship that are often proxy for debates about knowledge in the subject English (Yates et al. 2019) which attest to the continued importance of the literary in English, but do not capture, and instead often ignore, the significance of what teachers 'do' with texts in classrooms (Bacalja and Bliss 2019: 6) and what students build from their study.

These traditions of valuing literature, but being vague about its knowledge dimensions, are seen in the recent national Australian framework, *Australian Curriculum: English.* (ACARA 2016). The framework reinstates literature as a key Strand of the curriculum but does not develop in any clear or specific manner what constitutes literary knowledge. The overarching statement is that all students across the years of schooling are developing essential 'knowledge, understanding and skills' in its three Strands of Language, Literature and Literacy, but the detailed framework refers to 'knowledge' only in elaborating the Language Strand, and does not indicate how the different epistemological underpinnings of all Strands might be integrated (McLean Davies and Sawyer 2018).

In the following section, against this backdrop of historical and cultural indeterminacy about the epistemological purposes of literature in English, we will raise key themes concerning literary knowledge and ways of knowing to emerge from our longitudinal study regarding the kinds of expansive knowledges teachers imagine for their students in this subject, and the tensions they encounter in building the conditions for this knowledge to be created and mobilized.

Investigating Literary Knowledge in the Making of Australian English Teachers

Our project 'Investigating Literary Knowledge in the Making of English Teachers' commenced in 2016. Its central questions were:

- What role does literary knowledge have within secondary English curriculum and pedagogy?
- How do institutional and social contexts, such as tertiary study and teaching experience, shape early-career English teachers' literary knowledge?

The project took up these questions through a range of related inquiries. The first was a national online questionnaire of over 700 current English teachers. This included direct and indirect questions about how these teachers thought about knowledge in the context of English in general, and of literature in particular. A second and central component of the research was a semi-structured three-year study of twenty-four early-career teachers. This involved an annual interview with each teacher about their work, seeking to understand both their thinking about their field and how they had developed or modified their perspectives in light of the actual contexts (policy and institutional) in which they had worked. Participants wove their own literary education and institutional experiences into accounts of their classroom experiences and connected with, built on, reviewed or refuted previous interview conversations. Participant teachers were located in different states and education systems (Government, Independent, Catholic) and in diverse school contexts (in terms of socio-economic status, and ethnic and religious diversity). The project also included interviews with professors of literary studies, and representatives of curriculum authorities and teacher educators in this area, although we largely do not discuss these data in this chapter. The analysis of material from the project is in process, and this chapter is based on some initial findings related to the survey and to the first two years of the interviews with early-career teachers.

Concern about the Notion of 'Literary Knowledge'

An initial and striking finding arising from both the survey and many of the longitudinal study's first year of interviews was that teachers were reluctant to talk about 'knowledge'. While teachers were happy to talk about the value and purposes of literary study, they often resisted, or were uncomfortable using, the term 'knowledge'. Given the history of English we mapped earlier, this is perhaps unsurprising. Katya reflected:

> I don't really like the word 'knowledge' . . . there's some truth to be learnt that is teachable . . . but . . . 'literary knowledge' sounds to me like knowing the right things about the right books, and . . . that's simply not how I've found teaching

literature to be . . . if I think about literature [it is] more as like a way of being or a way of knowing.

Like Katya, many participants seemed reluctant to use the term, partly because it evoked for them propositional knowledge. They were also conscious of the vast, always growing, body of potential texts in English and the (inevitable) limitations of what they had read. In response to a direct question about how they understood 'literary knowledge', teachers often dwelt on what they saw as gaps in the amount and type of reading they had done (this was also the case in the pilot study for this project; see McLean Davies and Sawyer, 2020). Rebecca recalled anxiety about her own literary knowledge during her final practicum:

> I remember being terrified though because I was so worried that they'd find that . . . I didn't know as much as I should . . . just feeling like I hadn't read enough . . . and . . . even though I'd read heaps at Uni but still . . . feeling . . . unprepared in that way . . . because you know as a teacher . . . you've got to catch up really quickly, and as you get older you realise . . . nobody knows every single text, and you just sort of read it and get going, but as a student coming in there I was feeling . . . 'Oh you know I'm not ready for this', but trying really hard . . . to keep my head above water.

At the start of the project, another teacher, Debra, similarly felt a degree of anxiety about the gaps in her reading. However, at the end of the project, Debra thought that a teacher's literary knowledge is not something that can be measured by the number of books they have read and, further, that its attainability does not need to be 'complete' – and this offers a different dimension to Young's notion of powerful knowledge as stable and identifiable, and also departs from major twentieth-century approaches to literature promoted in the British Government Reports flagged earlier. This is just part of the sense that literary knowledge is dynamic and developing. The key tenets are for teachers to know what rich literary practices look like, to understand the importance of their students' contexts and to be able to supplement and extend their students' reading as appropriate.

Working in a classroom context with diverse students, Brittany was encouraged to broaden the range of texts she might use. But making her existing experience of literary studies and Western cultural values more accessible was not simply a pedagogical issue for her. Instead, it led her to question and then broaden her initial assumptions about what constituted the 'literary', to review and expand her thinking about epistemic quality, and to value a broad perspective on the literary field, understanding how literary 'value' and 'impact' issue from a range of different contexts. Her recounting of how she had never studied a writer such as Maya Angelou, despite being aware of her (Angelou's) work, also reminded us that literary studies, as a discipline, is experienced individually, often through a number of elective courses, rather than as a core body of content to be worked through in one's undergraduate years.

While Young and others argue that, at least in science, disciplines have internal structures that make them cohesive (Young and Muller 2010), we argue that in literary studies such coherence is created by the individual teacher and that, as teachers move into the classroom, this field of knowledge will shift and expand with experience and practice. Undergraduate literary studies can then be seen as sketching or gesturing towards the dimensions of the field, rather than defining the propositional field knowledge that future teachers will draw on in their work with students.

Literary Knowledge and the Canonical

For some participants, 'knowledge' in the initial interviews seemed to be associated with a traditional high-culture literary canon (i.e. being acquainted with particular books, especially Shakespeare), and many felt this emphasis was inappropriate in the diverse context of their school, in twenty-first-century Australia or, even, to the broadening purposes of literary study. Responding to cultural heritage arguments, and what we might see as the long shadow of Newbolt's arguments about distinction, Nicole stated:

> the literary knowledge I was talking about . . . which is like the literary canon, . . . I think that's class-based . . . I think it's white and very middle class . . . I think literary knowledge is important, but . . . I don't think anyone can say this is what everyone should know, and these are the texts that everyone should read. I think that instead . . . students should be exposed to a whole range of texts, and that we should aim to get them to be . . . critical thinkers who are empathetic and who are engaged in the world.

For Nicole, speaking in the first year of the interviews, the concept of literary knowledge belonged to a paradigm of English teaching that predated Dixon (1967/1975) and was actually irreconcilable with what she saw as the core business of teaching literary studies. Like many of our teacher participants, Nicole refined and revised her views over the course of the project. In the second year, after rereading her transcript, she reflected:

> I think I was a bit too prescriptive with what I considered literary knowledge then because I've realised that among English teachers we all have different types of literary knowledge . . . I think it depends on our personal reading preferences and interests and the types of culture we consume . . . we bring those interests and those strengths to the texts that we suggest and the way that we teach.

As she progressed, Nicole revised her initial response to the idea of 'literary knowledge' as meaning exposure to particular texts. Instead, she gave more emphasis to the type of teacher and student practices involved in working with literary texts to build knowledge, including a greater recognition that a diversity of interests was involved, and that building engagement was an intrinsic, rather than a peripheral, element of making knowledge in this area meaningful.

Like Nicole, Timothy was imbued with significant cultural and literary capital from his own secondary and tertiary education. At his first interview, Timothy described the autonomy afforded to his students by whole-Faculty practices of having students undertake conceptual inquiry based on a range of texts. During the course of the project, he moved to a new selective school and found himself needing to draw far more on his store of canonical knowledge (e.g. he saw the parents in his current school wanting their children 'to get . . . a canonical knowledge of literature'). Nevertheless, this new context modified his perspective on the purposes of the types of enquiry undertaken in his previous setting. In this new school, he found himself returning to the pedagogical and epistemological approaches to literature used in that previous school, in order to engage his current students:

> I turn [specific approaches to the canon] . . . into project-based learning units . . . that lead to student engagement. I think is more important than having this kind of canonical knowledge because I don't think that actually eventuates in a lot of circumstances . . . and I think you're more likely to have students leave high school [that] have a real interest in literature [if they] have agency in . . . finding texts and deconstructing texts and looking at the themes that they want to look at.

The comparison of his experiences of teaching in two quite different contexts helps Timothy to identify how his own literary education has been shaped, and to recognize that the literary experiences he has had do not simply need to be reproduced and that student engagement is an essential component of developing 'powerful' ways of literary knowing that extend beyond school.

An Expansive and Expanding Notion of Powerful Literary Knowledge

While many teachers in the study were concerned about the term 'literary knowledge', at least in their initial interviews, those who did use the word 'knowledge' in relation to literature in their initial interviews often gestured towards an understanding that was beyond the text itself, drawing on Dixon's concept of personal growth, and also Cox's formulation of critical engagement with the world (DESWO 1989: 21). In her first-year interview, Sophie said:

> I guess literary knowledge doesn't just come from looking at the book or the text or the poem or whatever, I think it comes from things that are outside it. So obviously looking at context, . . . and looking at how people who are reading it view it as well.

Echoing these ideas, Veronika suggested, 'maybe literary knowledge is the knowledge of how you read the world, and expanding your literary knowledge is expanding the ways in which you can read the world.' In a similar vein, Rebecca emphasized the importance of the experience of literature for the ability to see beyond the text, and to appreciate different ways of reading and seeing the world:

> I think literary knowledge is being able to see all those different perspectives and look at a text and see all different possibilities . . . it can't be measured because it is like a lens that you look through at the world and at texts and at ideas.

In fact, 'reading the world' turned out to be a strong justification across our early-career teachers for their work in teaching literature. When asked what they wanted their students to take away from the study of literature, our teachers specified knowledge about humanity and its worlds as conveyed in literary texts, as well as knowledge of the ideas and contexts that produced particular texts. Literature was also related to education of the emotions and to more general intellectual and philosophical growth, although each of these could be read as the outcome of those knowledges of 'the world'. These were not their only answers, of course, to questions of the value of literature, either individually or as a cohort, but constituted a common enough collective theme to justify us pursuing it here, and can be understood, we argue, as powerful knowledges in school English.

One way in which literary study and connections to such worldly concerns has historically been manifested in the English curriculum has been in treating literature as contributing to discussion around themes. In fact, treating literature by presenting groups of texts (or textual extracts) around specific (usually social justice-oriented) themes had a strong historical moment in the 1960s and 1970s in Australia and Britain, especially on the back of the *Reflections* series out of the Walworth school where John Dixon taught (Clements et al. 1963). The problem here, of course, is that literature is then seen as either in the service of, or itself being a version of, history/philosophy/social science or general personal development. Studying literature may still prioritize meaning, but without the central defining focus on language and, especially, on form and textuality, is it still 'English'? What *is* 'literary knowledge' in this view of the role of literature? Dixon conceded that his emphasis on pupil experience at the centre of English was often dismissed as 'sociology' (Dixon 1967/1975: 85). Quite contrary to recognizing the value which Dixon ascribed to literature, his notion of literature as 'bringing new voices into the classroom' was clearly read as prioritizing the theme over the literature – hence the early and persistent criticism of 'growth' as downgrading – even neglecting – literature (Allen 1980; Hansen 1979; Inglis 1975; Whitehead 1976).

Nevertheless, that does not seem to us the way in which our teachers saw literature. Veronika's description of the purpose of literature as a way of 'reading the world' seems to us to take account of textuality. Knowledge of *how* the world is read through texts implies knowledge of characteristic literary or textual practices. Indeed, for both Rebecca and Katya, greater experience of teaching encourages them to connect the high epistemic quality afforded by connecting literature with knowledge of the world, with what might be identified as the lower epistemic quality associated with reproducing particular forms and genres. While Rebecca retains an expansive understanding of the value and purpose of literary knowledge, in the final stage of the project she registers a connection between expansive literary experiences – knowing 'how' with the development of students' literacy skills, 'knowing that':

> [literary] analysis was my main focus . . . But now . . . I want them to be able to write so that they can express all that lovely analysis that we've done in class . . . obviously I still think it's [the teaching of literature] of value . . . it's something I think about a lot, and my classroom is still very discussion based . . . .. But . . . you know we can talk about it all we want but if we can't write it that's a problem.

Like Rebecca, Katya also highly valued her students' literary experiences at the commencement of the project, and her classroom experiences similarly led her to reassess her attitude to literacy and the teaching of knowledge about language and form:

there is some coherent value in our love of literature and . . . it's what builds community . . . *but* . . . we have a responsibility to help these children to be able to write . . . and it's not that I think they're at odds with each other, I actually think that the first one helps with the second one . . . they might verbally be able to do the appreciation, but I find it really hard to get them to write.

For both Rebecca and Katya, exploring questions of literary value and knowledge, and identifying what is powerful in this context, leads them to consider the kinds of propositional and pragmatic knowledge that enables higher-order thinking, and knowing. Importantly, rather than seeing these kinds of knowledge in a hierarchical relationship, for both Rebecca and Katya, they work together symbiotically, facilitating access to transformative education in English.

Conclusion

In this chapter, we argued that there is value in reconsidering the notion of powerful or significant knowledge in English, a subject undertaken by all students in Anglophone contexts, and which has historically to some extent 'tiptoed around' such interrogation. We contended that the assumptions of Young and others about propositional knowledge and disciplinary coherence do not apply as readily to the subject English, but argued that while teachers are reluctant, in some instances, to talk about knowledge, interviews with early-career teachers over time provide us with insights into the complexities of knowledge in this field. While the arguments of Young and others seek to identify what constitutes powerful knowledge in the discipline, with a view to ensuring that all students may have access to this, our research sees teachers implying that powerful literary knowledge in the subject English, the high epistemic quality apparent in being able to 'read' the world, can be animated only if students themselves are engaged in and with the process of knowledge production, and have the pragmatic and material means through which to engage in new understandings of texts. This suggests a connectedness between 'knowing how' and 'knowing that' (Winch 2013; Hudson 2018), enabled by attention to language and form, in this curriculum area.

It is also clear that conversations about knowledge in English, particularly literary knowledge, are valuable for teachers, and for pre-service teacher education. One interpretation of Young's argument is that academic disciplines provide the core knowledge for teachers, which they then learn to enact pedagogically in practice. Our research shows that, in the case of English teachers, their tertiary education provides key inputs into the development of new knowledge and understanding, but that this will continue to be developed, expanded and refined from the practice of their own teaching. Teacher education therefore plays an important role in supporting teachers to understand the distinctive and evolving nature of knowledge in English, and the connections between 'knowing how' and 'knowing that' in this curriculum area. Indeed, while attention is often paid in pre-service courses to identifying the tensions in English (Yates 2017), and to rehearsing notions of the subject English as unstable, and counter to other 'knowledge-based' subjects in secondary school, a more productive approach may be to explore the different ways powerful knowledge can and is being created in classrooms, the ways in which this diverges from subjects like the sciences, and teachers' key role in this.

As we have shown, conceptualizing literary knowledge as centrally concerned with ways of understanding and connecting the field, as in dialogue with other knowledges and skills within the larger subject of English, and as connecting texts, readers and reading, sees these early-career teachers nuancing and complexifying literary knowledge. This cluster of connections seems fundamental to how such teachers view epistemic quality. One key insight for policymakers who are increasingly disassembling the subject of English into 'literacy' (assessed through high-stakes standardized tests) and the 'teaching of texts' is this vital need for the connection of key aspects of the larger subject. Related to this is the importance of focusing on the connections between student engagement, pedagogy and literacy development in the context of student knowledge production around literature.

Acknowledgement

The project *Investigating Literary Knowledge in the Making of English Teachers* is funded by the Australian Research Council through its Discovery scheme (DP160101084). www.literaryknowledge.com.au

Notes

1 The 'Anglo-American Conference on the Teaching and Learning of English' convened at Dartmouth College, New Hampshire, in 1966 and hosted more

than fifty scholars from the United Kingdom, the United States and Canada. The seminar has remained highly influential in Britain and Australia as a touchstone for discussions on curriculum design, particularly through the account of the seminar written by John Dixon in *Growth through English* (1967/1975), which popularized the notion of the 'growth model' of English. The influence of Dartmouth in the United States has been more debatable (Brass 2016).

2   The Newbolt Report (Newbolt [1921]) was arguably the high point of the view that literature be the centre of the English curriculum in schools. The Newsom Report (CACEE 1963: 155) also argued for 'the civilising experience of contact with great literature'. The Bullock (DES, 1975) and Cox (DESWO, 1989) reports contained similar, although not identical, arguments. For Dixon, literature brings 'new voices into the classroom' and 'adds to the store of shared experience' (1967/1975: 13). See McLean Davies and Sawyer (2020).

References

Allen, D. (1980), *English Teaching Since 1965: How Much Growth?* London: Heinemann.

Australian Curriculum, Assessment and Reporting Authority (ACARA) (2016), *English Foundation to Year 12*. http://www.acara.edu.au/curriculum/learning_areas/english.html

Australian Institute for Teaching and School Leadership (AITSL) (2011), *Australian Professional Standards for Teachers*. https://www.aitsl.edu.au/teach/standards

Bacalja, A. and Bliss, L. (2019), *A Report on Trends in Senior English Text-Lists*, Melbourne: VATE.

Barrett, B., Hoadley, U. and Morgan, J. (2018), *Knowledge, Curriculum and Equity: Social Realist Perspectives*, London: Routledge.

Beavis, C. (2013), 'Literary English and the Challenge of Multimodality', *Changing English: Studies in Culture and Education*, 20 (3): 241–52.

Brass, J. (2016), 'Re-reading Dartmouth: An American Perspective', *English in Australia*, 51 (3): 52–7.

Britton, J. (1970), *Language and Learning*, London: Allen Lane.

Central Advisory Council for Education (England) (CACEE) (1963), *The Newsom Report: Half Our Future*, London: Her Majesty's Stationery Office.

Clements, S., Dixon, J. and Stratta, L. (1963), *Reflections (Walworth English course): An English Course for Students Aged 14–18*, London: Oxford University Press.

Department for Education (DfE) (2011), *Teacher Standards: Guidance for School Leaders, School Staff and Governing Bodies*. https://www.gov.uk/government/publications/teachers-standards

Department of Education and Science (DES) (1975), *A Language for Life: Report of the Committee of Inquiry by the Secretary of State for Education and Science under *the Chairmanship of* Sir *Alan Bullock FBA*, London: Her Majesty's Stationery Office.

Department of Education and Science and the Welsh Office (DESWO) (1989), *The Cox Report: English for Ages 5 to 16*, London: Her Majesty's Stationery Office.

Dixon, J. (1967/1975), *Growth Through English: Set in the Perspective of the Seventies* (3rd ed.), London: Oxford.

Doecke, B. (2016), 'History: Autobiography: Growth (Fifty Years since Dartmouth)', *English in Australia*, 51 (3): 33–9.

Doecke, B. (2017), 'What Kind of "Knowledge" is English? (Re-reading the Newbolt Report)', *Changing English*, 24 (3): 230–45. DOI: 10.1080/1358684X.2017.1351228

Doecke, B. and Mead, P. (2017), 'English and the Knowledge Question', *Pedagogy, Culture and Society*, 26 (2): 249–64. DOI: 10.1080/14681366.2017.1380691

Durrant, C. (2004), 'English Teaching: Profession or Predicament?', *English in Australia*, 141: 6–8.

Evans, C. (1993), *English People: Experience of Teaching and Learning in British Universities*, London: Open University Press.

Glazener, N. (2015), *Literature in the Making: A History of U.S. Literary Culture in the Long Nineteenth Century*, London: Oxford University Press.

Goodwyn, A. (2012), 'The Status of Literature: English Teaching and the Condition of Literature Teaching in Schools', *English in Education*, 46 (3): 212–27.

Goodwyn, A., Durrant, C., Sawyer, W., Scherff, L. and Zancanella, D. (eds) (2019), *The Future of English Teaching Worldwide: Celebrating 50 Years from the Dartmouth Conference*, London: Routledge.

Green, B. (2018), *Engaging Curriculum: Bridging the Curriculum Theory and English Education Divide*, London: Routledge.

Hansen, I. V. (1979), 'The Case for Literature Study in Secondary Schools: Some Difficulties', *The Teaching of English*, 36 (May): 3–16.

Hudson, B. (2018), 'Powerful Knowledge and Epistemic Quality in School Mathematics', *London Review of Education*, 16 (3): 384–97.

Hudson, B., Henderson, S. and Hudson, A. (2015), 'Developing Mathematical Thinking in the Primary Classroom: Liberating Students and Teachers as Learners of Mathematics', *Journal of Curriculum Studies*, 47 (3): 374–98.

Hudson, B., Tani, S., Randahl, A-C., Kristiansson, M. Crisan, C. Figueiredo, M. P. and Lofstron, J. (2019), 'Powerful Knowledge and Epistemic Quality across School Subjects and Teacher Education (Part 2)', *Symposium of the European Conference on Educational Research*, September, Hamburg.

Inglis, F. (1975), *Ideology and the Imagination*, Cambridge: Cambridge University Press.

Locke, T. (2007), 'Constructing English in New Zealand: A Report on a Decade of Reform', *L1 Educational Studies in Language and Literature*, 7 (2): 5–33.

McGowan, M. (2019, June 24), 'Wollongong University Intervenes to Approve Ramsay Centre Western Civilisation Degree', *The Guardian*. https://www.theguardian.com/

australia-news/2019/jun/24/wollongong-university-intervenes-to-approve-ramsay-centre-western-civilisation-degree

McLean Davies, L., Martin, S. K. and Buzacott, L. (2017), 'Worldly Reading: Teaching Australia Literature in the Twenty-first Century', *English in Australia*, 52 (3): 21–30.

McLean Davies, L. and Sawyer, W. (2018), '(K)now You See It, (K)now You Don't: Literary Knowledge in the "Australian Curriculum: English"', *Journal of Curriculum Studies*, 50 (6): 836–49. DOI: 10.1080/00220272.2018.1499807

McLean Davies, L. and Sawyer, W. (2020), 'On Being "Well Read"', in B. Marshall, J. Manuel, D. L. Pasternak and J. Rowsell (eds), *The Bloomsbury Handbook on Reading Perspectives and Practices*, 145–67, London: Bloomsbury.

Mead, P. (2011), 'What We Have to Work With: Teaching Australian Literature in the Contemporary Context', in B. Doecke, L. McLean Davies and P. Mead (eds), *Teaching Australian Literature: From Classroom Conversations to National Imaginings*, 52–69, Adelaide: AATE/Wakefield Press.

Medway, P. (1980), *Finding a Language: Autonomy and Learning in Schools*, London: Chameleon Books.

Medway, P. (1990), 'Into the Sixties: English and English Society at a Time of Change', in I. Goodson and P. Medway (eds), *Bringing English to Order: The History and Politics of a School Subject*, 1–46, London, New York and Philadelphia: The Falmer Press.

Medway, P. (2010), 'English and Enlightenment', *Changing English*, 17 (1): 3–12. DOI: 10.1080/13586840903556987

Misson, R. and Morgan, W. (2006), *Critical Literacy and the Aesthetic: Transforming the English Classroom*, Urbana, IL: NCTE.

Moore, R. (2013), 'Social Realism and the Problem of the Problem of Knowledge in the Sociology of Education', *British Journal of Sociology of Education*, 34 (3): 333–53. DOI: 10.1080/01425692.2012.714251

Moore, R. and Muller, J. (1999), 'The Discourse of Voice and the Problem of Knowledge in the Sociology of Education', *British Journal of Sociology of Education*, 23 (4): 189–206.

Muller, J. (2009), 'Forms of Knowledge and Curriculum Coherence', *Journal of Education and Work*, 22 (3): 205–26.

Muller, J. and Young, M. (2019), 'Knowledge, Power and Powerful Knowledge Revisited', *The Curriculum Journal*, 30 (2): 196–214. DOI: 10.1080/09585176.2019.1570292

Newbolt, H. (Chair), The Departmental Committee Appointed by the President of the Board of Education to Inquire into the Position of English in the Educational System of England (1921), *The Teaching of English in England*, London: His Majesty's Stationery Office.

Sawyer, W., McLean Davies, L., Gannon, S. and Dowsett, P. (2016), 'Mid-Atlantic Crossings: Some Texts that Emerged from Dartmouth', *English in Australia*, 51 (3): 40–51.

Squire, J. R. (ed.) (1968), *Response to Literature: Papers Relating to the Anglo-American Seminar on the Teaching of English (Dartmouth College, New Hampshire, 1966)*, Champaign, IL: National Council of Teachers of English.

West-Pavlov, R. (2018), *The Global South and Literature*, Cambridge: Cambridge University Press. DOI: 10.1017/9781108231930

Whitehead, F. (1976), 'The Present State of English Teaching: (1) Stunting the Growth', *The Use of English*, 28 (1, Autumn): 11–17.

Winch, C. (2013), 'Curriculum Design and Epistemic Ascent', *Journal of Philosophy of Education*, 47 (1): 128–46.

Yandell, J. (2017), 'Knowledge, English and the Formation of Teachers', *Pedagogy, Culture and Society*, 25 (4): 583–99. DOI: 10.1080/14681366.2017.1312494

Yates, L. (2017), 'History as Knowledge: Humanities Challenges for a Knowledge-based Curriculum', in B. Barrett, U. Hoadley and J. Morgan (eds), *Knowledge, Curriculum and Equity: Social Realist Perspectives*, London: Routledge.

Yates, L., Woelert, P., Millar, V. and O'Connor, K. (2017), *Knowledge at the Crossroads? Physics and History in the Changing World of Schools and Universities*, Singapore: Springer.

Yates, L., McLean Davies, L., Buzacott, L., Doecke, B., Mead, P. and Sawyer, W. (2019), 'School English, Literature and the Knowledge-base Question', *The Curriculum Journal*, 30 (1): 51–68. DOI: 10.1080/09585176.2018.1543603

Young, M. (2013), 'Overcoming the Crisis in Curriculum Theory: A Knowledge-based Approach', *Journal of Curriculum Studies*, 45 (2): 101–108. DOI: 10.1080/00220272.2013.764505

Young, M. and Muller, J. (2010), 'Three Educational Scenarios for the Future: Lessons from the Sociology of Knowledge', *European Journal of Education*, 45 (1): 1–27.

Young, M. and Muller, J. (2013), 'On the Powers of Powerful Knowledge', *Review of Education*, 1 (3): 229–50. DOI: 10.1002/rev3.3017

Young, M., Lambert, D., Roberts, C. and Roberts, M. (2014), *Knowledge and the Future School: Curriculum and Social Justice*, London: Bloomsbury.

7

Transforming Circular Economy Principles into Teachers' Powerful Professional Knowledge

Kalle Juuti and Niklas Gericke

Introduction – Why Teach about the Circular Economy?

Sustainability is strongly emphasized in international-level policies (European Commission [EU] 2019; United Nations [UN] 2015). Curriculum documents for compulsory schooling in many countries also frequently mention sustainability, for example, Finland and Sweden (Finnish Educational Agency 2015; Swedish National Agency for Education 2018). Sustainability is not a curriculum subject where time allocation, goal and content are stated clearly; however, knowledge of sustainability and the objective of learning sustainable ways of living are integrated into every school subject in the Finnish school curriculum. Similarly in Sweden, sustainability forms part of the general curriculum and should therefore be addressed by all teachers. This makes the inclusion of topics on sustainability challenging because it is situated outside traditional disciplinary content (Sund and Gericke 2020).

Typically, sustainability is divided into three main dimensions: environmental, social and economic. Yet, in the pursuit of sustainable development, these dimensions are regarded as interdependently and holistically intertwined (Giddings et al. 2002). It seems that environmental and societal dimensions are more emphasized than the economic dimension by teachers in the classroom (Berglund and Gericke 2018). This is not optimal when the environmental and social message is that natural resources are being overused and that economic growth requirements have led to global and inter-generational inequities.

This chapter addresses the question of how to include the economic dimension in teacher education in a way that promotes education for sustainability. The question that then emerges is: What should the focus be when teaching the economic dimension? Namely, the chapter deals with the third KOSS network research question on the nature of teachers' powerful professional knowledge in this context and considers the implications for teacher education policy and practice.

In the committee paper *Our Common Future* by Brundtland (1987) for the UN's World Commission for Environment and Development, which sparked the inclusion of sustainability in policy documents worldwide, the term 'sustainable development' was used instead of 'sustainability'. The concept of sustainable development is polysemous in the sense that it includes the seemingly contradictory goals of 'sustainability' and 'development', whereas sustainability is often understood to refer to the preservation of natural resources, while 'development' is seen as synonymous with economic growth (Atkinson et al. 2007), which introduces tension between environmental, social and economic sustainability (Giddings et al. 2002). However, according to many policy documents (e.g. Brundtland 1987), in terms of sustainable development, economic growth is essential to the social dimension of poverty reduction, especially in developing countries. This interpretation of sustainability has been heavily criticized; for instance, questions have been asked whether human capital can replace natural capital in economic growth (Neumayer 2003). Spangenberg (2005) notes there are constraints on economic growth: (1) the economy should not threaten the natural system's sustainability; environmental sinks and sources are indispensable to an economically sustainable economy; (2) the economy should not undermine the sustainability of the institutional system of society or undermine the system of human sustainability; every economy needs suitable institutional conditions and human resources to be economically sustainable; and (3) the economy should not risk its economic sustainability. This means the economy must be environmentally and socially sustainable.

When transforming sustainability or sustainable development into sustainable education and education for sustainable development (ESD), this perspective on the economy must be taken into account. It has been argued that it is necessary to integrate a view of sustainability which considers the tension between environmental, social and economic sustainability (Berglund and Gericke 2016). In this chapter, the *circular economy's* potential to respond to the call for the integration of the economic aspects of sustainable development into the teaching curriculum and take account of the constraints outlined by Spangenberg (2005) is considered. However, it is important to recognize that the circular economy is a policy concept established within the EU's European Green Deal framework, which states:

It [the European Green Deal] is a new growth strategy that aims to transform the EU into a fair and prosperous society, with a modern, resource-efficient and competitive economy where there are no net emissions of greenhouse gases in 2050 and where economic growth is decoupled from resource use. (EU 2019: 2)

Hence, the European Green Deal document is essentially a strategy for economic growth in a new format. It basically strives for the integration of economic, social and environmental sustainability by valuing a fair and prosperous society and establishing tangible constraints on the depletion of natural resources. Therefore, the European Green Deal policy requires changes to the economy in line with the circular economy. The EU (2019), national governments and independent foundations, like Sitra (2016) in Finland and the Ellen McArthur Foundation (2019) in the UK, promote the circular economy tenet as a solution to managing the overconsumption of natural resources to mitigate global warming and the mass extinction of species reflected by the linear extract-produce-use-dump material and energy flow model to which the modern economy adheres. The circular economy is described as restorative by design and aims to ensure that products, components and materials are constantly kept at the highest utility levels and value. Still, it should not be viewed as a specific technique or process; instead, it is a way of thinking and organizing economic activities (Webster 2017: 17). Thus far, this chapter has addressed the rationale for teaching the circular economy (i.e. as a contribution to ESD by integrating the environmental, social and economic dimensions).

However, the definition of a circular economy remains unclear; it holds political connotations and comprises separate ideas (Korhonen et al. 2018). In addition, it is not connected to any specific traditional academic discipline or school subject. The reason for including the circular economy in the school curriculum relates to European policy. Nonetheless, teaching is not the same as policy. This means it is crucial to consider and discuss the transformation process when new content knowledge is transformed from the intended curriculum into an enacted curriculum, and this transformation process becomes even more complex because a topic like the circular economy is multidisciplinary in nature and not part of traditional disciplinary content knowledge.

Powerful disciplinary knowledge is specialized knowledge that exceeds everyday knowledge and provides the cognitive tools for participation in discussions on social, cultural, economic and environmental issues and an evaluation of the trustworthiness of the arguments (Lambert et al. 2015; Young and Muller 2015). Powerful knowledge gives the tools to act more intelligently than would be possible by only applying everyday knowledge and provides an understanding of the mechanisms involved in how the world works (Arthur 2009).

In this chapter, the circular economy is viewed as a powerful concept in ESD with the potential to empower adolescents to act in sustainable ways. However, authoritative knowledge on the policy level outside the school institution might not be the same as that taught and learnt in the classroom, which needs to be adapted to students' pre-knowledge levels and the way the teaching is performed (Gericke et al. 2018). The content-selection decision-making process is intertwined with the question of how to teach, and the epistemic quality (Hudson 2018) of the content must also be considered while deliberating on this (Sund Gericke and Bladh 2020). In the transformation process, the question therefore does not pertain to the delivery of content in parts for acquisition by the students, but to why these practices are authentic from a disciplinary perspective. Accordingly, the question pursued in this chapter is similar to that proposed by Deng (2020: 32): 'How would content [that relates to the circular economy] be interpreted and transformed in ways that allow content to open up manifold opportunities for the cultivation of human capabilities or powers (abilities, dispositions, ways of thinking, understanding worlds) for all students?' Hence, this chapter discusses the ways and manner in which the circular economy can be transformed into powerful professional knowledge for teaching in teacher education. The context of teacher education is chosen because, while seeking to establish new teaching practices, it is important to bring about the professional development of teachers (Furlong and Whitty 2017).

What to Teach: Circular Economy-Related Strategies

The core idea of a *circular economy* is to close loops in natural resources (Stahel 2016). Optimally, all material resources circulate between production and consumption, and no waste is produced. Stahel (2016) estimates that implementation of a circular economy holds the potential of cutting emissions by up to 70 per cent, increasing the workforce, and significantly reducing the level of waste. Circular economies have been adopted in large industries; in addition, a growing number of small- to medium-sized enterprises are incorporating the circular economy concept into their business plans (Sitra n.d.). The type of circular economy content, namely what to include in the school curriculum and teacher education and content that responds to societal change, is discussed due to its importance for society. Stahel (2016) defines a circular economy according to three closed loops. The first loop is reuse, repair and remanufacture. The owner controls how the goods are used, but the user does not necessarily have to be the owner. The producer of the goods may retain ownership of them and rent or sell them as a service. The second loop is the 'take back' of goods while the third loop is the recycling of materials. The renewal of used products or materials reduces the need to make new products or use virgin materials. These loops connect the use, manufacturing and distribution of goods. The idea is that if the ownership can be transferred directly from the manufacturer to the user, the amount of waste will be reduced.

A circular economy not only involves recycling but also gives emphasis to renewable energy sources and cradle-to-cradle designs. With the latter, biological and technical materials are placed in different cycles. Their separation means that the biological materials can be fed back into the natural material cycle via composting or anaerobic digestion. Finally, digitalization supports the transition from a linear economy to a circular one by, for example, promoting dematerialization (Ellen MacArthur Foundation 2019) through better data management, an enhanced production process design and rapid prototyping. Increased demand for music and television streaming services compared to the delivery of music via a physical artefact (e.g. CDs and LPs) may be an example of dematerialization. The objective of a circular economy is to ensure that 'the product value chain and life cycle retain the highest possible value and quality as long as possible and is also as energy efficient as it can be' (Korhonen et al. 2018: 38). Thus, the circular economy relates to sustainable development. The objective of ensuring environmental sustainability in a circular economy can be achieved by relying on material loops and renewable energy production. Social sustainability can be realized by sharing resources and increasing employability and participative decision-making. In addition, economic sustainability can be better accomplished through cost reduction rather than through the purchase of virgin materials, especially for innovative new product designs.

Thus, a circular economy is eclectic. Hawken et al. (1999) introduced four strategies to enable countries, communities and companies to consider environmental, social and economic sustainability from a circular economy perspective. These strategies focus on radical resource productivity, biomimicry, a service and flow economy, and investment in natural capital. Webster (2017) interpreted these strategies as shifts in economic and consumer behaviours. The first strategy is to make design changes to recover, disassemble and remanufacture materials and develop cleaner material flows.

The second strategy supports the idea that there is no waste, only resources. The 'everything is food' idea is adopted from living ecosystems. The third and fourth strategies aim to change consumer behaviour and ownership patterns by placing emphasis on services (Stahel 2010) and the shared economy (Ertz et al. 2019; Hamari et al. 2015) in which the consumer has a two-sided role as a receiver and provider of goods/services. Especially in relation to the third and fourth strategies, digitalization has enabled economic activities by providing platforms for individuals to provide and receive resources and services (Kenney and Zysman 2016).

Even though a circular economy holds promise in terms of its ability to foster sustainable development, Korhonen et al. (2018) argued that the concept is political, superficial and a collection of vague and separate ideas. Policy and business reports give an idealistic view of the strengths of a circular economy for sustainable development. Korhonen et al. (2018) summarized the physical, economic, managerial and sociocultural limitations of a circular economy. The laws of thermodynamics set major limits on closed material and energy loops. A totally closed material–energy loop is impossible owing to the law of entropy. In addition, with recycling, material loss occurs and enormous amounts of energy are required. The circular economy project or initiative should be evaluated in terms of its global and temporal influence. A more sustainable product may eliminate the immediate problem by pushing it forward for later consideration or shifting it to a different location, likely a developing country. Korhonen et al. (2018) noted that it is very difficult to evaluate the impact of temporal and global influences on the economy. For example, it is not necessarily optimal to make a product that is long-lasting because new products in the future might be more energy-inefficient or emit fewer emissions.

Economic limitations can also have a rebound effect. When production costs decline, the price of the product also decreases. This boosts consumption and increases the energy and material resources used. The crucial question is how resources can be conserved in a circular economy when innovative product designs are needed to promote sustainable consumption practices: '[I]f the current consumption culture will not change, [the] CE [circular economy] will remain as a technical tool that does not change the course of the current unsustainable economic paradigm' (Korhonen et al. 2018: 44). If the circular economy is going to be part of the school curriculum and teacher education, the problematic and critical perspectives on the circular economy should be included and, together with policy ideas, should constitute the basis for the transformation of powerful knowledge into taught knowledge.

The Transformation of Circular Knowledge into Powerful Knowledge

The preceding section describes the establishment of a *circular economy* at the policy level based on the needs of society, but not adequately developed based on the needs of a discipline. It is thus proposed that this concept should comprise part of the teaching content in schools. The question posed is: Who should teach this content in a subject-driven curriculum? Practically speaking, a multidisciplinary approach is required when teachers of different specializations participate because the content stems from several disciplines. A second question: How to identify the powerful knowledge of this 'non-disciplinary' content? Young (2015) defined powerful knowledge as subject-specific, coherent, conceptual disciplinary knowledge that, when learnt, empowers students to make decisions and become competent in ways that influence their lives positively. The description of a circular economy does not correlate with the first part of this definition since it is not subject-specific conceptual knowledge, nor is it coherent; rather, it is eclectic and context-specific. Yet, policy documents throughout Europe (EU, 2019) claim that the circular economy fulfils the latter part of Young's definition (i.e. it provides possibilities for action by learners that positively influence their lives). We suggest that this is possible only if the challenges relating to this eclectic concept are also included when the content is transformed into taught knowledge.

Circular economy strategies comprise a tentative framework of knowledge to be taught in teacher education and schools as a means for achieving transformation (see columns 1 and 2, Table 7.1). These strategies constitute a basic version of those proposed by Hawken et al. (1999). The strategies are suggested ways of organizing knowledge regarding what should be taught and the content to be learnt. Yet, as stated, circular economy strategies are eclectic and context-dependent. If they are taught without reflection, several unintended consequences may be emphasized (Korhonen et al. 2018). It is therefore proposed that these unintended consequences be also addressed when teaching students about the circular economy (see column 3, Table 7.1).

The strategies presented in Table 7.1 were applied during a teacher education course that focused on the circular economy in Finland, described in more detail by Juuti et al. (2019), in which a multidisciplinary perspective was taken (see examples in column 4, Table 7.1). While transforming circular

Table 7.1 Circular Economy Strategies Adopted in Teacher Education

Strategies	Desired Achievements	Unintended Consequences	Examples*
From disposable to fixable (radical resource productivity)	Lengthening the lifespan of a product by improving its quality and by paying particular attention to reparability	May shift sustainability-related challenges to a different setting in time or space	Modular furniture expands the lifespan of the product by using exchangeable parts
From waste to raw material (biomimicry)	During the product's lifetime, technical and biomaterial cycles are separated	New uses of waste may result in unsustainable production	A company turns old batteries into fertilizer that can be used in agriculture
From product to service (service and flow economy)	When a commodity is available as a service, there is no need for everyone to own everything	An increased number of services may increase total consumption	Professionals arrange a desired solution for lighting instead of purchasing lamps
From owning to sharing (investing in natural capital)	People share material resources via Internet platforms	People may purchase new products to share	Short-term property rentals

*Examples of vignettes analysed during a teacher education course that considered the circular economy in Finland. Source: Juuti et al. 2019.

economy strategies into taught knowledge, it is important to recognize that the students are probably unfamiliar with these concepts (Lommi et al. 2019). We would argue that such strategies (Hawken et al. 1999) and the associated limitations (Korhonen et al. 2018) marshal powerful professional disciplinary knowledge of the circular economy, here referred to as an aspect of *powerful professional knowledge*, a term coined by Furlong and Whitty (2017). This approach considers the transformation challenge and the fact that the school content might draw on different disciplines and practices, in contrast with Young's (2015) description of powerful knowledge as disciplinary and without recognition of the transformation process that teachers must consider. Therefore, in this study, powerful professional knowledge is a suitable concept with respect to the use and understanding of the circular economy and its role in teacher education.

To evaluate the trustworthiness of arguments on circular economy strategies and their limits, powerful professional knowledge is required of several disciplines, such as physics, chemistry, biology, the social sciences, psychology and economics. The process of choosing what to teach from each discipline is the subject specialist teacher's task. For example, in physics, the conservation law of energy and the principle of entropy are essential to designing and critically evaluating resource productivity. Knowledge of biology and chemistry facilitates the ability to judge material selection and the safety of waste usage, for instance, how it could be made safe when using municipal waste-based fertilizers. In addition, psychology-based knowledge could be used to determine why people are reluctant to reduce the number of objects they own and when designing business models that motivate people to buy services instead of products. Similarly, the social sciences could help in evaluating the advantages and disadvantages of local and global equity products. Thus, circular economy-based strategies require conceptual tools from different disciplines to identify the opportunities to create powerful citizens who live in line with circular economy principles.

How to Teach: Invention Making by Students

In disciplinary education, determining what to teach is intertwined with deciding on the teaching method. The nature of the discipline is essential to how the subject is taught (Bladh et al. 2018). However, the nature of teaching may vary depending on the goals. In science education, Roberts (2007) referred to a *vision I* perspective of teaching where the goal was to provide the subject concepts in preparation for further studies, in contrast to a *vision II* perspective that addressed the use and application of contextual knowledge by citizens from an everyday perspective. From a vision I perspective, concepts are taught in a way that is supposed to mimic authenticity in relation to the subject. Simultaneously, concepts and disciplinary practices constitute the content (i.e. what to teach and how to teach it) emphasized by Krajcik and Shinn (2015) with regard to teaching scientific practices. Taught content can thus be idealized as being of high epistemic quality when the domain is presented in an authentic way having been transformed from a discipline into teacher education and schools. Concepts and procedures in teaching are considered to have epistemic similarity with the data gathering, analysis and justification used in the methods of the mother discipline, science.

By contrast, in education for sustainability development, which includes the circular economy, the overarching goal is to address real-life problems of a multidisciplinary nature that are not situated within a single discipline (Sund and Gericke 2020). Here, the goal of teaching is more in line with the vision II perspective, according to the typology of Roberts (2007), where the goal is to apply knowledge to real-life situations. In the teaching context, the epistemic logic also differs and better correlates with what can be achieved with knowledge. Hudson (2018) argues that high epistemic quality in mathematics education shows mathematics content as fallible, refutable and uncertain. Further, he claims that high epistemic quality mathematics education promotes problem-solving, critical thinking, creative reasoning, the generation of multiple solutions and learning from mistakes. Thus, from this perspective, high epistemic quality is not only embedded in the structure of the discipline but is also associated with the execution of teaching and how it is performed. In the current study, it is argued that the same situation exists when teaching a multidisciplinary topic like the circular economy. It is important to teach the circular economy using a multidisciplinary approach that draws on several disciplines to establish powerful professional knowledge. Simultaneously, the teaching should address real-life sustainability challenges pertaining to the circular economy using teaching strategies of high epistemic quality. An emerging question then pertains to how circular economy should be taught. In the previous section, a framework of strategies, comprising the core content when teaching the circular economy, was proposed and unintended consequences were highlighted. Here, the teaching approach to use is discussed because much of what is found in the literature regarding the circular economy stresses the importance of innovation. The focus is hence on the application of disciplinary knowledge to new situations rather than any reproduction of already established disciplinary knowledge. Identifying how to teach the subject matter links substantially to determining which subject matter should be taught when teaching the circular economy.

Webster (2017) suggested that innovations are pivotal to a circular economy. Ollikainen and Pohjola (2013) argued that economic growth does not necessarily require an increase in the use of natural resources, but should be built on innovations. Sustainable inventions in the circular economy are therefore seen as separate from the use of natural resources. Making inventions is not only essential to the circular economy; doing this is (or should be) an essential part of sustainability science in general (Miller 2015). Making inventions is considered an authentic practice in a circular economy (i.e. of high epistemic quality).

Therefore, to transform the circular economy into teacher education and school teaching while ensuring high epistemic quality, the teaching methods must represent the authentic practices of the circular economy, in line with previous arguments in relation to other school subjects (Hudson 2018; Krajcik and Schin 2015). As a consequence, when teaching and learning about the circular economy students should be motivated to make inventions, which relates to how this should be performed. For example, a circular economy project at school could focus on how school tablets could be effectively shared and how to maintain them. This would avoid the need to purchase more equipment. From a broad perspective, sustainability in science motivates student inventions, thereby providing an answer to the question of how to teach.

Here, in terms of transformation, when students engage in making inventions, they learn to understand how the world works, which includes complex and unexpected influences that might induce changes in consumer behaviour, as discussed previously when considering what to teach (Korhonen et al. 2018). Making inventions is thus both the content and method of circular economy when transformed into teacher education as school knowledge and practice. The introduced strategies may be understood as design principles to guide the process or teaching design and learning process and possible constraints. For example, in visual arts at primary school, students typically create a card for Mother's Day. As a design principle, they could design a card that does not use any material. A design constraint could be that it must be possible to disassemble the card. The same constraints could apply to a craft while the students design artefacts for everyday use.

In general, making inventions is a collaborative and iterative design process in which knowledge and skills are applied to create novel and practical solutions to fulfil real-world needs and address effective resource sharing. Inventions are novel and appropriate solutions to open-ended tasks. Through inventing, pupils learn to identify needs; frame problems; explore solutions; consider alternatives; communicate their ideas verbally, visually, and materially; and collaborate (Kangas et al. 2013). Making inventions is an archetypical form of knowledge-creation learning that promotes existing knowledge and provides opportunities to create something new. Accordingly, inventing, as a form of learning, requires: (1) engaging pupils in complex open-ended problem-solving beyond the classroom; (2) focusing enquiries on parallel work with material, digital and conceptual artefacts that are 'hands on' and 'minds on'; (3) persuading pupils to cross community boundaries and (4) catalysing pupil–specialist collaboration to provide students access to specialist knowledge practices (Kangas et al. 2013).

The invention process, we argue, invites students to consider and revisit circular economy strategies, what could be achieved, any unintended consequences and how to avoid them. The circular economy is not a coherent independent body of knowledge; instead, it comprises strategies to integrate and employ different disciplinary learning knowledge to achieve sustainability goals.

Seitamaa-Hakkarainen et al. (2001) conceptualized a collaborative design model that can be seen as an example of how to structure students' invention processes in the classroom. The model illustrates the nature of innovations. Seitamaa-Hakkarainen et al. (2001) identified seven phases of invention: (1) elaborating on the design ideas and re-designing and creating the design context; (2) defining the design task and design constraints; (3) creating conceptual and visual design ideas; (4) evaluating the design ideas and constraints; (5) connecting to expert cultures and data collection; (6) experimenting and testing the design ideas (sketching and prototyping); and (7) assessing the prototype function. In a transformation of the circular economy during a teachers' education course, we used these phases while teaching the students about inventions (Juuti et al. 2019) and we believe they could be used to teach the circular economy in schools as well.

A key element of the model – distributed expertise – is that the process is open, inclusive and collaborative. In particular, disciplinarily specialist knowledge is needed to manage the complex design process of the circular economy. Sormunen et al. (2020) summarized the key elements required for the invention process. The invention process commences with an orientation phase where emphasis is placed on building a creative atmosphere and trust between group members. The invention challenge (the problem to be addressed by the invention) is defined in the second phase. In the third phase, the focus is on the production of ideas, making enquiries and assessing ideas. This phase is crucial from a disciplinary knowledge point of view. Depending on the problem and ideas needed to solve the problem, the students make enquiries into the topic. These enquiries follow subject-specific trajectories. A scientific enquiry is different from a social sciences enquiry. This is exemplified by the fact that the students can conduct a chemistry experiment to determine the most optimal material for a certain product, or they can organize an interview to identify the values and preferences of a group of people to optimize the service to be designed. The fourth phase involves testing the ideas and selecting the best one. The key concept is evaluated in the fifth phase. The sixth phase – modification – involves prototyping and producing and, typically, this takes the most time in the classroom. During this phase, the students test their concept to obtain feedback, make iterations and revert to the ideation phase if the innovation does not address the invention challenge. The end of the invention process concerns the presentation of the product or concept. Products that resolve the challenge are publicly accessible representations of the students' learning during the teaching and learning process.

Based on our own experiences with the integration of the circular economy into teacher education, the student teachers experienced difficulty guiding the invention process. Our experiences show that certain aspects need special attention when teaching the circular economy in teacher education, for example, how to facilitate the students to create ideas, test them, conduct enquiries, obtain new knowledge, test prototypes or concepts, and learn how to utilize feedback. Teaching the circular economy in this way is challenging. Yet, Härkki et al. (2020) found that shared values were a defining feature of highly functional collaboration while working with design and inventions. If teachers trust each other, share values and are committed to developing teaching, the invention process will often be successful. In the case of the circular economy and education for sustainable development, collaboration among teachers of different subjects is required. Thus, the need for shared values and the intention to develop teaching is likely to be pivotal when incorporating circular economy principles into teacher education.

Conclusion: Powerful Professional Knowledge of the Circular Economy

The concept of a circular economy was described in this chapter and a way was proposed to transform the concept into teachable content in teacher education and schools. This involved integrating what to teach with how to execute it using multidisciplinary circular economy inventions while addressing real-world problems. Thus, when teaching sustainability, the economic dimension can be integrated with environmental and social dimensions. The argument as to why to teach the circular economy in school is based on European-level policies for resource-efficient and competitive economies, which stress the need to decouple economic growth from resource use (EU 2019). To achieve this ambitious goal, there is a need to implement circular economy principles early on in school teaching, and teacher education is a suitable vehicle for this as it creates common powerful professional knowledge among teachers. As outlined in this chapter, the circular economy is a way of rethinking current ways of living and, by inventing new teaching practices that adhere to the four identified circular economy strategies, the status quo in this regard can be challenged. The conjecture for transforming the circular economy into teacher education is that while engaging in the process of making circular economy inventions or guiding pupils during the process, student teacher interns should be equipped and committed to embedding sustainability in their teaching.

We have problematized the writings of the policy documents with a view to achieving this ambitious goal. Conceptually, the circular economy has been criticized for being political and constituting a collection of separate ideas (Korhonen et al. 2018). Conversely, policy papers have shown the circular economy to be a 'magic bullet' that can be used to achieve a sustainable, fair and prosperous society (Ellen MacArthur Foundation 2019; EU 2019; Sitra 2016). Thus, there is a risk of oversimplifying complex problems relating to sustainability. Teaching that uses a critical approach, including the amalgamation of multidisciplinary perspectives that draw on subject specialist knowledge, is therefore recommended, while ensuring authenticity in relation to real-life problems concerning sustainability. Using our suggested teaching approach, circular economy strategies and invention practices should not be separated; they should be seen as intertwined. Deng (2020) stresses that content needs to be interpreted and transformed in a way that allows for the cultivation of students' capabilities. We support this deduction.

Making inventions is an essential aspect of the circular economy (Webster 2017) and, when transformed into teacher education, it integrates the teaching parameters (what should be taught) with the methods (how it should be taught) (i.e. knowledge and pedagogy are transformed and merged into a conglomerate that is difficult to separate but, in combination, creates high epistemic quality teaching). In addition, the topic is multidisciplinary since it draws on the knowledge and practices of several disciplines, which means that the research objective can be drawn from society and everyday life. Thus, powerful, professional knowledge emerges when all of these aspects are considered in the teaching process.

Developing powerful professional knowledge among teachers of different school subjects is important because sustainability issues, such as a circular economy, are the responsibility of teachers regardless of the subjects in the national curriculum (Finnish Educational Agency 2015; Swedish National Agency for Education 2018). Teachers are required to organize and enact multidisciplinary teaching as per these steering documents. Yet, research has shown that multidisciplinary teaching is challenging (Kervinen et al. 2016) and teachers often feel uncomfortable teaching outside of their disciplinary tradition (Gericke et al. 2020; Oulton et al. 2004). Hence, it is important to create learning opportunities for subject-specific teacher students to ensure they are exposed to these teaching experiences during teacher education and in so doing can develop powerful professional knowledge.

Acknowledgements

We thank the Finnish innovation fund SITRA, the Helsinki Institute for Sustainability HELSUS and the Erasmus+ project 'Schools Educating for Sustainability: Proposals for and from In-service Teacher Education' for supporting the development of circular economy for teacher education.

References

Arthur, W. B. (2009), *The Nature of Technology: What It Is and How It Evolves*, New York: Simon and Schuster.

Atkinson, G., Dietz, S. and Neumayer, E. (2007), 'Introduction', in G. Atkinson, S. Dietz and E. Neumayer (eds), *Handbook of Sustainable Development*, 1–23, Cheltenham: Edward Elgar Publishing.

Berglund, T. and Gericke, N. (2016), 'Separated and Integrated Perspectives on Environmental, Economic, and Social Dimensions—An Investigation of Student Views on Sustainable Development', *Environmental Education Research*, 22 (8): 1115–38.

Berglund, T. and Gericke, N. (2018), 'Exploring the Role of the Economy in Young Adults' Understanding of Sustainable Development', *Sustainability*, 10: 2738. DOI: 10.3390/su10082738

Bladh, G., Stolare, M. and Kristiansson, M. (2018), 'Curriculum Principles, Didactic Practice and Social Issues: Thinking Through Teachers' Knowledge Practices in Collaborative Work', *London Review of Education*, 16 (3): 398–413.

Brundtland, G. H. (1987), *World Commission on Environment and Development: Our Common Future*, The World Commission on Environment and Development. https://sustainabledevelopment.un.org/content/documents/5987our-common-future.pdf

Deng, Z. (2020), *Knowledge, Content, Curriculum and Didaktik: Beyond Social Realism*, London: Routledge.

Ellen MacArthur Foundation (2019), *Completing the Picture: How the Circular Economy Tackles Climate Change*. https://www.ellenmacarthurfoundation.org/assets/downloads/Completing_The_Picture_How:The_Circular_Economy-_Tackles_Climate_Change_V3_26_September.pdf

Ertz, M., Durif, F. and Arcand, M. (2019), 'A Conceptual Perspective on Collaborative Consumption', *AMS Review*, 9: 27–41.

EU (2019), *The European Green Deal*. https://ec.europa.eu/info/sites/info/files/european-green-deal-communication_en.pdf

Finnish Educational Agency (2015), *Core Curriculum for Basic Education*, Helsinki: Finnish Educational Agency.

Furlong, J. and Whitty, G. (2017), 'Knowledge Traditions in the Study of Education', in J. Furlong and G. Whitty (eds), *Knowledge and the Study of Education: An International Exploration*, 13–57, Oxford: Symposium Books.

Gericke, N., Hudson, B., Olin-Scheller, C. and Stolare, M. (2018), 'Powerful Knowledge, Transformations and the Need for Empirical Studies across School Subjects', *London Review of Education*, 16 (3): 428–44.

Gericke N., Huang, L., Knippels, M. C., Christodoulou, A., Van Dam, F. and Gasparovic, S. (2020), 'Environmental Citizenship in Secondary Formal Education: The Importance of Curriculum and Subject Teachers', in A. Hadjichambis et al. (eds), *Conceptualizing Environmental Citizenship for 21st Century Education*, 193–212, Cham, Switzerland: Springer.

Giddings, B., Hopwood, B. and O'Brien, G. (2002), 'Environment, Economy and Society: Fitting Them Together into Sustainable Development', *Sustainable Development*, 10: 187–96.

Hamari, J., Sjöklint, M. and Ukkonen, A. (2015), 'The Sharing Economy: Why People Participate in Collaborative Consumption', *Journal of the Association for Information Science and Technology*, 67 (9): 2047–59.

Härkki, T., Vartiainen, H., Seitamaa-Hakkarainen, P. and Hakkarainen, K. (2020), 'Co-teaching in Non-linear Projects: A Contextualized Model of Co-Teaching to Support Educational Change', *Teaching and Teacher Education*. Available online 9 September 2020, 103188. In press. DOI: 10.1016/j.tate.2020.103188

Hawken, P., Lovins, A. and Lovins, L. H. (1999), *Natural Capitalism: Creating the Next Industrial Revolution*, New York: Little Brown and Company.

Hudson, B. (2018), 'Powerful Knowledge and Epistemic Quality in School Mathematics', *London Review of Education*, 16 (3): 384–97.

Juuti, K., Lommi, H. and Turkkila, M. (2019), *The Inventions for Circular Economy in the Classroom*, The University of Helsinki. https://blogs.helsinki.fi/inventionsforcirculareconomy/

Kangas, K., Seitamaa-Hakkarainen, P. and Hakkarainen, K. (2013), 'Design Thinking in Elementary Students' Collaborative Lamp Designing Process', *Design and Technology Education: An International Journal*, 18 (1): 30–43.

Kenney, M. and Zysman, J. (2016), 'The Rise of the Platform Economy', *Issues in Science and Technology*, 32 (3): 61–9.

Kervinen, A., Uitto, A., Kaasinen, A., Portaankorva-Koivisto, P., Juuti, K. and Kesler, M. (2016), 'Developing a Collaborative Model in Teacher Education—An Overview of a Teacher Professional Development Project', *LUMAT*, 4 (2): 67–86.

Korhonen, J., Honkasalo, A. and Seppälä, J. (2018), 'Circular Economy: The Concept and its Limitations', *Ecological Economics*, 143: 37–46.

Krajcik, J. and Shin, N. (2015), 'Project-based Learning', in K. Sawyer (ed), *The Cambridge Handbook of the Learning Sciences*, 275–97, New York: Cambridge University Press.

Lambert, D., Solem, M. and Tani, S. (2015), 'Achieving Human Potential Through Geography Education: A Capabilities Approach to Curriculum Making in Schools', *Annals of the Association of American Geographers*, 105 (4): 723–35. https://www.tandfonline.com/doi/full/10.1080/00045608.2015.1022128

Lommi, H., Turkkila, M. and Juuti, K. (2019), 'Alkuopetuksen oppilaiden käsityksiä kiertotaloudesta ['Pupils' Views on Circular Economy']', in M. Kallio, H. Krzywacki and S. Poulter (eds), *Arvot ja arviointi*, 208–24, Helsinki: Suomen ainedidaktinen tutkimusseura.

Miller, T. (2015), *Reconstructing Sustainability Science: Knowledge and Action for a Sustainable Future*, London: Routledge.

Neumayer, E. (2003), *Weak Versus Strong Sustainability: Exploring the Limits of Two Opposing Paradigms*, Cheltenham: Edward Elgar Publishing.

Ollikainen, M. and Pohjola, M. (2013), *Talouskasvu ja kestävä kehitys* [Economic Growth and Sustainable Development], Helsinki: Suomalainen Tiedeakatemia.

Oulton, C., Day, V. J. Dillon, J. and Grace, M. 2004. 'Controversial Issues—Teachers' Attitudes and Practices in the Context of Citizenship Education', *Oxford Review of Education*, 30 (4): 489–507.

Roberts, D. (2007), 'Scientific Literacy/Science Literacy', in S. K. Abell and N. G. Lederman (eds), *Handbook on Research in Science Education*, 729–80, Mahwah, NJ: Lawrence Erlbaum Associates.

Seitamaa-Hakkarainen, P., Raunio., A.-M., Raami, A., Muukkonen, H. and Hakkarainen, K. (2001), 'Computer Support for Collaborative Designing', *International Journal of Technology and Design Education*, 11: 181–202.

Sitra (2016), *Leading the Cycle—Finnish Road Map to a Circular Economy 2016–2025*. https://media.sitra.fi/2017/02/28142644/Selvityksia121.pdf

Sitra (n.d.), *The most interesting companies in the circular economy in Finland*. https://www.sitra.fi/en/projects/interesting-companies-circular-economy-finland/

Sormunen, K., Seitamaa-Hakkarainen, P., Kangas, K. and Korhonen, T. (2020), Keksintöprojektien jäsentäminen ja suunnittelun lähtökohdat [Basics for Planning Invention Projects], in T. Korhonen and K. Kangas (eds), *Keksimisen pedagogiikka*, 26–47, Jyväskylä: PS-kustannus.

Spangenberg, J. (2005), 'Economic Sustainability of the Economy: Concepts and Indicators', *International Journal of Sustainable Development*, 8: 47–64.

Stahel, W. R. (2010), *The Performance Economy*, London: Palgrave Macmillan.

Stahel, W. R. (2016), 'Circular Economy', *Nature*, 531: 435–8.

Sund, P. and Gericke, N. (2020), 'Teaching Contributions from Secondary School Subject Areas to Education for Sustainable Development—A Comparative Study of

Science, Social Science and Language Teachers', *Environmental Education Research*, 26 (6): 772–94.

Sund, P., Gericke, N. and Bladh, G. (2020), 'Educational Content in Cross-Curricular ESE Teaching and a Model to Discern Teacher's Teaching Traditions', *Journal of Education for Sustainable Development*, 14 (1): 78–97.

Swedish National Agency for Education (2018), *Curriculum for the Compulsory School, Preschool Class and School-Age Educare 2011: Revised 2018*. https://www.skolverket.se/getFile?file=3984

UN (2015), 'Transforming Our World: The 2030 Agenda for Sustainable Development', Resolution 70/1 adopted by the General Assembly on 25 September 2015. http://www.un.org/en/ga/70/resolutions.shtml (accessed 18 April 2019).

Webster, K. (2017), *The Circular Economy: A Wealth of Flows*, Cowes: Ellen MacArthur Foundation.

Young, M. (2015), 'Powerful Knowledge as a Curriculum Principle', in M. Young, D. Lambert, C. Roberts and M. Roberts (eds), *Knowledge and the Future School: Curriculum and Social Justice*, 65–88, London: Bloomsbury Academic.

Young, M. and Muller, J. (2015), *Curriculum and Specialization of Knowledge: Studies in the Sociology of Education*, London: Routledge.

8

Teachers as Curriculum Makers for School Mathematics of High Epistemic Quality

Brian Hudson

Introduction

This chapter focuses on the change in teachers' practice and their experiences of the impact on student learning that arose from a research and development project on developing mathematical thinking in the primary school classroom. In particular, it draws on outcomes from the project supported by the Scottish Government (2010–12) called *Developing Mathematical Thinking in the Primary Classroom* (DMTPC) conducted in the context of the Scottish *Curriculum for Excellence* reform and reported on in Hudson et al. (2015). It does so by revisiting empirical data from the original study, mainly drawn from post-trial interviews with and action research reports by the participants. The analysis of the data is informed by a theoretical framework that combines the ideas of epistemic quality as discussed in Hudson (2022), of 'teachers as curriculum makers' (Lambert and Biddulph 2015) and of teachers' 'powerful professional knowledge' (Furlong and Whitty 2017). The DMTPC project was based at the University of Dundee and carried out in collaboration with a group of primary school teachers ($n=24$) and Local Education Authority (LEA) advisory staff members across several LEAs in North East Scotland. The project's overall aim was to develop and implement a postgraduate course for serving teachers on developing mathematical thinking in the primary school classroom. The project as a whole was established within a design research framework, which aimed to promote curriculum development through the process of classroom-based action research on the part of participants and also research and evaluation with respect to the project as a whole. A 'Curriculum for Excellence' development partnership group was established at the outset of the project, including teachers from each of the Local Education Authorities (LEA) together with LEA advisory staff and members of the university project team. The design of the course of study was based on developing an 'open collective cycle' model of a professional learning community (Huberman 1995) enhanced by blended learning through use of a technology-supported online learning environment. In conclusion, this chapter especially focuses on KOSS research question 3 by addressing the question of *how the nature of teachers' powerful professional knowledge in school mathematics can be characterized* with reference to the field of subject didactics. Finally, consideration is given to the implications for innovation in teacher education policy and practice.

Theoretical Framework

Epistemic Quality

This chapter draws on the discussion in Hudson (2022) in relation to evaluating epistemic quality in primary school mathematics. The term 'epistemic' is concerned with the knowledge involved in a didactical or teaching-studying-learning situation (Hudson et al. 2022). In turn, the term 'epistemic quality' refers to the quality of what students come to know, make sense of and are able to do in school. The concept of epistemic quality arose from a perspective informed by concepts drawn from the field of subject didactics (Hudson et al. 2015; Hudson 2016) and is seen as a way of thinking that helps articulate aspects of what we mean by 'powerful knowledge' (Young 2013, 2015). It is also seen as a way of making quality education visible and as of particular significance while addressing the challenges of UN Sustainable Development Goal 4 to ensure inclusive and equitable quality education for all (UN 2015). It is especially significant as it concerns the need to maximize the chances that all pupils will have *epistemic access* (Young 2013: 115; Morrow 2008) to powerful knowledge through the curriculum which is regarded as 'access to the best knowledge in any field of study they engage in' (Young 2013: 115). In Hudson et al. (2015), low epistemic quality is characterized by an approach that presents school mathematics as infallible, authoritarian, dogmatic, absolutist, irrefutable and certain, while also entailing an overemphasis on memorization, rule-following of strict procedures, and right or wrong answers. This is described as *mathematical fundamentalism* (2015) and contrasted with *mathematical fallibilism*, which is based on a heuristic view of mathematics as a human activity

(Lakatos 1976). The latter involves an approach that presents mathematics as fallible, refutable and uncertain, and which promotes critical thinking, creative reasoning, the generation of multiple solutions and learning from errors and mistakes. The concept arose from a perspective informed by concepts drawn from the field of subject didactics, particularly from a consideration of the transformation process of didactic transposition (Chevallard 2007), which recognizes that knowledge is not something that is to be taken as simply given and to be explained but rather that it is potentially encapsulated in situations, and it is in going through those situations that the pupil, or whoever, can learn. This view of learning as 'learning from the situation' sees knowledge as built up and transformed or *transposed* in didactic situations.

The concept of epistemic quality is discussed further in Hudson (2022) by considering it in relation to that of *epistemic ascent* (Winch 2013) as concerns subject expertise. This is based on a continuum that reflects a trajectory in the development of subject expertise from that of the novice towards that of an expert in the subject. By drawing on Winch (2013: 129), attention is paid to three distinct, yet related, kinds of knowledge: *knowledge by acquaintance*, propositional knowledge or *knowledge that* and procedural knowledge or *knowledge how*. The primary mode of *knowledge by acquaintance* is seen to be through the senses so that one may be acquainted with objects, events, processes, states and persons. In turn, it is argued that *knowledge that* cannot consist solely in the identification of true, though isolated, propositions, but is embedded in a conceptual structure, which is itself embedded within further related propositions. Finally, as concerns *knowledge how*, it is argued that knowing how to do something is an epistemic capacity related to *knowledge by acquaintance* and *knowledge that*, given that knowing how to do something typically requires elements of the other two kinds of knowledge. In developing subject expertise, it is viewed as crucial for enhancing the ability to understand and to make inferences (Brandom 2000) by employing the concepts embodied within the subject matter. It is also stressed that it is necessary to be able to distinguish within the subject between claims that can be counted as knowledge and those that count simply as beliefs. This distinction can be especially hard for a novice because the source of such beliefs is authoritative testimony. Beginning to learn a subject involves starting to use the language associated with the concepts of the subject, and this is primarily a practical ability that is learned. Accordingly, a central dimension of learning about a subject is learning to take part in conversations and discussions that employ those concepts. This aspect is developed further in the following section with reference to the discussion by Lambert and Biddulph (2015) about the dialogic space offered by curriculum-making in the process of learning to teach and the creation of a progressive knowledge-led curriculum.

Teachers as Curriculum Makers

In their discussion on the process of learning to teach, Lambert and Biddulph (2015) argue that the curriculum-making process is a 'signature part' of a teacher's identity. Referring to Hart (2001), they emphasize the complexity of the teacher's role and argue that teachers need to hold three interrelated priorities in balance. The first priority relates to the needs, prior knowledge and experiences of students; the second to the nature and purposes of the discipline, and the third to the understanding and performative craft of pedagogic technique. From this perspective, curriculum-making is seen as curriculum thinking in practical action, taking on a 'trinity of educational practice' (2001) that involves subject, child and teacher. This way of thinking resonates strongly with the Continental European tradition of didactics and corresponds closely with the idea of 'holding complexity' (Hudson 2002: 53; Hudson 2016: 112) as being a central part of a teacher's reflective practice and highlights the way in which curriculum and pedagogy effectively merge at the classroom level. A key tool for the analysis of the complex relations between teacher, student and the content in the teaching-studying-learning process is the didactic triad. The didactic triad should be treated as a whole, although this is almost impossible to do in practice. The most common approach is to take the *pedagogical relation* between the teacher and the student(s) as a starting point. The pedagogical relation between the teacher and the student is taken as the significant starting point in *Geisteswissenschaftliche*, that is, human science pedagogy. In their discussion of the didactic relation in the teaching-studying-learning process, Kansanen and Meri (1999) draw attention to the influence of the thinking of Herman Nohl and also to the writing of Klafki (1970: 55–65) who summarized this relation by stating that it is important to consider from the point of view of a young person and it aims to draw out his or her best. They highlight that the content of this relation must be thought through in each situation, and that it must be interactive in nature such that a student cannot be compelled or forced into it. Moreover, they stress that it is not a permanent relation, but one from which the young person gradually grows out of as that individual develops their own independence. They also highlight the way in which this relation also gradually takes shape since the development of the young person brings different perspectives along with it. Further they argue that this characteristic has often been referred in pedagogical discussions to as 'the pedagogical suicide of the teacher' or the 'pedagogical paradox', with reference to Immanuel Kant. The relation is illustrated in Figure 8.1 based on the figure in Hudson (2016: 112).

However, the relationship between the teacher and the content must also be considered, thereby bringing the teacher's competence into focus. It should also be noted that teaching in itself does not necessarily imply learning and that the term 'studying' therefore provides a more accurate description of the activities of students. It is through studying that the instructional process can be observed, while the invisible part of this relation may be learning. Accordingly, a key aspect of the teacher's role is guiding this didactic relation, as shown in Figure 8.2 similar to the earlier one based on the figure in Hudson (2016: 112).

Further, it is important to stress the way in which this analysis takes place within a school and societal context, as emphasized in Hudson and Meyer (2011: 8). In expanding the perspective, the first step is to bring the classroom situation into focus, while the second step in widening the vision is to consider the school as

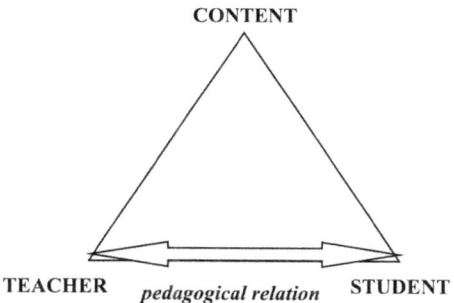

Figure 8.1 The pedagogical relation in the didactic triad.

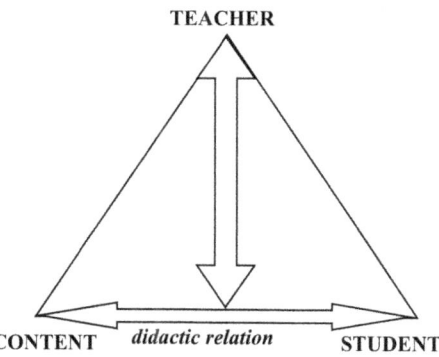

Figure 8.2 The didactic relation in the didactic triad.

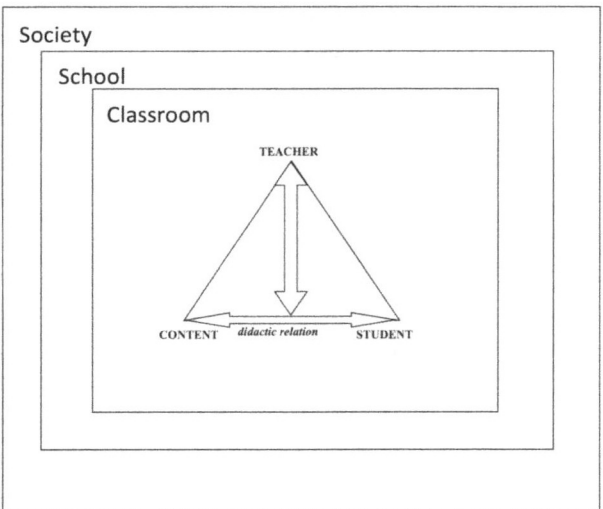

Figure 8.3 The didactic triad within the wider school and societal context.

a subsystem of wider society which in turn reflects broader societal changes as illustrated in Figure 8.3 and adapted from the figure in Hudson (2016: 112). This framework reflects that of Gericke et al. (2018), who describe processes of knowledge transformation that occur on societal, institutional and classroom levels.

In their discussion, Lambert and Biddulph (2015) draw attention to the dialogic space offered by curriculum-making in the process of learning to teach and the creation of a progressive knowledge-led curriculum. This space is seen as the basis for dialogic teaching that involves ongoing talk between teachers and students such that teachers can build on the everyday knowledge that students bring into the classroom. As indicated earlier, there is a strong correspondence with the emphasis placed by Winch (2013) within the framework of *epistemic ascent* on the importance of inferential relationships. These inferential relationships are important for the development of both *knowledge how* and *knowledge that* and for the interrelationships between them. Accordingly, use of the language associated with the concepts of the subject is a crucial aspect of the process of beginning to develop expertise in that subject, and this is primarily a practical ability that is learned by taking part in conversations and discussions which employ those concepts. Lambert and Biddulph (2015) also highlight a set of principles as a means to guide students' collaboration with each other, with their teachers and with the discipline in their reflections on the Young People's Geography project. Central to these is the principle of 'valuing conversation', involving the use of conversation between teacher–student, student–student, and teacher–teacher as a basis for curricula possibilities and knowledge building. In relation to this aspect, they define conversation in a broader sense as 'dialogue between student and teacher, teacher and subject, experience and disciplined thought, curriculum and pedagogy, school and everyday' (2015: 220). They also draw attention to the potential for creating dialogic spaces for young people in the school curriculum and also to how such spaces illustrated the way in which students can be part of the curriculum-making process as a result. In turn, this example is seen as an illustration of where curriculum meets pedagogy.

Powerful Professional Knowledge

The aim of supporting the development of teachers as curriculum makers holds implications for the knowledge base of teachers, in turn raising the question of what may constitute the *powerful professional knowledge* required for teacher education (Furlong and Whitty 2017: 47–51). In their discussion (Furlong and Whitty 2017: 47–51), they refer to the work of Young and Muller (2010) in reasserting the importance of disciplinary knowledge in professional contexts. Yet, they argue that they do not necessarily exclude other knowledges and emphasize there is a critical pedagogical element to this. They also highlight a key challenge for professional disciplines as being the need to establish precisely how disciplinary knowledge, that is epistemologically strong, articulates with other forms of knowledge and how it can thereby impact practice. In turn, they ask how can disciplinary knowledge and other external knowledges be brought together with professionals' reflective practice and practical theorizing in professional arenas to produce really powerful professional knowledge and learning. This leads to one of the key KOSS research questions addressed by this book in terms of how the nature of teachers' powerful professional knowledge can be characterized and what the implications are for teacher education policy and practice.

Following the work of Furlong and Whitty (2017) in the same volume, Tatto and Hordern (2017) write about the configuration of teacher education as a professional field of practice through a comparative study of mathematics education. In their study, they analyse the role of educational studies in the secondary teacher education curriculum in Germany, Poland, Singapore and the United States. The data come from an analysis of syllabi from cross-national representative samples of pre-service programmes. The analysis focuses on knowledge of the discipline, knowledge of the school curriculum for the discipline, the pedagogy of the discipline, the general pedagogy and the practicum. The authors use Bernstein's sociology of knowledge as a theoretical framework to discuss the differential emphasis given to these five domains within and across countries 'as an expression of the re-contextualisation of knowledge from singulars to regions' (2017: 255) in relation to how the foundation disciplines and elements of mathematical knowledge are decontextualized to address the preparation of knowledgeable mathematics teachers.

Their approach to the analysis reflects the curriculum tradition's influence through the very constructive way in which they draw on Schulman's (1987) typology in teacher education programmes related to mathematics. This enables them to differentiate between mathematical content knowledge (MCK) and general pedagogical knowledge (GPK). This then leads to a focus on mathematical pedagogical content knowledge (MPCK) that 'involves multiple forms of knowledge contextualisation, including knowledge of the discipline, the curriculum and instruction, and of students thinking' (1987: 259). In their study, the MPCK assessment framework includes three sub-themes in order to address the complexity of learning to teach mathematics and the role of teacher education in the process. These three themes are *mathematics curricular knowledge, knowledge for planning mathematics teaching and learning*, and *enacting mathematics for teaching and learning*.

The analysis leads to a number of significant points regarding the configuration of mathematics teacher education in different national contexts. Notably, it highlights the contrast between a narrowly conceived technical model of teacher education and broader more disciplinary-based forms of education studies. They conclude that where broader pedagogic norms persist and there are strong traditions of educational theory there may be greater openness to extending the teacher's role in order to develop research-capable practitioners with pastoral and counselling skills. Still, the system-level approach in their analysis means no comparison is made of the differences in approaches to classroom practice across the four countries. In particular, the very significant role of subject didactics in Germany is overlooked in this analysis. This chapter accordingly aims to address this gap by considering the question of how the nature of teachers' powerful professional knowledge can be characterized from the perspective of subject didactics.

Background to the Study

The research study associated with the DMTPC project (Hudson et al. 2015) was carried out with serving teachers and built on an earlier study involving students in initial teacher education that addressed the question of the nature of subject content knowledge in mathematics (Henderson and Hudson 2011). The DMTPC study mainly focused on the teachers' confidence, competence, attitudes and beliefs in relation to teaching mathematics. As outlined in the introduction, the project's overall aim was to develop and implement a postgraduate course for teachers on the theme of developing mathematical thinking in the primary classroom. The project was based at the University of Dundee and carried out in collaboration with a group of teachers ($n=24$) and Local Education Authority (LEA) advisory staff members across several LEAs in North East Scotland. The design of the course of study was based on developing an 'open collective cycle' (OCC) model of a professional learning community (Huberman 1995) enhanced by blended learning through use of a technology-supported online learning environment. The framing of the project as a whole was established within a design research framework (Bannan-Ritland 2003), which aimed to promote curriculum development through the process of classroom-based action research on the part of participants and also research and evaluation of the project overall. The Curriculum for Excellence Development partnership group that planned the course included teachers with one from each of the Local Education Authorities (LEA) together with LEA advisory staff members and members of the university project team. An important aspect of the case made for support in the grant application was the fact that most mathematics lessons at that time in Scotland still tended to feature some form of teacher-led demonstration followed by children practising skills and procedures from a commercially produced scheme (Scottish Executive Education Department 2005). The more recent Scottish Survey of Literacy and Numeracy reported the activities in which the highest percentage of pupils reported that the ways in which they had participated 'very often' were to 'listen to the teacher talk to the class about a topic' (62 per cent in P4 and 64 per cent in P7 and S2) and to 'work on your own' (between 55 and 61 per cent) (Scottish Government 2012: 13).

The course of study was structured around three main questions, two core texts and an action research project. The key questions were:

1. What is mathematics?
2. What is mathematical thinking?
3. What is good mathematics teaching?

As part of the module assessment, participants designed an action research project that would consider the implications of current literature on the development of mathematical thinking; identify the strategies, skills and attitudes to be enhanced; identify methods of data collection and analysis that provide evidence of impact; be feasible and realistic in terms of the resources available in school; pay consideration to progression and assessment and identify the issues which emerged from the study.

The Study

This chapter focuses on the change in the teachers' practice and their experiences of the impact on student learning by revisiting empirical data from the original study. In particular, it addresses the KOSS research question of how the nature of teachers' powerful professional knowledge in school mathematics can be characterized. The data are mainly drawn from post-trial interviews with four of the participants and action research reports completed by another four group members. The initial phase of the design research framework took place in the first year of the project and involved the informed exploration and design of instruments and tools to gather the data. This was carried out alongside the processes of curriculum development and recruiting the participants. Further phases that ran parallel to this involved the enactment of the module and subsequently the action research projects carried out by the participants on the classroom level.

Data Analysis

The data from the post-trial interviews with the course participants ($n=24$) were revisited by reading them through the lens of the theoretical framework outlined in this chapter with particular attention to concepts of *epistemic quality, teachers as curriculum makers*, and *powerful professional knowledge*. This entailed rereading the interview transcripts in the first stage and coding the data for incidences that related to 'epistemic quality', 'teachers as curriculum makers' and 'powerful professional knowledge'. The coding process was based on a deductive approach involving these three categories and led to the emergence of several subcategories or themes discussed here. The second stage involved rereading the action research reports written by four participants according to the same approach. The results of these processes are discussed in the following sections.

Stage 1 Data Analysis: Post-trial Interviews

The most frequently recurring theme while analysing the interview data related to the importance of language and classroom talk, both of which are central to the theoretical framework in relation to *developing the dialogic space in the classroom and the epistemic quality of classroom interaction*. The second-most frequently recurring theme concerned the importance of *developing the dialogic space with colleagues*. The third theme related to *developing the practice of teacher as curriculum maker* and involved the role of time and the development of a variety of methods against the background of the Curriculum for Excellence in particular. Several more issues that emerged are clustered around the fourth theme concerned with *developing the epistemic quality of the content*. It became clear during this process that all of these four themes related in some way to the development of powerful professional knowledge, with this aspect being returned to in the final discussion. With this in mind, each theme is discussed further here and illustrated with examples of what the participants stated in the interviews.

Developing the Dialogic Space in the Classroom and the Epistemic Quality of Classroom Interaction

The most frequently recurring theme in the analysis of the interview data related to the importance of starting to use the language associated with the concepts of the subject and to take part in conversations and discussions that employ those concepts, namely, a central dimension of the previous discussion on the epistemic quality of the classroom interaction. This aspect corresponds with the emphasis placed by Lambert and Biddulph (2015) concerning the dialogic space at the classroom level. All interviewees referred to the importance of developing their practice of teacher questioning in relation to this aspect.

For example, in commenting on the change in her practice and the impact on student learning, Alice highlighted the change in her practice and the resulting impact on her students in terms of motivation:

> I've changed the way I teach maths, again, it's away from . . . we were very much of the textbook and, you know, worksheets etc. and I am very much into more questioning, I have more group sessions, we'll do a lot more oral work, practical work than we ever did in the past . . . they're actually almost excited to be working together in maths.

While reflecting on a recent lesson observation by her deputy head teacher, Bridget said:

> I was using my questioning skills . . . to actually develop their thinking even further and I got a really good feedback from that lesson so yeah, I think I had the skill of questioning but I think it's kind of confirmed it and probably pushed on my confidence more because I know I'm doing it right.

Bridget also highlighted the impact on her students of greater emphasis on conversation in terms of motivation:

> Oh, I think that they have probably seen a kind of revival within me . . . when we're doing the thinking skills, they really enjoy it and they like the fact that they're working together or they can work on their own and they can actually come up with any kind of method that they think that they've used and then they can explain it and they like going up to the board and explaining it to everybody how they got this, that and the other.

In her responses, Caroline emphasized the change in her practice, her students' increased levels of engagement as a result as well as the students' use of language:

> the main difference in my teaching is now I do more asking than telling, do you know . . . and to give the children something to start with and then to let them almost tell you what maths is it they need to know . . .
>
> . . . I did ask them the question last week; I said what would someone say if they came into our classroom when we're doing maths, what do you think they would say? and that straight away the kids were saying 'oh, they would say good group discussions, they would say that we're listening to one another, they would say that we're sharing our ideas and that we're talking about the strategies'.

Caroline also reflected on the development of her practice in terms of the balance between providing knowledge and experience for her students in relation to this aspect:

> I think I've been getting a good mix between, you know, giving them the, sort of, knowledge and letting them have experience, if that makes sense?

With regard to Denise's responses, she emphasized that her questioning was the most significant aspect of her practice to change and also noted the importance of building her confidence to make this change.

> I've found is that my questioning is the biggest thing that has changed and it's changing and it's . . . confidence yes and questioning without a doubt has been a big thing.

In addition, she highlighted how this had an impact on her students' attitudes and levels of motivation:

I would certainly say that there seems to be quite high motivation and little anxiety which I suppose is what we're aiming for.

Developing the Dialogic Space with Colleagues

Three of the four interviewees also referred to the importance of a dialogic space with peers and more widely. This corresponds with the broader sense of the term 'conversation' as used by Lambert and Biddulph (2015) as involving dialogue between student and teacher, teacher and subject, experience and disciplined thought, curriculum and pedagogy, school and everyday.

For example, Alice referred to the importance of colleagues sharing their experiences, resources and practices for her own professional learning:

> drawing upon other people's experiences in discussion groups and seeing, finding out about resources that are out there, finding out about other peoples' methodology. I think that aspect I've benefitted from.

In her responses, Caroline pointed to the role of the online environment for sharing resources and developing a dialogic space with her peers:

> I like how everything is done, you know access to everything online . . . I love it, it's so accessible, having the discussion forums . . . and I think people are great people who really are willing to share everything and people are posting their things up and they're putting on their documents. Yeah, I think there's very much a sense of we're all in this together so, yeah. Very positive, very, very positive.

In relation to Denise's response, she stressed the importance of the key texts and the dialogue between experience and disciplined thought through reading and reflection on practice:

> I think by reading these quite academic texts there have been quite a few, sort of, light bulb moments, it's like 'oh yeah, ok, I understand that, I can see that happening' and I think through talking with S (University tutor) as well I think what's really come over is how taking very small steps, very slowly is actually ok because I think we get there in the end and we get there with more understanding in the end as well.

Developing the Practice of Teacher as Curriculum Maker

With regard to the practice of becoming teacher as curriculum maker, the role of time and the development of a variety of methods was emphasized by interviewees against the background of the Curriculum for Excellence.

For example, Alice stressed how the interaction between the course and the Curriculum for Excellence had led to a change in her practice, and she also highlighted the importance of time and the development of a variety of methods:

> I think it is a combination of the being part of the group doing the study and also the introduction of Curriculum for Excellence, they both impacted . . .
>
> I think being allowed to actually take time over a piece of mathematics . . . I'll maybe find some games that they can work on just to better their understanding . . . I am using different methods, a variety of methods.

Developing the Epistemic Quality of the Content

Several more issues that emerged are clustered around the aspect of developing the epistemic quality of the content. These included placing an emphasis on the purpose of mathematics, real-life applications of the subject, and breaking down concepts in the subject.

Alice's responses show the importance of both the need to break down the mathematical concepts and to think about the purpose, as illustrated here:

> I think in breaking things down a bit more, it's almost like getting to the nitty gritty of it, I think, but the purposes behind maths, the how it came about, I suppose the history of the maths and the necessity of it, why we actually do it . . . It's breaking down the mathematical concepts . . . it's helping children to enjoy mathematics and to see the purpose behind it and to see how enjoyable it can be as well.

On this aspect, Bridget stressed real-life applications, the changes in her practice and the impact on her students:

> I've also looked at literature for real life maths and things like that and actually being able to, you know, include that into my teaching as well . . . I think it's changed them . . ., I think doing this course has made me look at it in a different way to real life so then they actually see more of a purpose to what they are doing.

Bridget also commented on the impact on her own thinking about and attitude to the subject:

> I think it's kind of reignited my interest in maths and . . . backed up my feeling that actually yeah that was my stronger subject and I do enjoy it.

In relation to Caroline's response, she emphasized the way in which she was paying greater attention to building on her students' prior knowledge:

had really begun to think more about the cycle of talking to the kids, actually finding out what it is they know before you then, sort of, move on rather than just, sort of, ploughing on relentlessly, do you know, we're in this term we have to be doing fractions or now we have to be doing multiplication or whatever.

With regard to Denise's responses, she stressed the way in which she had placed greater emphasis on sharing the learning intentions of the lessons with her students in a way that was also resonant with the idea of students as curriculum makers:

I'm far more aware of sharing the learning intentions with the children . . . I completely understand learning intentions, I know how to set learning intentions, I know about success criteria but was I actually using them? Probably not, no. Sharing that with the children and then, having high expectations of what they will then achieve but in a low stress way.

Stage 2 Data Analysis: Action Research Reports

The second stage involved rereading action research reports written by four participants based on the same approach outlined above. The four themes that emerged in the analysis of the interviews were also evident while analysing the action reports. However, in overall terms more attention was given to the detail of the mathematical content in the action research reports. For example, in her conclusion Anna underscored the value of a topic-based approach for teaching new concepts and the importance of vocabulary in this process. Elsa's project focused on how her questioning could impact the mathematical thinking of her students in relation to the topic of time and in particular the distinction between analogue and digital representations. In her report, she emphasizes how a shift towards group work and discussion led to increased levels of confidence and motivation as well as improved attitudes to mathematics. The project conducted by Florence involved the teaching of odd and even numbers in which she commented on her greater awareness of the need for children to have the *time* to expand their thinking – whether alone or with others. She also observed that her students were beginning to use the mathematical language modelled by the teachers, for example 'match', 'pair' and 'even'. Gabrielle's project also concentrated on children's understanding of odd and even numbers. In her reflections, she also stressed how the Curriculum for Excellence was seen to allow more time to be spent teaching mathematics and in empowering teachers to engage in activities involving spatial representations that aim to develop deep understanding. Finally, she expressed her strong commitment to principles of inclusion arguing that:

> as pupils are involved in all activities; they have a better share of power within lessons – the environment for learning is one of trust where pupils are confident about articulating their thinking without fear of being wrong . . . As making conjectures is a key principle of mathematical thinking, it is of paramount importance that pupils feel secure about guessing/estimating or offering responses to be further explored.

Discussion

As discussed, this chapter aims to address the question of how the nature of teachers' powerful professional knowledge can be characterized from the perspective of subject didactics. This approach recognizes the complexity of the teacher's role as highlighted by Lambert and Biddulph (2015), the complexity of learning to teach as emphasized by Tatto and Hordern (2017), and builds on the idea of 'holding complexity' as being a central part of a teacher's role as already referred to elsewhere (Hudson 2002: 53; Hudson 2016: 112). Considering the role of the teacher from the perspective of subject didactics brings a focus onto the didactic triad, particularly the didactic relation. As mentioned, a key aspect of the teacher's role relates to guiding this didactic relation that is a relation to another relation, that is, the relation between the student and the content. Thus, one focus in this *set* of relationships is on the core of a teacher's professionalism, and, in view of the complexity of this set of relations as manifested in any situation, it is difficult to think that the didactic relation could be organized universally, or according to a set of recipes or technical rules. Teachers' own practical theories and pedagogical thinking are consequently seen to be vital. The tradition of didactics hence provides a framework that places the teacher at the heart of the teaching-studying-learning process. Moreover, it provides a framework for teachers' thinking about the most basic how, what and why questions concerning their work, and strongly resonates with the work of Shulman (1987).

In considering the four themes emerging from this study, we can see how these map onto various aspects of Shulman's model overlaid onto the didactic triad in Figure 8.4 which is adapted from that illustrated in Hudson (2016: 113). In particular, there is a close correspondence between the didactic triad

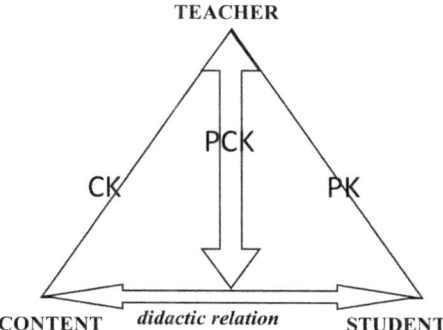

Figure 8.4 Mapping Shulman's categories onto the didactic triad.

and Shulman's (2016: 113) concept of pedagogical content knowledge (PCK), which can be seen as the professional knowledge required by teachers in guiding the didactic relation. This also helps to distinguish between the associated pedagogical knowledge (PK) which relates to the pedagogical relation that is distinct from the content knowledge (CK) required and which maps onto the teacher's relation with their subject-specific content knowledge.

With regard to the theme of *developing a dialogic space in the classroom and the epistemic quality of classroom interaction*, we can see how this maps onto the pedagogical relation associated with pedagogical knowledge (PK). The focus of this aspect emerging from this study is the development of teachers' *knowledge how* as exemplified in the emphasis given to developing teacher questioning skills and student group working, promoting thinking skills and the students' use of language and building their confidence.

In relation to *developing the epistemic quality of the content*, this is clearly associated with the content knowledge (CK) of the teacher. The study participants stressed the purposes of mathematics, the value of drawing on real-life applications of the subject and breaking down the concepts in the subject. The latter aspect of breaking down concepts reflects a process evident in the work of most of the teachers. It is the reverse of knowledge building and is referred to as 'decompression' by Ball and Bass (2000: 99) in their work on interweaving content and pedagogy in relation to teaching and learning to teach mathematics. This kind of *knowledge how* is not necessarily the kind of understanding a mathematician would possess. Rather, it involves the ability to deconstruct one's own mathematical knowledge into a less polished and final form, in which elemental components are accessible and visible. In contrast, while most personal knowledge of subject matter in mathematics is highly compressed, in this form it might be completely inadequate for teaching. The polished and compressed form of mathematics as a discipline can actually obscure the ability to discern how learners are thinking at the roots of that knowledge. Teachers of mathematics must therefore be able to work backwards from a mature and compressed understanding of the content in order to unpack its constituent elements.

The remaining two themes of *developing the practice of teacher as curriculum maker* and *developing the dialogic space with colleagues* can be seen as related to the didactic relation and teachers' pedagogical content knowledge (PCK). In considering the former, we can see how the introduction of the Curriculum for Excellence enabled these teachers to take the time to develop a variety of methods as they interweaved content and pedagogy in relation to teaching and learning to mathematics. This involved the development of activities that reflected the importance of developing a mathematical vocabulary in this process and specific examples like addressing the distinction between analogue and digital representations of time, beginning to use the mathematical language modelled by the teachers such as 'match', 'pair' and 'even', and understanding the concept of odd and even through pedagogical activities based on spatial representations. This dialogical process lies at the heart of the didactic relation and the development of teachers' pedagogical content knowledge (PCK). Further, a vital aspect in developing this *knowledge how* was the process of *developing the dialogic space with colleagues* that involved sharing experiences, resources and practices in addition to reading and reflection on practice.

In this chapter, it has been argued that the concept of epistemic quality helps articulate aspects of what we mean by powerful knowledge. It is especially significant in relation to the need to maximize the chances that all pupils will have *epistemic access* (Young 2013: 115; Morrow 2008) to powerful knowledge through the curriculum, which is seen as 'access to the best knowledge in any field of study they engage in' (Young 2013: 115). It follows that teachers who are able to develop powerful professional knowledge will demonstrate the abilities to support their students in developing knowledge of high epistemic quality. This is central to ensuring inclusive and equitable quality education for all (UN 2015) and in maximizing the chances that all pupils will have *epistemic access* to powerful knowledge through the curriculum. In relation to the question of how the nature of teachers' powerful professional knowledge can be characterized, this study has illustrated some aspects of such powerful professional knowledge being enacted by teachers as curriculum makers in teaching primary school mathematics. The study has highlighted the associated *knowledge how* in particular through the

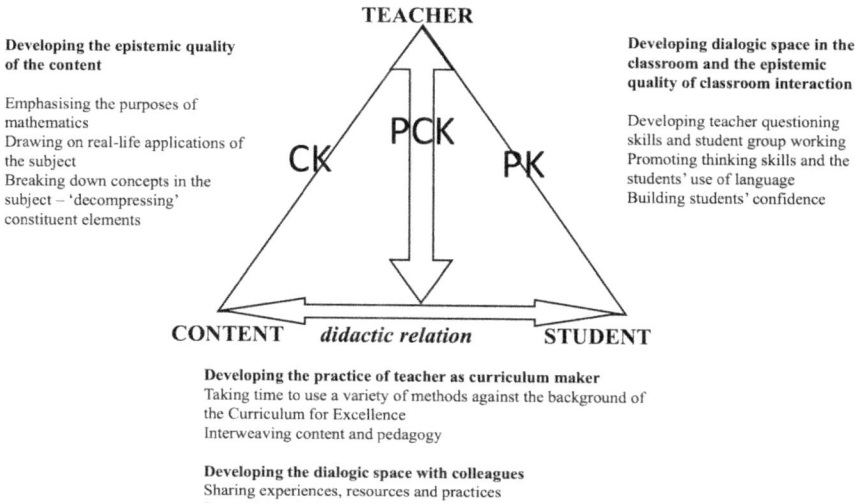

Figure 8.5 Mapping the emerging themes onto Shulman's categories and the didactic triad.

four themes of *developing the dialogic space in the classroom and the epistemic quality of classroom interaction, developing the epistemic quality of the content, developing the practice of teacher as curriculum maker* and *developing the dialogic space with colleagues* (Figure 8.5). With regard to the question of epistemic access, Gabrielle's comments in the conclusion of her action research report are especially powerful in which she argues for her pupils to have a better share of power within lessons and stresses the environment for learning as one of trust in which pupils are confident about articulating their thinking without fear of being wrong.

Finally, in relation to the implications for innovation in teacher education policy and practice this study reveals several significant issues. A major implication relates to recognizing teacher education as a lifelong process that entails initial teacher education, induction and continuing professional development. The design of the course of study had the aim to develop an 'open collective cycle' model of a professional learning community, enhanced by blended learning through use of a technology-supported online learning environment. This aspect was central to the success of the course in terms of enhancing the practice of teacher as curriculum maker and in supporting that process by developing a dialogic space with colleagues. In a post Covid-19 world, the potential of technology to support professional learning in this way has become self-evident. A second major implication relates to the importance of addressing the development of mathematics as a subject at primary school level, which is a highly formative stage in terms of developing attitudes and beliefs in relation to the subject. The importance of Subject-Specific Educational Content Knowledge (SSECK) across school subjects in general is highlighted in the final chapter of this book (Stolare et al., this volume). The challenge for teacher education policy making in relation to school mathematics is to ensure that the development of SSECK is an essential dimension of teacher education in order to support the development of such teachers as curriculum makers in relation to subject-specific education in mathematics at all stages of the lifelong process of teacher education.

References

Ball, D. L. and Bass, H. (2000), 'Interweaving Content and Pedagogy in Teaching and Learning to Teach: Knowing and Using Mathematics', in J. Boaler (ed.), *Multiple Perspectives on the Teaching and Learning of Mathematics*, 83–104, Westport, CT: Ablex.

Bannan-Ritland, B. (2003), 'The Role of Design in Research: The Integrative Learning Design Framework', *Educational Researcher*, 32 (1): 21–4.

Brandom, R. (2000), *Articulating Reasons: An Introduction to Inferentialism*, Cambridge, MA: Harvard University Press.

Chevallard, Y. (2007), Readjusting Didactics to a Changing Epistemology. *European Educational Research Journal*, 6 (2): 131–4.

Furlong, J. and Whitty, G. (2017), 'Knowledge Traditions in the Study of Education', in J. Furlong and G. Whitty (eds), *Knowledge and the Study of Education*, 13–57, Oxford: Symposium Books.

Gericke, N., Hudson, B., Olin-Scheller, C. and Stolare, M. (2018), 'Powerful Knowledge, Transformations and the Need for Empirical Studies Across School Subjects', *London Review of Education*, 16 (3): 428–44. https://doi.org/10.18546/LRE.16.3.06

Hart, T. (2001), 'From Information to Transformation: Education for the Evolution of Consciousness', in J. L. Kincheloe and S. R. Steinberg (eds), *Counterpoints: Studies in the Postmodern Theory of Education*, Vol. 162, New York, NY: Peter Lang.

Henderson, S. and Hudson, B. (2011). 'What is Subject Content Knowledge in Mathematics? On the Implications for Student Teachers' Competence and Confidence in Teaching Mathematics', in E. Eisenschmidt and E. Löfström (eds), *Developing Quality Cultures in Teacher Education: Expanding Horizons in Relation to Quality Assurance*, 175–94, Estonia: Tallinn University.

Huberman, M. (1995), 'Networks that Alter Teaching: Conceptualizations, Exchanges and Experiments', *Teachers and Teaching: Theory and Practice*, 1 (2): 193–211.

Hudson, B. (2002), 'Holding Complexity and Searching for Meaning – Teaching as Reflective Practice', *Journal of Curriculum Studies*, 34 (1): 43–57. DOI: 10.1080/00220270110086975

Hudson, B. (2016), 'Didactics', in D. Wyse, L. Hayward and J. Pandya (eds), *SAGE Handbook of Curriculum, Pedagogy and Assessment*, 107–24, London: Sage Publications.

Hudson, B. (2022), 'Evaluating Epistemic Quality in Primary School Mathematics', in B. Hudson, N. Gericke, C. Olin-Scheller and M. Stolare (eds), *International Perspectives on Knowledge and Curriculum: Epistemic Quality across School Subjects*, London: Bloomsbury Publishing.

Hudson, B., Gericke, N., Loquet, M., Olin-Scheller, C., Stolare, M. and Wegner, A. (2021), 'Epistemic Quality and Powerful Knowledge: Implications for Curriculum Innovation and Teacher Education Policy and Practice', Panel Discussion at European Conference on Educational Research (ECER 2020), University of Geneva, 6–10 September 2021.

Hudson, B., Henderson, S. and Hudson, A. (2015), 'Developing Mathematical Thinking in the Primary Classroom: Liberating Teachers and Students as Learners of Mathematics', *Journal of Curriculum Studies*, 47 (3): 374–98. DOI: 10.1080/00220272.2014.979233

Hudson, B. and Meyer, M. A. (eds) (2011), *Beyond Fragmentation: Didactics, Learning, and Teaching*, Opladen and Farmington Hills: Verlag Barbara Budrich.

Kansanen, P. and Meri, M. (1999), 'The Didactic Relation in the Teaching-Studying-Learning Process', in B. Hudson, F. Buchberger, P. Kansanen and H. Seel (eds), *Didaktik/Fachdidaktik as Science(-s) of the Teaching Profession?*, 2 (1): 21–36. TNTEE Publications. DOI: 10.13140/RG.2.1.2646.4726

Klafki, W. (1970), 'Das pädagogische Verhältnis', in W. Klafki et al. (Hrsg.), *Erziehungswissenschaft 1. Eine Einführung*, 55–91, Frankfurt am Main: Fischer Bücherei.

Lakatos, I. (1976), *Proofs and Refutations*, Cambridge: Cambridge University Press.

Lambert, D. and Biddulph, M. (2015), 'The Dialogic Space Offered by Curriculum-Making in the Process of Learning to Teach, and the Creation of a Progressive Knowledge-Led Curriculum', *Asia-Pacific Journal of Teacher Education*, 43 (3): 210–24.

Morrow, W. (2008), *Bounds of Democracy: Epistemological Access in Higher Education*, Pretoria: HSRC Press.

Scottish Executive Education Department (2005), *Assessment of Achievement Programme: Seventh Survey of Mathematics 2004*, Edinburgh: Scottish Executive Education Department.

Scottish Government (2012), *Scottish Survey of Literacy and Numeracy 2011 (Numeracy)*. http://www.scotland.gov.uk/Publications/2012/03/5285/downloads#res390565

Shulman, L. S. (1987), 'Knowledge and Teaching: Foundations of the New Reform', *Harvard Educational Review*, 5 (1): 1–22.

Tatto, M. T. and Hordern, J. (2017), 'The Configuration of Teacher Education as a Professional Field of Practice: A Comparative Study of Mathematics Education', in J. Furlong and G. Whitty (eds), *Knowledge and the Study of Education*, 255–74, Oxford: Symposium Books.

UN (2015), 'Transforming our World: The 2030 Agenda for Sustainable Development', https://sustainabledevelopment.un.org/?menu=1300

Winch, C. (2013), 'Curriculum Design and Epistemic Ascent', *Journal of Philosophy of Education*, 47 (1): 128–46.

Young, M. (2013), 'Overcoming the Crisis in Curriculum Theory: A Knowledge-based Approach', *Journal of Curriculum Studies*, 45 (2): 101–18. http://www.tandfonline.com/doi/full/10.1080/00220272.2013.764505

Young, M. (2015), 'Powerful Knowledge as Curriculum Principle', in M. Young, D. Lambert, C. R. Roberts and M. D. Roberts, *Knowledge and the Future School: Curriculum and Social Justice*, 65–88, 2nd edn, London: Bloomsbury Academic.

Young, M. and Muller, J. (2010), 'Three Educational Scenarios for The Future: Lessons from the Sociology of Knowledge', *European Journal of Education*, 45: 11–27.

Establishing Links to Specialized Knowledge in Social Studies Teaching

Ann-Christin Randahl and Martin Kristiansson

Introduction

Formal education plays an essential role for people to acquire knowledge resourceful for understanding different aspects of the world and to act in it wisely. In a late modern world of high complexity, resourceful knowledge often emerges as 'specialised knowledge' from the work of researchers in different disciplines (Young and Muller 2013). This kind of knowledge is resourceful because, if attained through learning, it takes pupils 'beyond their experience in the most reliable ways we have' (Young 2014: 67). To make this happen, teachers need to establish a strong link between specialized knowledge and what is learned in school (Gericke et al. 2018; Young and Muller 2013).

In this chapter, we discuss a Swedish project about migration in which social studies teachers in middle schools collaborate with researchers to transform specialized knowledge and make it accessible for pupils. Theoretically, the chapter is based on Bernstein's pedagogic device (see Singh 2002, further developed by Maton 2014) and the notion of cumulative knowledge building within the framework of LCT – Legitimation Code Theory (Maton 2013). The pedagogic device consists of three fields; production, recontextualization, and reproduction. In the fields of recontextualization, which are emphasized here, specialized knowledge is selected, rearranged and transformed into school knowledge and pedagogic discourse. This converted knowledge is finally realized in the fields of reproduction, where pupils meet teachers, to learn about the world.

Social studies in the earlier years in Sweden share a problem found in other countries by having a weak link to specialized knowledge, for two main reasons. First, social studies often have low priority compared to the 'core' subjects of first language and maths, making social studies count on routine and tradition (see, for instance, Brophy et al. 2009; Stolare 2016). Over time, this weakens the link to specialized knowledge. Second, schooling in earlier years is often learner-oriented, focusing on the everyday knowledge pupils bring to school as a motivating factor (Kristiansson 2018). However, for pupils to develop resourceful knowledge, everyday knowledge must be connected to specialized knowledge, through teaching and learning in the classrooms. Maton (2013) approaches this connection semantically, where specialized knowledge (and language) is unpacked by connecting it to everyday knowledge and repacked again by connecting it to specialized knowledge to create what he calls 'semantic waves'. This process of knowledge building through unpacking and repacking is argued to take pupils beyond their everyday experience. Yet, creating semantic waves presupposes that teachers have access to specialized knowledge.

The aim of this chapter is to explore teachers' knowledge-building processes to strengthen the link between everyday and specialized knowledge. The context provided to explore the transformation of knowledge is a peer discussion about migration among three middle-school teachers and two teacher students, moderated by two researchers. The site is chosen for three reasons. First, the peer discussion makes transformation processes visible since they can be traced by the participants' utterances. Second, peer discussions as a site for professional development is an arena of interest for contemporary school development. Third, peer discussions as a site for recontextualization is less explored than, for example, policy documents or curricula.

We start the chapter by briefly describing the project, putting the first phase up front to give a context to our aim. The analytic tools used to explore how the un- and repacking of the first phase worked are then described. In the third section, we discuss some of the most important findings of our analysis. We end the chapter by discussing these findings in relation to teacher education and the implications they might hold for teachers' professional development.

Developing Teaching in Three Phases

The peer discussion is part of a project constructed as a so-called research-development-circle or an RD-circle (Bladh et al. 2018). This circle has three main phases. In the first phase, there is a focus on building a deeper understanding of migration, based on specialized knowledge. The second phase concentrates on planning for teaching. The third phase focuses on testing and evaluating the planned teaching in different classrooms. In each phase, the unpacking and repacking between specialized and everyday knowledge is key to reaching the main objective of strengthening the link to specialized knowledge in middle-school social studies teaching.

The overall design of the RD-circle is inspired by educational design research (EDR) (e.g. McKenney and Reeves 2019; Plomp and Nieeven 2013). EDR conducts interventions in the often messy and complex classroom settings in order to develop teaching and learning as well as to give research contributions based on these developmental efforts. Before entering the classrooms, one carefully investigates what is going to be developed and the problems, needs and contexts connected to that. Based on this knowledge, prototypes are constructed for classroom-testing. This prototype-building includes acquiring input from different experts and pilot-tests with smaller groups of pupils. It also involves theoretical framing of the problem, the prototype and how to develop it, as well as framing the analysis of the prototype and its processing. Changes are made based on these preparations, making it ready for the classroom-testing. When ready, an iterative testing process begins that puts the prototype into action, analysing its shortcomings and making revisions until it is robust enough to be practical as well as effective for actual teaching and learning.

Following the basic ideas of doing EDR-research, the project departed from the problem of social studies resting weakly on specialized knowledge as a resource to understand the social world and cope with its issues. Migration, as a social studies content, was chosen because humans have always, and will probably always, migrate, making it a social phenomenon well worth understanding. Migration also involves contemporary and future issues connected to both its causes and consequences which are important to understand and handle. Finally, migration has been studied systematically from which specialized knowledge has emerged as a resource to take pupils beyond their everyday experience of migration and its issues. Since social studies in the earlier years generally have a weak connection to this kind of knowledge, the first phase of the project concentrated on developing the teachers' content knowledge about migration as a precondition for developing knowledge about teaching this content. The first phase was followed by a second one of constructing a module on migration consisting of different teacher and pupil activities. This construction was tested and evaluated for practicality and effectiveness in the third phase. The two first phases each lasted one semester, while the third phase lasted two semesters.

In relation to the pedagogic device, the first phase highlights the fields of recontextualization, focusing the transformation of disciplinary knowledge and how to teach this knowledge. Like the second phase, it is located in the fields of recontextualization. However, the link to the fields of reproduction is more emphasized due to the construction of the teaching material. The third phase is more clearly placed in the fields of reproduction, concentrating on how teaching affects pupils' meaning making, using specialized knowledge as a resource. The remaining part of this chapter focuses on the first phase of the project, presenting analysis of the knowledge-building process about migration and how to teach this content in a peer discussion.

In the first phase, the group of teachers and researchers came together six times to learn from the first two chapters of a popularized research review on human migration (Hanlon and Vicino 2014) and to discuss how to teach this content. The review as such can be seen as recontextualizing specialized knowledge, making migration as a phenomenon more comprehensible for the lay person. Further, the researchers mediated the content in video-recorded, explanatory PowerPoint presentations for the teachers to watch before reading the mentioned chapters. The researchers moderated the discussions during the meetings. Each meeting lasted two hours and the teachers were given three hours of preparation before the meetings.

Focusing on Semantic Shifts to Analyse Knowledge Building

To gain access to the theoretical knowledge of a discipline or field, the understanding and use of concepts are crucial. Concepts are used to describe and generalize lived experience. When related to other concepts, they build constellations or webs of meanings that form the base of a subject area. Within the framework of legitimation code theory (LCT), it is argued that knowledge building is promoted through semantic shifts between disciplinary and everyday knowledge (Maton 2013, 2014). By analysing these shifts, one can trace transformation processes.

To describe semantic shifts, two modalities are used: semantic density and semantic gravity. Both modalities can be analysed along a continuum where the semantic density and gravity can be relatively weaker or stronger. The stronger the semantic density, the more the meaning is condensed. The stronger the semantic gravity, the more the meaning is tied to or dependent on the context (Maton 2013).

Two different analytic tools are used to analyse the semantic shifts in the discussion: a semantic plane (Shay 2013) and semantic waves (Maton 2013).

In the semantic plane, semantic density and semantic gravity form two axes (see Figure 9.1). These axes create four quadrants, where a different kind of knowledge is in focus. When the semantic density is strong and the semantic gravity is weak, theoretical knowledge is in focus. In this study, for example, the meaning of different concepts is discussed. When semantic density as well as semantic gravity is strong, professional knowledge is being focused on. This is the case, for example, when teachers discuss what to teach about, that is, questions about selection (Singh 2002). When both semantic density and semantic gravity are weak, general knowledge is in focus. Here, questions about migration are discussed in everyday language. Instead of talking about what causes migration, teachers talk about why people move. When semantic density is weak and semantic gravity is strong, practical knowledge is in focus. In this case, for example, when teachers discuss classroom activities or tasks in everyday language.

The semantic plane as an analytic tool makes it possible to plot what is going on in the different peer discussions of the RD-circle getting an overview of how the knowledge building efforts are semantically distributed.

The semantic wave as an analytic tool (see Figure 9.2) aims to capture the process of the semantic shifts, where disciplinary knowledge is connected to everyday knowledge and a disciplinary discourse is connected to everyday language (the dotted line). When knowledge building as a process is working,

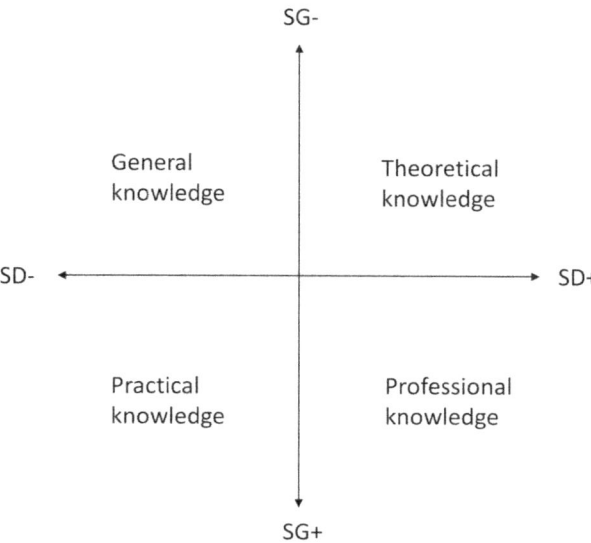

Figure 9.1 The semantic plane.

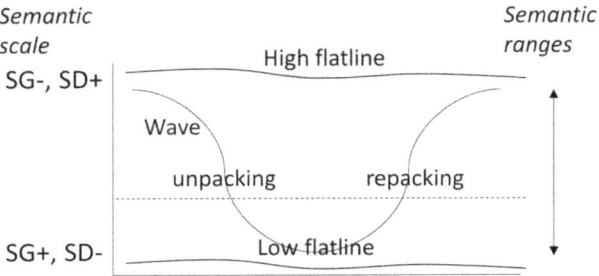

Figure 9.2 Semantic profiles (adapted from Maton 2013: 13).

it may be identified as semantic waves of downward and upward shifts. In a downward shift, concepts are unpacked into more familiar common-sense or everyday language and scientific knowledge connected to concrete phenomena. In an upward shift, the concrete example is generalized or connected to the theoretical field, whereby the concept is reconnected to its web of meaning. If there is a high flat line within the disciplinary discourse, theoretical or technical concepts are discussed in relation to each other, without connection to the lived world, experiences or specific examples. Scholars within a discipline can argue about different perspectives along a high flat line, for example. If there is a low flat line, no disciplinary knowledge is developed, nor a language that can work as a means to generalize experiences (Maton 2013).

The analysed data of the knowledge building within the RD-circle consists of the second peer discussion in the first phase of the circle. Three middle-school teachers, two teacher students and two researchers participated in this discussion. As preparation, the teachers read the two first chapters of a research overview about migration (Hanlon and Vicino 2014). In these two chapters, concepts are defined, causal factors pointed out and patterns of migration described. Further, the reading was scaffolded by a recorded summarizing PowerPoint presentation. The discussion had the dual aim of developing both knowledge about migration and knowledge about how to teach about migration. We regard the former goal, building knowledge about migration, as a more context-independent activity, where the knowledge developed serves as a general knowledge base for the participating teachers. The latter goal, building knowledge about how to teach about migration, is considered more context-dependent, where the knowledge developed serves as a basis for teaching in a certain situation. This means that gravity weakens when general knowledge building is being focused on and strengthens when teaching is being focused on in the discussion.

Analytical Process and Considerations

Whether focusing on general knowledge or teaching practice in the discussion, the participants might use more scientific language or more everyday language. Ideally, one would find a discursive mobility (Nygård Larsson 2011) between a more scientific and more everyday language. This move along the semantic continuum may be seen as a resource for knowledge building, connecting an everyday language to a scientific language (and thereby an everyday understanding to a more scientific understanding). In the peer discussion under study, scientific language is above all manifested in the use of scientific concepts related to migration. When a concept is used, it opens up a possibility to relate this concept to other concepts that are linked to the field of migration. For example, it seems to matter whether the participants choose to talk about *migration* or *movement*:

> R1: what is the difference between to migrate and to move
>
> [...]
>
> T1: well, I suppose there is no difference really, or I think it is about a voluntary or an involuntary...
>
> T3: yeah and
>
> T1: ...migration

The example illustrates how the use of *migrate* instead of *move* leads to a distinction being made between voluntary and involuntary migrants, referring to the research overview about migration, which emphasizes this division: 'Within the category of migrants, there is often a distinction made between voluntary migrants and involuntary migrants' (Hanlon and Vicino 2014: 5).

In another example on the same topic, one researcher questions whether he had migrated when he moved from a city to the countryside. The researcher moderating the discussion uses the question to distinguish internal and external migration. These two types of migration are also the starting point of the research overview (Hanlon and Vicino 2014: 3-4).

> R1: Well I moved from the city to an old house in the countryside. Could you call that movement a 'migration'
>
> T1: To migrate, hum, that sounds more like a statement
>
> R2: If you think in terms of internal migration, i.e. you move inside the country, you've made an odd migration. Most people move from the countryside to the city

[...]

R2: But if I would check the official statistics on migration

R1: I would probably be visible there

Table 9.1 Analytical Tool

Knowledge focused	Semantic relations	Indicators	Example quotes from empirical data
Theoretical knowledge	SD+, SG−	Knowledge building about migration Participants using concepts from the field of migration	Well, there is the difference, if you are a voluntary migrant, then you have an opportunity to move back. Mostly, that is not the case, if you are an involuntary migrant. Then, most often you can't return.
Professional knowledge	SD+, SG+	Knowledge building about the teaching of migration Participants using concepts from the field of migration	I have talked about these concepts push and pull in relation to migration (in her teaching: our clarification). Why do they move? We have touched upon that.
General knowledge	SD−, SG−	Knowledge building about migration Participants using everyday language	That you build small communities, to make it easier for your family or other fellows to move in, that's something I hadn't reflected upon earlier.
Practical knowledge	SD−, SG+	Knowledge building about the teaching of migration Participants using everyday language	In my opinion, pupils find these think-about questions hard, like imagine you are living in a country with a large population...

Examples like these influenced our decision to analyse utterances or turns containing concepts from the field as an indicator strengthening the semantic density, even if the syntactic and/or semantic context displays more of an everyday discourse.

These considerations about semantic gravity and semantic density guiding the coding procedure are captured in Table 9.1.

In the second peer discussion in phase one of the RD-circle, there are a total of 440 turns or utterances, minimal response or support excluded. The analytical tool is used to assess each of the 440 turns in relation to gravity – is the focus on teachers' general knowledge building or on educational practice – and in relation to density – are there any concepts used? Six of the 440 turns are judged irrelevant, consisting of five utterances concerning administration of data in the project and one utterance which is inaudible. Our findings from the analytical process are presented in the next section.

Findings

To obtain an overview of how the second peer discussion is semantically distributed, the turns are displayed in the semantic plane (see Figure 9.3). Most of the interaction (49 per cent) takes place in the SD-, SG+ area, where teaching about migration is discussed using everyday language. In 7 per cent of the turns where teaching is in focus, the participants use concepts from the field of migration. A little less than half of the interaction (44 per cent) concerns knowledge building about migration, that is, definition of concepts and causal factors. The relatively equal distribution of turns between the two upper quadrants indicates a discursive mobility (Nygård Larsson 2011), connecting everyday language to a more theoretical language (the arrow in the plane), and thereby possibly bridging the gap between a more scientific understanding and an everyday understanding of migration. Compared to the teachers, the researchers use concepts with a higher density and more often in the interaction (in bold in the plane).

Whether the semantic shifts in the discussion support the transformation of knowledge or not can be revealed by semantic profiles, where a semantic wave is desirable. In relation to concepts, unpacking is used as a resource to connect concepts to an everyday understanding and language and repacking as a resource to generalize concrete examples relate them to the field of knowledge

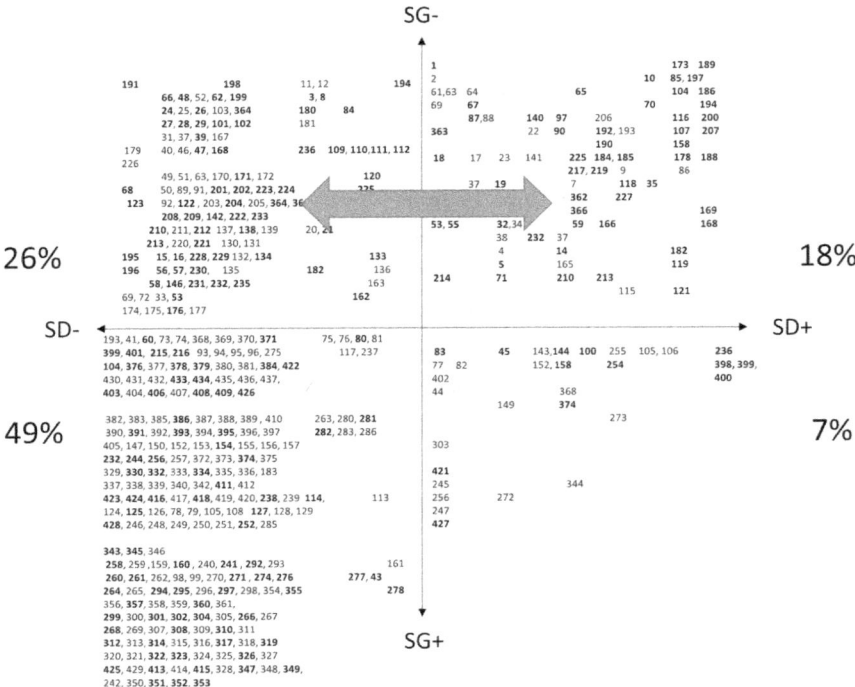

Figure 9.3 Turns distributed in the semantic plane.

and to other concepts. Participating teachers as well as researchers unpack concepts. However, the repacking is mostly carried out by one of the researchers, who moderates the discussion. In the following example, the concept 'migrate' is unpacked in turn 150 (why people choose to move). The reasons that people migrate (people are forced to, people have different possibilities) are repacked in turn 158 by the concept of voluntary and involuntary, which is further linked to push-and-pull factors:

> 149: [T3] well, maybe it is a good idea to give the pupils different identities. For example, someone from Sweden, someone from Syria and someone from Africa. And then, the pupils try to figure out which possibilities these people have to **migrate** and why they choose to **migrate**. And so on
>
> [R2] exactly
>
> 150: [T1] and the pupils get a better understanding about why people really choose to
>
> 151: [T3] move

[T1] move

[T3] yes

152: [T1] and it might be, well you are forced to, or you do it **voluntarily**

153: [T3] yes, and as you said, what limits us

154: [R1] Exactly, for us it is easy to say, well it is a matter of will or something

[T3] yes, exactly

[T1] yes

155: [T3] who come from Sweden compare to, hum

156: [T1] a girl from Zimbabwe or

157: [T3] exactly, that's how things are. But I think it was interesting, and that it could be a way to engage the pupils and help them to see how things differ

[R1] yes, exactly

[T3] ...different possibilities so to speak

[R1] mm

158: [R2] well then, the theme could be **voluntary and involuntary**. You could have that as a starting point for different reasons than...

[T1] mm

[T2] ...why you move, I suppose...

[T1] absolutely

[R2] ...Now we are approaching these **push and pull factors**

This discursive mobility forms a functional wave (Nygård Larsson and Jakobsson 2017). Further, there is a two-step process with nominalizations supporting this shift (c.f. Gibbons 2010). In the excerpt, the following nominalizations can be identified:

- Upward shift: pupils can figure out which *possibilities* people have to migrate
- Downward shift: pupils obtain a better *understanding* of why people really choose to move
- Upward shift: it could be a way to engage the pupils and help them see how things differ, different *possibilities*...

Transferred into a diagram, the semantic wave is shaped in the following way (see Figure 9.4).

There are also other semantic profiles. In a second example, a low flat line is illustrated. No concepts are used. Instead, deictic pronouns are common. In the excerpt, two student teachers are asked by a researcher to elaborate on the question being discussed concerning who is a migrant. Unlike the teachers, the

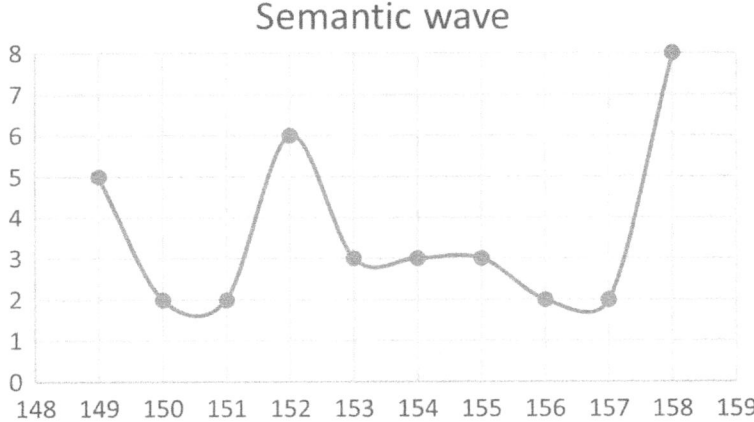

Figure 9.4 Semantic wave.

students have had no theoretical input prior to the meeting. They have not read the two chapters in the research overview or seen the PowerPoint presentation, where one of the researchers mediates the content. No semantic shifts are identified; instead, the turns become stuck in everyday language.

> 73: [TS2] well, I have only considered **the notion** at large...
>
> [R2] yes
>
> [T2] yes
>
> [TS2] ... that you, well, come from another country or...
>
> [R2] yes
>
> [TS2] ... that you kind of...
>
> [T1] mm
>
> [TS2] ... not what it means if you scan it...
>
> [R1] no, hum
>
> [TS2] ... but you must know **it**, if you have to explain the word to the pupils, because they want to know exactly what **it** means...
>
> [T3] mm
>
> [R2] ... what
>
> 74: [TS1] well yes, but at the same time, they seem to have an opinion about **it** already, as they get onto well...
>
> 75: [T1] well refugees
>
> 76: [TS1] yes, exactly. They already have kind of an idea about **it**

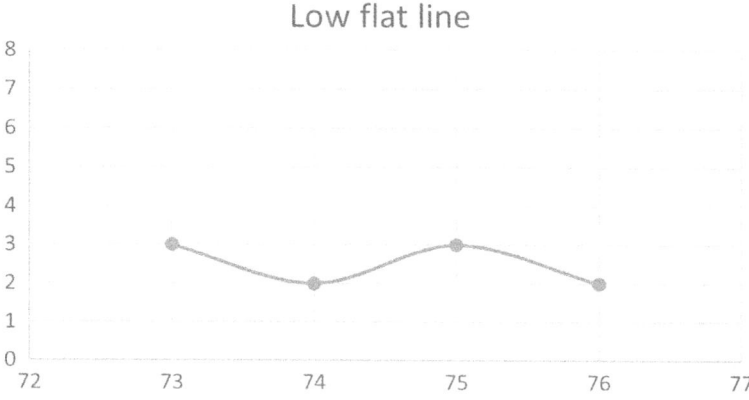

Figure 9.5 Low flat line.

Transferred into a diagram, this semantic profile is shaped in the following way (see Figure 9.5).

Not only does a low flat line seem to interrupt the transformation process, but there also seems to be a semantic limit, an Icarus effect, manifested in a high flat line. In the next excerpt, two researchers discuss different theoretical perspectives due to migration. No teacher gives even a minimal response or support during this part of the discussion. At a research seminar, this kind of discussion is relevant, but in the context of a research and development circle the aim is to build knowledge about migration and how to teach. Related to Bernstein's pedagogic device, this could be an example of where scholars position themselves in the fields of production instead of in the fields of recontextualization or reproduction:

> 196: [R1] well, because in other **scientific literature** I know they separate this rather distinct, and if you look at it historically...
>
> 197: [R2] ... we can identify a critique against **rational**, hum, this **rational economic choice** thing, but I did not consider it had something to do with **push and pull**, but
>
> 198: [R1] well it does, because it relates quite obviously to, well because it is such a **model**
>
> 199: [R2] well okay, I thought it was an overarching **principle**, when there is **gravity**, there is also **pressure** somehow
>
> 200: [R1] Well, yes and no, but from **a Marxist perspective** it is not a question of minus and plus, it concerns **power relations**

Transferred into a diagram, this semantic profile is shaped in the following way (see Figure 9.6).

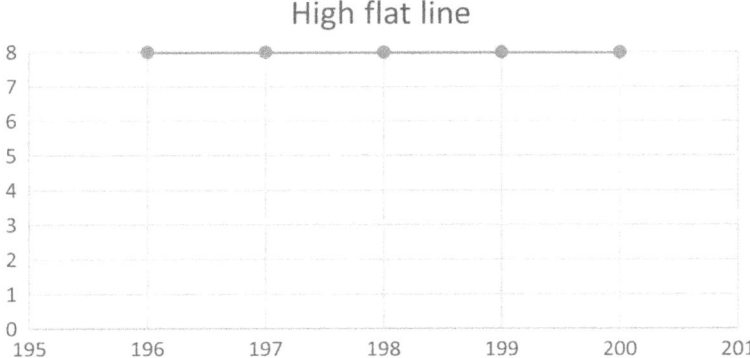

Figure 9.6 High flat line.

Different examples of semantic profiles identified in the second peer discussion are described earlier. To summarize, transformation processes occur more frequently in the discussion where knowledge building about migration is being focused on. Specialized knowledge about migration is connected to everyday knowledge, accomplished through a discursive mobility, where concepts are scrutinized and linked to each other. However, two risks were identified during this part of the meeting. First, there is a risk of becoming stuck in everyday language with few possibilities of cumulative knowledge building. As this data set suggests, it is caused by a lack of theoretical and linguistic input. Second, there is the risk of an Icarus effect where the two researchers leave the school context in favour of the research context and cause a high flatline, with few possibilities for transformation.

In the second part of the discussion, where teaching about migration is in focus, the interaction is laden with practical issues more than content. Connections to specialized knowledge about migration are thereby downplayed. Questions about selection or what to teach are rare. This was an unexpected result, discovered mainly by the use of the semantic plane as an analytical tool.

The RD-circle serves its goals in many respects, first and foremost by scaffolding the cumulative knowledge building. Yet, in other respects the setup seems insufficient to fulfil its goals – at least at this early point of the RD-circle. The transformation process, that is, the adaptation of knowledge for educational purposes in the fields of reproduction, seems to require a higher amount of scaffolding than is being offered at this stage.

Strengths and challenges in the RD-circle are elaborated on in the following discussion. Further, implications for professional development programmes and teacher education in social studies are proposed.

Implications

In a professional development perspective, the results indicate that this kind of RD-circle can be an effective means to increase teachers' knowledge base. Through consciously moderated peer discussions, teachers strengthen their understanding of migration as concerns, for example, causes and effects. The role of the moderator, taking on an epistemic responsibility, seems to be crucial. From the perspective of the analytical framework, the moderator often makes the semantic upward shift, repacking the content by using or referring to concepts. This causes semantic shifts where the semantic density strengthens and the semantic profile gains the shape of a wave, argued to ease cumulative knowledge building. However, this role is not performed in the same manner when the focus moves to classroom practice. Mostly, the peer discussion becomes stuck in a low flat line, suggesting that successful knowledge building about migration does not automatically ignite professional knowledge building of what it means to teach about migration, based on classroom-practice experience. This discovery pinpoints the complexity of making specialized knowledge, even if one knows it well, suitable for pupils' learning in a classroom setting – that is, of reproducing specialized knowledge. Teachers and researchers coming together, for instance, in a RD-circle, exploring and digging deep into this problem, can support professional learning and development by both contributing to the participating teachers' professional repertoire and teachers' professional reservoir by spreading the knowledge built together (Bernstein 1999).

From a teacher education perspective, the findings may serve to highlight two important relationships for successful student teacher learning – to connect theory to practice and specialized knowledge to the teaching of specialized knowledge. To make this happen, it is essential that a teacher educator establish the link between specialized knowledge and what it means to teach this. The results partly visualize how to bridge courses about specialized knowledge to courses about pedagogy, often described as too distant from each other. Also, it could bring theory closer to practice, pointing at fruitful collaborations between teachers and researchers.

Being able to transform specialized knowledge is even more emphasized in today's school, resting on a research-informed paradigm. Further, today's teachers are expected to develop practice through peer-collaboration and with researchers (Olsson 2018). But to trust this kind of collaboration, it needs to be scrutinized. An important aspect of this is to use fruitful tools to analyse its processes and outcomes. Viewing it as collaborative cumulative knowledge building that can be captured through semantic analytic tools, this chapter has shown that tools like these are important. It could even be worth the time of teacher education to have student teachers analysing different aspects of teaching and learning using these tools. In themselves, they could be used as didactic tools to develop pupils' knowledge resting more firmly on specialized knowledge as well as tools to evaluate the quality of teaching, aiming for more resourceful ways for pupils to understand the world and cope wisely with its issues.

References

Bernstein, B. (1999), 'Vertical and Horizontal Discourse: An Essay', *British Journal of Sociology of Education*, 20 (2): 157–73.

Bladh, G., Stolare, M. and Kristiansson, K. (2018), 'Curriculum Principles, Didactic Practice and Social Issues: Thinking Through Teachers' Knowledge Practices in Collaborative Work', *London Review of Education*, 16 (3): 398–413.

Brophy, J., Alleman, J. and Knighton, B. (2009), *Inside the Social Studies Classroom*, New York: Routledge.

Gericke, N., Hudson, B., Olin-Scheller, N. and Stolare, M. (2018), 'Powerful Knowledge: Transformations and the Need for Empirical Studies across School Subjects', *London Review of Education*, 16 (3): 428–44.

Gibbons, P. (2010), *Lyft språket, lyft tänkandet: språk och lärande* [English Learners, Academic Literacy, and Thinking] (1. uppl.), Uppsala: Hallgren and Fallgren.

Hanlon, B. and Vicino, T. J. (2014), *Global Migration: The Basics*, New York: Routledge.

Kristiansson, M. (2018), 'Principer för samhällsrelevant SO [Guiding Principles for Selection in Social Studies Teaching]', *SO-didaktik*, 6: 34–7.

Maton, K. (2013), 'Making Semantic Waves: A Key to Cumulative Knowledge-building', *Linguistics and Education*, 24: 8–22.

Maton, K. (2014), *Knowledge and Knowers: Towards a Realist Sociology of Education*, London: Routledge.

McKenney, S. and Reeves, T. (2019), *Conducting Educational Design Research*, London: Routledge.

Nygård Larsson, P. (2011), *Biologiämnets texter: text, språk och lärande i en språkligt heterogen gymnasieklass* [Texts in the Subject of Biology: Text, Language, and Learning in a Linguistically Heterogeneous Class in Secondary School], Diss. Lund: Lunds universitet, Malmö.

Nygård Larsson, P. and Jakobsson, A. (2017), 'Semantiska vågor: elevers diskursiva rörlighet i gruppsamtal [Semantic Waves: Students Discursive Mobility in Group Conversations]', *NorDiNa: Nordic Studies in Science Education*, 13 (1): 17–35.

Olsson, D. (2018), *Improving Teaching and Learning Together: A Literature Review of Professional Learning Communities*, Karlstad: Karlstad University Studies.

Plomp, T. and Nieveen, N. (2013), *Educational Design Research: Part A, An Introduction*, Enschede: SLO.

Shay, S. (2013), 'Conceptualizing Curriculum Differentiation in Higher Education: A Sociology of Knowledge Point of View', *British Journal of Sociology of Education*, 34 (4): 563–82.

Singh, P. (2002), 'Pedagogising Knowledge: Bernstein's Theory of the Pedagogic Device', *British Journal of Sociology of Education*, 23 (4): 571–82.

Stolare, M. (2016), 'En massa innehåll: Lärare talar om sin undervisning i SO och historia på mellanstadiet [A Lot to Cover: Middle School Teachers' Talk About Teaching Social Science and History]', in Maria Olson och Sara Irisdotter Aldenmyr (eds.), *SO-ämnen och tematiker för lägre åldrar*, 123–40, Lund: Gleerup.

Young, M. (2014), 'Powerful Knowledge as a Curriculum Principle', in M. Young and D. Lambert (eds), *Knowledge and the Future School: Curriculum and Social Justice*, 65–88, London: Bloomsbury.

Young, M. and Muller, J. (2013), 'On the Powers of Powerful Knowledge', *Review of Education*, 1 (3): 229–59.

10

Supporting Teachers' Professional Development in Social Studies Education

Martin Stolare, Gabriel Bladh and Martin Kristiansson

Introduction

The discussion taking place in the sociology of knowledge about 'powerful knowledge' as a curriculum principle has been an important contribution to the ongoing debate on knowledge, curriculum and the future school (Young and Muller 2016).

It has been emphasized that linking to the *didaktik* tradition can be a way of discussing how powerful knowledge can be understood in the context of education (Deng 2018; Gericke et al. 2018; Bladh 2020). The powerful knowledge approach stresses the importance of pupil encounters with specialized knowledge and the transparent relationship of school subjects to the particular quality of knowledge that the academic disciplines represent (Nordgren 2017). We have previously shown the potential of relating powerful knowledge to Klafki's theory of categorial *Bildung* (formation) (Bladh et al. 2018). In this way, by combining the Anglo-Saxon curriculum tradition with German and Scandinavian *didaktik* theory, questions on the selection and transformation of content and subject matter can be better understood. In this chapter, we want to deepen the discussion on knowledge in education in relation to teachers' professional development and the role of specialized knowledge. All this will be done by relating to the subject-*didaktik* theory of *didaktical* reconstruction (Kattman et al. 1997).[1] As our empirical context, we will use an ongoing, collaborative and design-research-inspired curriculum research and development project addressing teaching about social issues, specifically migration. The project's focus is the investigation and problematization of how teaching about migration in upper primary school (years 4–6) can be connected to specialized knowledge, with an emphasis on the role of content selection and transformation.

The theme of this chapter is models for curriculum development within the framework of professional development processes (Prediger et al. 2017, 2019). In their 3-T model, two different, yet complementary, implementation strategies for teaching innovations – material- and community-based strategies – are discussed in research on professional development (Prediger et al. 2017; Prediger, Roesken-Winter and Leuders 2019). These types of strategies were both used in the research and development circle where we, as researchers, together with primary teachers for two years, developed and tested concrete lesson plans dealing with the social issue of migration. A starting point for the circle was the opportunities and challenges of designing teaching plans and teaching artefacts on specialized knowledge. In this chapter, the work in the circle of constructing lesson plans and artefacts is analysed using the *didaktical* reconstruction model. The outcome of the analysis is viewed in the context of professional development, for the school as well as for teacher education.

Our *didaktical* analysis opens a discussion on the role that educational design – the construction of lesson plans and artefacts – might have on processes of professional development and how these processes can contribute to the development of the teachers' powerful professional knowledge (Furlong and Whitty 2017). The latter naturally leads to reasoning about not only the character of the professional knowledge that teachers need to acquire and continuously develop through their professional career but also the conditions making the development possible. Aspects of the selection and transformation of subject matter become a possible point of departure for discussing teachers' professional knowledge and to what extent one can speak of it as being powerful.

The overarching research question is: *What characterizes the process of selection and transformation of a subject matter by in-service teachers, and what implications might this hold for teacher education policy and practice?*

Social Realism and the *didaktik* Tradition

By focusing on the role of knowledge in education, the social realism perspective – to which the powerful knowledge approach is connected – has productively opened up new links to the tradition of *didaktik* and, more specifically, subject didactic research. As stated by Muller (2016), a positive effect of the 'knowledge turn' has been to 'demonstrate the difference that disciplinary difference can make to the learning process'. The continental and Nordic tradition of *didaktik* discerns content and subject matter as a starting point in a related way. Michael Young (2014) uses the idea of powerful knowledge as a curriculum principle. Fundamental to the *didaktik* tradition is the understanding of the relations between the teacher, subject matter and pupils as the three corners of the *didaktical* triangle. The relational approach also points to the necessity that the *didaktical* questions – why, what, how and for whom – are seen in relation to each other. In his work on categorial *Bildung*, the German educationalist Klafki identified this ideal by relating material *Bildung* theories (objective, knowledge-focused content; *Bildungsinhalt*) to formal *Bildung* theories (student-focused content; *Bildungsgehalt*). Categorial *Bildung* represents the objective and subjective side of *Bildung*, dialectically in combination (Meyer and Meyer 2007; Willbergh 2016). Young's 'powerful knowledge' as a curriculum principle has, above all, the character of a basic material formation theory in which content structure, central concepts, 'big ideas' and perspectives are highlighted. The formal perspective on content knowledge, what knowledge can do for students, is more implicitly stated. Compare Deng (2020), who also problematizes the focus on knowledge in Young's powerful knowledge concept and urges a deeper interrogation with a theory of content. Klafki's *didaktik* model, on the other hand, emphasizes the educational potential as a vital selection principle. When teachers make their didactical choices in their 'curriculum thinking', the educational potential of the content (seen as its exemplary, contemporary and future significance for the learner) is an essential principle of selection (Bladh et al. 2018). When Young and Muller (2019) revisit the idea of powerful knowledge, they discuss the connection of the concept to two different aspects of power, which has not been clearly elaborated. They state (2019: 4): 'our efforts at clarification had taken their primary task to be elucidating power as a "socio-epistemic property" of knowledge, rather than on power as "potential or capacity" for social actors to do something' (compare Maude 2016). This discussion on the 'objective' and the 'subjective' sides of powerful knowledge are in line with Klafki. The idea of categorial *Bildung* in *didaktik* would imply a dialectic meeting between 'curriculum' and 'pedagogy' when teachers make a selection and transformation of their content and subject matter in their curriculum planning. This relational perspective of *didaktik*, heavily drawing on Klafki's ideas of categorial *Bildung*, is further developed in the subject-*didaktical* models of *didaktical* reconstruction to which we will return.

Two Strategies for Professional Development

Migration as a social issue is the theme of our project. The purpose of this project is to investigate, among other things, the potential of specialized knowledge in social studies education in upper primary school (years 4–6).[2] The project is inspired by an educational design research approach in which we develop and try out different teaching plans and artefacts in an iterative process (van den Akker et al. 2006; McKenney and Reeves 2012). The platform for this work is a research and development circle. Within the framework of the circle, we as researchers worked together with three social studies teachers. In the circle, we collectively discussed teaching plans and artefacts that were tested in the teachers' classroom. A research and development circle can be understood as an arena for teachers and researchers to meet, functioning as a platform for professional development. The idea is that commitment and activity in the circle should not be too intensive, thus making it possible for the circle to be an integrated part of the teachers' workday. This also indicates that the theme, problem or question addressed in the circle should be in line with the teachers' professional context and formulated in collaboration between teachers and researchers.

The local context is a factor that becomes a natural dimension of the work and discussions in the circle representing a community strategy for professional development. An inductive community-strategy approach, in which the work in the circle is built from below based on the local conditions, is combined with a deductive material strategy (Prediger, Roesken-Winter and Leuders 2019). The material-strategy implies that there were pre-designed ideas on how to teach about migration that did not grow out of the unique conditions prevailing on the site. These ideas were expressed in various teaching prototypes based on specialized knowledge, subject-disciplinary as well as subject-specific educational. It is not uncommon for the researchers to introduce these ideas and initial prototypes in the meetings.

These two strategies can be considered in light of the *didaktik* tradition. Where the deductive material-strategy relates to *Materiale-Bildung*, to speak in terms of German *Bildung* theory (Jank and Meyer 2002), with a focus on the subject matter and the *didaktical* question *what*. The subject matter representing specialized knowledge is introduced from 'above' and thus not contextually rooted. The inductive community strategy is linked to the specific situation and by extension is connected to the pupils – to the *didaktical* question of *whom* – and *Formale-Bildung*.

The teaching artefacts developed within the framework of the circle are thereby the outcome of an interplay between community and material strategies. In Klafki's terms, these are strategies making categorical *Bildung* possible (Klafki 1985/2001). The discussion of the two strategies can be related to the 3-T model of Prediger et al. (2017; Prediger, Roesken-Winter and Leuders 2019) for professional development. This model highlights the relationship between different levels in a system of professional development (PD). The research and development circle represents the PD level of the model, while the teachers' experience, the actual educational practice, represents the classroom level.

The link between the two levels in the process of professional development is central to the above model. Here the *didaktical* triangle has developed into a tetrahedron emphasizing the importance teaching artefacts have in the *didaktical* process. The teachers' experiences and the researchers' more or less empirically grounded notions of the classroom level, of an educational practice, constitute the main content of the discussion and learning that takes place at the level of professional development. It also means that the content focused on at the level of professional development is more complex than the content at the classroom level. At the level of professional development, not only the subject matter content is addressed, but the educational practice of the classroom level as a whole. The deductive perspective expressed in the material strategy can

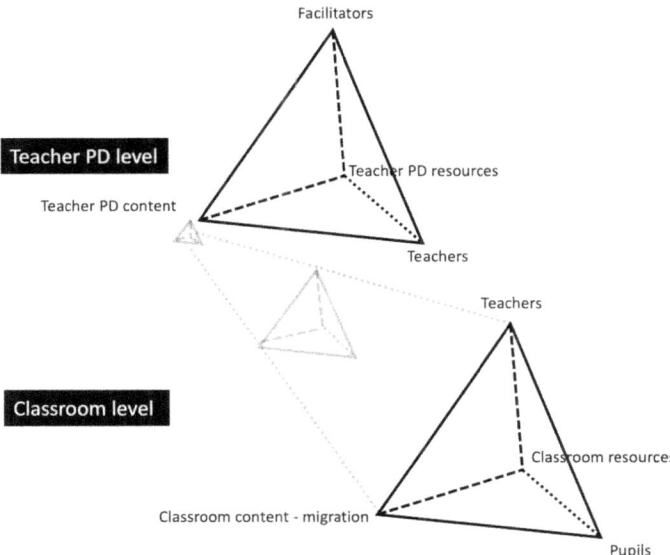

Figure 10.1 Adaptation of the 3-T model PD research (Prediger et al. 2017; Prediger, Roesken-Winter and Leuders 2019).

be knowledge contributions and suggestions for solving or highlighting the problems and challenges on the local level. The model with these two different, but in this case, complementary, strategies also captures the challenges that there may be in boosting the powerful knowledge approach in the context of professional development. Questions about the significance (what?) need to be combined with aspects of relevance (why? and for whom?). It is essential to consider these questions relationally in a didactical analysis of educational practice (Bladh, Stolare and Kristiansson 2018).

The Model of *didaktical* Reconstruction

We have previously stressed the possibility of linking the discussion regarding powerful knowledge and specialized knowledge to Klafki's theory of categorial *Bildung* (Bladh, Stolare and Kristiansson 2018). The categorial theory of *Bildung* constitutes the foundation of the model of *didaktical* reconstruction. Developed in the context of science education, this model has contributed to further deepening the subject didactic perspectives of the categorial *Bildung* theory and, therefore, to also qualify the perspectives on selection and transformation (Kattman et al. 1997; Duit et al. 2012).

Kattman et al. (1997), who, together with Duit and others developed the model of *didaktical* reconstruction, stress the importance of focusing on the precise nature of the content, from both the objective material side (specialized knowledge) and subjective formal side (pupils' conceptions of the knowledge),

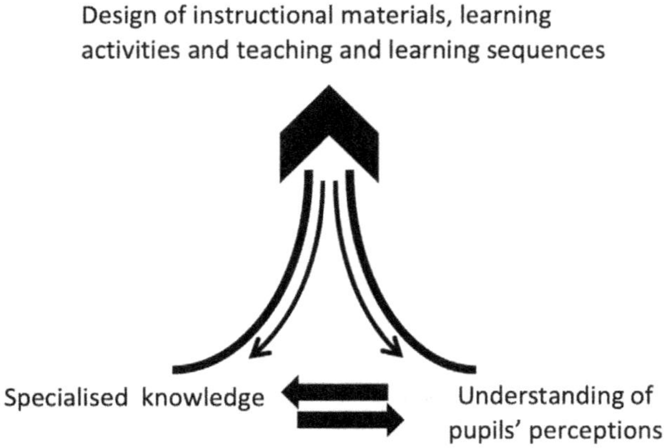

Figure 10.2 The model of *didaktical* reconstruction. Adapted from Kattman et al. 1997.

while planning or making a didactical analysis. The *didaktical* triangle, seen as the interaction between teacher–pupil–subject matter and the *didaktical* questions – why, what, how, for whom – permeates the model. While guiding the teacher in the process of planning and evaluating the teaching, the model of *didaktical* reconstruction can function as a framework in subject didactic research.

The transformation of specialized knowledge in a school context should not be considered as an easy task. In the model of *didaktical* reconstruction, this challenge is captured by the concept of elementarization, building on Wolfgang Klafki's discussion of the elementary (Klafki 1995: 185; Jank and Meyer 2002: 219). Fundamental here is the notion that school subject matter needs to have a different structure than the specialized knowledge developed by scholars. The complexity of the latter must be reduced – clarification is needed. Further, this should be accomplished without simplifying or distorting the knowledge (Kattman et al. 1997; Duit et al. 2012). In the clarification process, is it essential, according to the model of *didaktical* reconstruction, to determine the central building blocks, the elements of the knowledge area, that pupils need to acquire in order to gain knowledge of what they are supposed to learn. The clarification of the knowledge is done in relation to the perception of the pupils' understanding of the knowledge area. Once this deconstruction of the specialized knowledge is complete, it is necessary to assemble – reconstruct – the elements into what can be described as *educational pathways*. It is through using these pathways that pupils can learn the clarified but nonetheless complex subject matter. Thus, the model of *didaktical* reconstruction points to three different but intertwined activities that are all related to the aim of education: clarification (from special knowledge to subject matter), recognition of the pupils' perspectives (the pre-instructional views of the pupils) and *didaktical* structuring (designing and developing of teaching, making lesson plans) (Reinfried et al. 2009).

Although not explicitly stated, *didactical* reconstruction can be understood as a model in which the teacher is the prime agent. The teacher's understanding of the specialized knowledge and of the pupils' perceptions is central to the process of selecting and transforming the knowledge that the pupils are to learn. In a sense, the construction of lesson plans becomes not only a question of *how* – a practical methodological concern – but also of *what* and *why*. The what-question relates to the pupils, with the idea that the subject matter in school should not be a direct reflection of the academic discipline (Kattman et al. 1997). The specialized knowledge needs to be reconstructed, expressed in teaching artefacts, learning activities and learning sequences. Accordingly, the model of *didaktical* reconstruction has a stance on the question of how the relationship between discipline and school subject should be perceived, as well as on the interaction between the processes of selecting and transforming subject matter in relation to pupils' understanding.

The model of *didaktical* reconstruction constitutes a fruitful framework for contextualizing the processes of teaching and learning. In the following, the model will be used to frame an empirical didactical analysis of our work in the research and development circle, focusing on the selection and transformation of knowledge while planning teaching on the topic of migration. In the subsequent discussion, we will return to the implications our analysis hold for teachers' professional development and teacher education.

Example 1: The Selection of Specialized Knowledge

The research and development circle, comprising three teachers and two researchers, met approximately every eight weeks, sometimes more often, for a little more than three semesters. The work in the circle was divided into three phases. During the first phase, current research on the topic was read and discussed. The second phase was devoted to teaching development, which was then tested during the third phase of the circle.

State-of-the-art disciplinary research on migration formed the basis for the first six meetings constituting the first phase of the research and development circle. The ambition of the research project was to explore the challenges and possibilities of building on specialized knowledge in social studies education. It also meant that the question of selecting subject matter was addressed from the very start in the circle. The *didaktical* questions *why and what* played a central role in this context. In preparing for the meetings of the first phase, the participants were requested to read parts of the book *Global Migration: The Basics* (Hanlon and Vicino 2014). This book covers central themes on the topic of migration, including different perspectives in migration theory, explaining migration on societal, group and individual levels; global migration patterns and their changes; and the impact of migration on communities. This meant that the starting point in the circle was taken from relevant specialized knowledge and that the issue of powerful knowledge was explicitly addressed. In our previous experience of working with research and development circles, we noted that questions of subject matter selection can easily fall into the background. Instead, the formation of concrete teaching plans – prepared or executed – often tend to dominate the discussions. These perspectives are essential and logical but can also threaten to displace other issues altogether. In organizing the first six meetings as a study circle, we aimed to devote due time to content and selection questions.

The first empirical example is taken from the second meeting of the circle. The analysis focuses on the teachers' arguments regarding the selection of subject matter. This means that the issue of significance becomes essential – namely, what knowledge is considered important in the context of the teachers, and how is it justified?

Significance directs the attention to the subject matter itself with the underlying question of *When you know things about migration, what is it you know?* In an educational context, however, significance cannot be discussed concretely without linking it to aspects of relevance.

Relevance goes in two directions. First, there is relevance in relation to society, the present and the future, in terms of being able to manage one's role as a citizen. Relevance can also be directed internally, meaning what pupils themselves perceive as relevant. Here, relevance is linked to the pupils' life world. The interaction between significance and relevance is captured in the *didaktical* reconstruction model: the dialectical interaction between the teachers' knowledge of the subject area and students' performances is signalled. In this way, the *didaktical* question of the selection of subject matter becomes relational. The point is that, in an educational context, no issues of significance and relevance are decoupled from each other. This is also something that becomes clear in the discussions in the circle displayed below.

How do the teachers then reason about the selection of specialized knowledge and its connection to the teaching? What can be characterized as an 'aha!' experience is indicated when the teachers are to specify the subject matter they want to highlight. In their reading of the research, they were especially interested in (to them) previously unknown aspects of the topic of migration. The fact that there is a clear gender dimension in migration and how that has changed over time was a novelty to the teachers. They therefore believe that it is especially important to raise gender, as well as sexuality, as factors in the migration process. In the conversation in the circle, the teachers also expressed their surprise at the role and significance of the money shipments migrants send to their home countries. Aspects of the 'brain-drain' were something they raised as paradoxical and talked about in terms of an 'aha!' moment. The rationale behind the 'aha!' experience as a selection principle is that this is knowledge which has the power to be an eye-opener for the pupil. Such knowledge can challenge pupils' established perspectives and conceptions. There is thus a *didaktical* and rhetorical point in raising new and unknown perspectives on what is being studied.

> Teacher 3: I also find this [connection between] migration and sexuality interesting. The idea that you don't necessarily migrate due to war or work, that sexuality and [the freedom to] be yourself can also be a reason for migration. Something we view as a right in Sweden is not so elsewhere. I think the kids will be hooked by that idea too.

When the teacher above singles out the connection between migration and sexuality, it is not solely based on the notion that this new knowledge is significant and relevant to them from a knowledge perspective. Instead, the teacher's orientation to the new, unexpected knowledge perspectives is done with one eye on the intended pupils. The pupils are present in the selection process. In this way, significance and relevance are intimately associated with teachers' motives for the subject matter selection.

Even more prominent in the teachers' discussion of selection is their experience with pupil misconceptions. By highlighting specific subject matter, teachers recognize opportunities to challenge pupils' misconceptions. It becomes evident that teachers see it as important to try to change pupils' understanding of what drives migration and who migrants are. One such misconception that teachers see as necessary to confront is the pupils' simplified view that a migrant and a refugee are practically synonymous.

> T3: I think there will be very interesting discussions with the pupils when addressing voluntary and involuntary migration and what it leads to.
>
> Researcher 1: And what is voluntary in this context, yes?
>
> T3: Yes, and what life looks like for someone who chooses and those who have no choice. These are two completely different lives as well.
>
> [...]
>
> T3: I got a little stuck on what I read in the book, just that…
>
> R2: There is something that you think is extra interesting?
>
> T3: There are so many different things, yes. There are so many different types of migration, and you don't always think about it. The first thing that comes to mind is those who are forced to flee.
>
> R1: I think of the boats across the Mediterranean.

Migration is today a contentious social issue. Strong values are associated with migration, which means that the topic could be considered controversial in a school context. This is also evident in the teachers' reasoning. There is a value-oriented goal linked to migration as a topic.

> T3: No, but just that you. No, I'm just wondering if you might assign pupils some form of identity. You might take ... Yes, someone who lives in Sweden and someone who comes from Syria, and then you have someone from Africa and then maybe someone from Asia – so they [the pupils] get it. And then you work from that, and you see what opportunities you have for migration. Why do I migrate as a Swede, and why do you migrate in Syria? And from there, create some identity around this
>
> R2: Yeah, that's it.
>
> T1: And pupils gain a greater understanding of why people actually do...
>
> T3: move
>
> T1: move

The teachers stress the importance of pupils practising perspective recognition since it might open their eyes up to the different dimensions and driving forces of the migration process (Barton and Levstik 2004). They express the urge to challenge the pupils' simplified comprehension of migration and to create a more sophisticated understanding of the phenomenon. In order to achieve this, a certain part of the subject matter needs to be emphasized. Here, the teachers' argumentation relates to the process of elementarization, as their recognition of potential subject matter can be explained by a deeper disciplinary understanding.

It is apparent that teachers in the circle allow their experiences of pupils' understanding and ability to acquire knowledge to be a crucial factor in the choice

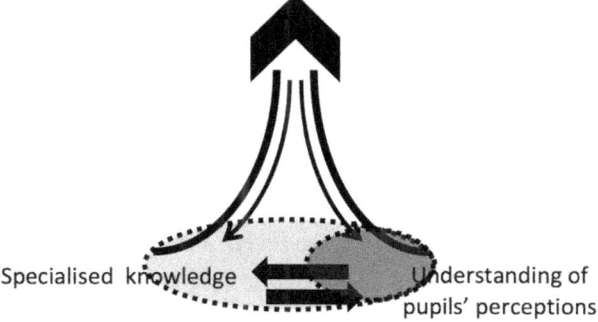

Figure 10.3 Migration and the selection of specialized knowledge.

of specialized knowledge and subject matter. The emphasis lies on the right side of the model of *didaktical* reconstruction. It is also interesting to highlight what is not said in the circle. The teachers make few references to the themes they usually highlight while teaching about migration. It thus seems that the literature reading in the circle has changed their orientation of the field, a fact expressed in their use of 'aha! experiences as a strategy to select significant and relevant subject matter.

Example 2: Transformation of Specialized Knowledge

Teaching plans and tasks were produced during the second phase of the circle. The process of development was rooted in the discussions in the first phase, where, as described above, the challenges of selecting significant and relevant specialized knowledge and subject matter were highlighted. In the second phase, the efforts were directed to transforming the designated specialized knowledge in such a way that it should be possible for the pupils to comprehend and learn. The teachers' line of reasoning about the transformation process is illustrated in the following empirical example.

There are reasons to reconnect to the model of *didaktical* reconstruction and the concept of elementarization (see Figure 10.2). The latter stresses the need to avoid oversimplifying the specialized knowledge that subject matter represents. The first step is the deconstruction of the specialized knowledge into its fundamental elements. In the next step, these elements are put together in a process of reconstruction expressed in learning pathways which can help pupils to acquire the knowledge. The actual teaching – symbolized by the arrowhead of the model – can be perceived as the result of the transformation, of the interaction between the selection of specialized knowledge, the structure thereof and the teacher's perception of the pupils' conceptions of the area that the specialized knowledge represents. This interaction is clarified and specified in the teaching plans and teaching artefacts.

The empirical example here is from the final meeting of Phase Two, which took place a couple of weeks before the developed teaching plans and tasks were to be tested. The topic of the meeting was addressing the question of why people migrate. What defines individuals' decisions to migrate, and what are possible obstacles to migration? Introduced and discussed at this meeting was a teaching artefact that draws attention to these particular issues. The teachers had previously used teaching artefacts that paid little or no attention to the obstacles and difficulties that can influence the decision to migrate.

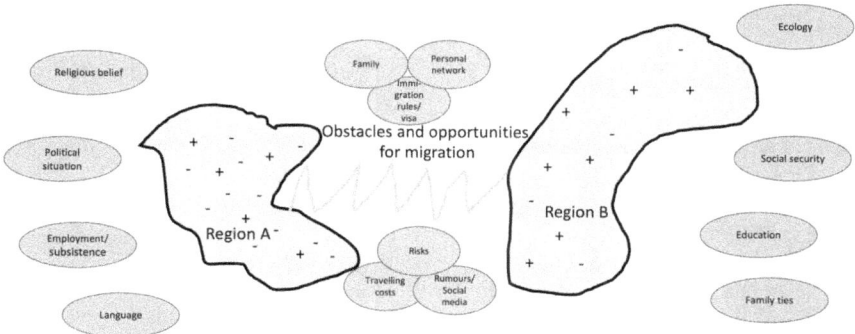

Figure 10.4 The model for explaining processes of migration.

The ambition of this particular task was to help pupils recognize the structural and institutional perspectives on migration, which had been so fundamental in the literature studied in the first phase of the circle. Talking about obstacles and restrictions was then understood as necessary for grasping the complexity of migration as a social phenomenon.

A classic way of explaining migration is to refer to the so-called push-and-pull model (Lee 1966). This model is organized around the idea that there are factors which push people away from their place of emigration and, simultaneously, factors that pull people to their place of immigration.

With the aim of fostering a nuanced, rather than a mechanical, understanding of migration, the push-and-pull model was used to develop a teaching artefact integrating dimensions of obstacles and institutional situations (cf. Lee 1966). The outlined model in Figure 10.4 lay before us during the conversation at that meeting. It was around this image that the discussion was oriented.

Initially, the teachers responded positively to the teaching artefact, commenting that it was transparent and could help pupils understand what causes individuals to migrate and the factors considered in those situations. Teacher 3 states that the idea of making a list of the positive and negative aspects of the place in which they live and the one to where they migrate would make sense for the pupils.

However, after five minutes, the view slowly seems to change. Teacher 1, who will be the first to try out the teaching plans, begins to wonder. There are things about the task she does not understand.

T1 (Teacher): But the restrictions, where do they come into this? Is it too. . .?

R2 (Researcher): Good! Then maybe they should not be here?

T3: No, then, I think.

R2: To cock things up.

T3: Hmm...

T1: Then, one question has to address the restrictions, in such a case, I think. For this, of course, advantages and disadvantages.

R2: Yes.

T1: To me... But...

R2: Great, T1.

L1: The obstacles; here they are.

R2: They will not be included.

T3: There could be a question: What are the restrictions and opportunities?

R2: Yes, would that work?

T3: Because then it becomes an analytical question for them.

T1: I just see my [pupils], sitting there like question marks, not knowing what to do.

T3: Yes, yes.

Teacher 1 continues to express her concern regarding how the teaching artefacts will function in her class. The task is too complicated. She is afraid that her pupils will not know what to do. The task needs to be simplified. The teaching practice and her perceptions of the pupils' understanding shape what she recognizes as possible to do, knowledge-wise. The line of reasoning can be related to the process of elementarization. Teacher 1 believes that it is essential to sharpen the description of the task and thus make the subject matter less complex. To her, further clarification is necessary. A little later in the conversation, Teacher 2 proposes a solution. Her idea is that the task could be presented in different steps. She thereby points to a possible learning pathway. Her proposal for a solution is something that the members of the circle support. The following conversation is mainly about what can be done to simplify or clarify the task.

Teacher 3, however, reasons in a slightly different way. Her position can be detected in the above quote, where she points out that the task can help pupils ask analytical questions. Here, the teaching artefact becomes a tool for opening up the specialized knowledge or further problematizing it. This is what Teacher 3 does by relating the teaching artefact, which is intended to discuss external migration to issues around internal migration. In the conversation Teacher 3 sheds light on the differences that can exist between internal and external migration.

Teacher 3 challenges the conclusion that the teaching artefact needs to be simplified and the subject matter clarified. Migration is a complex issue, and this complexity has to be reflected in the teaching artefact.

> T3: If you are moving to the United States, it [getting a visa] can be a huge obstacle. If you want to work or whatever, then a visa can be...
>
> R2: That was what Researcher 3 wanted, because it seems that everyone can move anywhere.
>
> T3: And that is not true.
>
> [Imperceptible chatter]
>
> T3: It becomes evident that not everything is so black and white.
>
> R2: And that was what was to be caught [by doing the task].
>
> T3: Yes.
>
> R1: This is also the thing with going further than the push-and-pull model.
>
> R2: And then it becomes a little unclear for the pupils. Something they have to handle.
>
> T3: Yes, but yes, that is the way it is. It is not black or white.

The fact that the teaching artefact is somewhat confusing and that no definite answers can be given is because migration is not a simple issue, and there is no single answer to why people migrate. According to Teacher 3, the complexity is something the pupils must experience because that is how things are in the real world.

Teachers 1 and 3 express divergent views in the conversation. Their line of reasoning can be related to the model of *didaktical* reconstruction. However, it is not a matter of either/or. It is more like a different centre of gravity. Teacher 1 is clear in allowing pupils' opportunities to understand and learn the subject matter guide how she perceives the task and the changes that need to be made. She is also the first to try out the task; she wants it to work. The situation for Teacher 3 is different; the time pressure is not as intense. Her line of reasoning also shows the possibilities that a detailed discussion about teacher artefacts may have in order to open up perspectives on specialized knowledge.

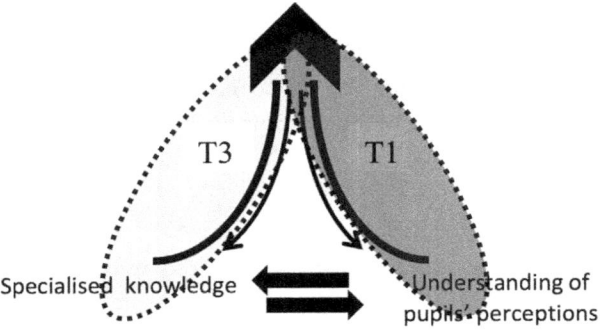

Figure 10.5 Migration and the transformation of specialized knowledge.

Discussion: Implications for Teacher Education

The approach here has been to use the model of *didaktical* reconstruction to uncover possible lines of argumentation when primary teachers in social studies education discuss questions about selection and transformation in relation to a specific teaching area – in this case, migration. It is obvious that the perception of pupils' understanding and opportunities greatly influenced how the conversation was conducted. This applies not only to the teachers but also to us researchers who were members of this circle. This is most evident when it comes to the issue of transformation.

If a reconnection is made to Prediger's model and discussion about professional development (Prediger et al. 2017; Prediger, Roesken-Winter and Leuders 2019), is it clear that community-rooted perspectives provided a framework for the work in the circle. Yet, it is also important to emphasize that the conscious strategy of focusing on specialized knowledge in the first phase of the circle, which may represent Prediger's material strategy, had a definite impact on the question of the selection of subject matter. Raising new and, for them, unknown, 'aha!' perspectives was perceived as an opportunity by the teachers. The teachers thus attributed a certain power to specialized knowledge and its opportunities to develop teaching and perhaps break free from dependency on a traditional path in a subject when it comes to the question of selection.

The model of *didaktical* reconstruction can be recognized as an illustration of the building blocks of teachers' subject-*didaktical* knowledge base (compare Komorek and Kattman 2009; Duit et al. 2012). Teachers need deep knowledge of the potential of relevant specialized knowledge. However, they also have to be connected to educational research addressing pupils' preconditions for learning. A third part of the knowledge base concerns the practical implementation of teaching. The model points out that a relationship exists between the different parts of the knowledge base. The teachers not only should have knowledge of the different parts but also need to develop procedural knowledge expressed in an ability to relate the three parts to each other in practical work and do so with an analytical gaze. One conclusion could be that initial teacher education needs to be organized to support the development of this subject-*didaktical* capability in student teachers. In this scenario, subject-*didaktik* should be the core of teacher education as well as an approach on which professional development is built. This conclusion does not only apply to initial teacher education; it also needs to be part of the systematic work with teachers' professional development. Here, the 3-T model of Predigers et al. (2017; Prediger, Roesken-Winter and Leuders 2019) shows the complexity of the task. We recognize that research and development circles fit well with this model as a way to scale up and make professional development subject didactically relevant.

So, what about powerful professional knowledge? Furlong and Whitty (2017) raise the perspective that teachers must deal with different knowledge traditions. Superficially, this division of knowledge traditions can be traced in the model of *didaktical* reconstruction. On one hand, there is specialized knowledge, developed in a scholarly context, which needs clarification in order to become subject matter. On the other hand, there is the knowledge of the pupils, perhaps less systematic and more experience-based. The relational perspective permeating the *didaktik* tradition gives an idea of how to think about powerful professional knowledge. Rather than being understood as knowledge of specific disciplinary content, it could be described as a 'knowing' (Carlgren 2020). A subject-specific 'knowing', somewhat simplified, can be described as the ability to create learning environments based on a dialectical relationship between the clarification of specialized knowledge and an understanding of the pupils' relationship to the potential subject matter. In concrete terms, it might mean that the teacher in the process of the subject-matter selection has the ability to balance aspects of significance and relevance and thus link the matter (*Bildungsinhalt*) to meaning (*Bildungsgehalt*) in the issues addressed in class (Hopmann 2007).

We have tried to demonstrate the empirical potential of the *didaktical* reconstruction model while addressing questions of selection and transformation. The model can be understood as a subject-*didaktical* specification of Klafki's model of categorial *Bildung*. Similarities but also differences between powerful knowledge and *didaktik* reconstruction have been touched upon. A unifying line is the role of specialized knowledge, but here we stress the selection and transformation to content (Deng 2020). The relational idea is a central feature of *didaktical* reconstruction that differs from the powerful knowledge approach, although we believe that Young and Mueller (2019), in their later articles, relate more clearly to pupils in their discussion of powerful knowledge as a curriculum principle.

Finally, a knowledge field such as migration in social studies is connected to a changing world and to partly changing specialized knowledge, which became obvious in the discussion in the research and development circle. An important point from social realism is that knowledge is not static and given, and particularly in a context such as social sciences, which attempts to make a changing world understandable, it is important to relate to up-to-date specialized knowledge. This is a fundamental understanding. If the education system is to respond to the social issues of today and tomorrow, it is necessary to consider the dynamic nature of specialized knowledge. This is true in the context of professional development and perhaps even more so in the construction of powerful teacher education.

Notes

1 We chose to name the model '*didaktical* reconstruction' instead of 'educational reconstruction' when translating from German to English as we see the need to stress the relational dimensions of the model.
2 Social studies is a label that captures the subjects geography, history, civics and religious education. In primary school these subjects have often been thought about thematically. However, since introduction of the latest curriculum, Lgr 11, subject-specific perspectives have become more prominent in primary school.

References

Barton, K. C. and Levstik, L. S. (2004), *Teaching History for the Common Good*, Mahwah, NJ: L. Erlbaum Associates.

Bladh, G. (2020), 'GeoCapabilities, Didaktical Analysis and Curriculum Thinking – Furthering the Dialogue between Didaktik and Curriculum', *International Research in Geographical and Environmental Education*, 29 (3): 206–20. DOI: 10.1080/10382046.2020.1749766

Bladh, G., Stolare, M. and Kristiansson, M. (2018), 'Curriculum Principles, Didactic Practice and Social Issues: Thinking Through Teachers' Knowledge Practices in Collaborative Work', *London Review of Education*, 16 (3): 398–413. DOI: 10.18546/LRE.16.3.04

Carlgren, I. (2020), 'Powerful Knowns and Powerful Knowings?', *Journal of Curriculum Studies*. DOI: 10.1080/00220272.2020.1717634

Deng, Z. (2018), 'Bringing Knowledge Back In: Perspectives from Liberal Education', *Cambridge Journal of Education*, 48 (3): 335–51.

Deng, Z. (2020), *Knowledge, Content, Curriculum and Didaktik*, Abingdon: Taylor and Francis.

Duit, R., Gropengießer, H., Kattmann, U., Komorek, M. and Parchmann, I. (2012), 'The Model of Educational Reconstruction – a Framework for Improving Teaching and Learning Science', in: D. Jorde and J. Dillon (eds), *Science Education Research and Practice in Europe: Cultural Perspectives in Science Education*, vol. 5, 13–37, Rotterdam: SensePublishers.

Furlong, J. and Whitty, G. (2017), 'Knowledge Traditions in the Study of Education', in G. Whitty and J. Furlong (eds), *Knowledge and the Study of Education: An International Exploration*, 13–57, Oxford: Symposium Books.

Gericke, N., Hudson, B., Olin-Scheller, C., Stolare, M. (2018), 'Powerful Knowledge, Transformations and the Need for Empirical Studies across School Subjects', *London Review of Education*, 16 (3): 428–44. DOI: 10.18546/LRE.16.3.06

Hanlon, B. and Vicino, T. J. (2014), *Global Migration: The Basics*, New York: Routledge.

Hopmann, S. (2007), 'Restrained Teaching: The Common Core of Didaktik', *European Educational Research Journal*, 6 (2): 109–24.

Jank, W. and Meyer, H. (2002), *Didaktische Modelle* (5, völlig überarb. Aufl.), Berlin: Cornelsen Scriptor.

Kattmann, U., Duit, R., Gropengießer, H. and Komorek, M. (1997), 'Das Modell der didaktischen Rekonstruktion – Ein Rahmen für naturwissenschaftsdidaktische Forschung und Entwicklung', *Zeitschrift für Didaktik der Naturwissenschaften*, 3 (3): 3–18.

Klafki, W. (1995), 'Didactic Analysis as the Core of Preparation for Instruction (Didaktische Analyse als Kern der Unterrichtsvorbereitung)', *Journal of Curriculum Studies*, 27 (1): 13–30.

Klafki, W. (1985/2001), *Dannelseteori och Didaktik – Nye studier*, Aarhus: Klim.

Komorek, M. and Kattmann, U. (2009), 'The Model of Educational Reconstruction', in S. Mikelskis-Seifert, U. Ringelband and M. Brückmann (eds), *Four Decades of Research in Science Education – From Curriculum Development to Quality Improvement*, 171–88, Münster: Waxmann.

Lee, E. (1966), 'A Theory of Migration', *Demography*, 3 (1): 47–57.

Maude, A. (2016), 'What Might Powerful Geographical Knowledge Look Like?', *Geography*, 101: 70–6.

McKenney, S. E. and Reeves, T. C. (2012), *Conducting Educational Design Research*, New York, NY: Routledge.

Meyer, M. and Meyer, H. (2007), *Wolfgang Klafki: Eine Didaktik fur das 21. Jahrhundert?* Weinheim: Belitz.

Muller, J. (2016), 'Knowledge and the Curriculum in the Sociology of Knowledge', in D. Wyse, L. Hayward and J. Pandya (eds), *The SAGE Handbook of Curriculum, Pedagogy and Assessment*, 92–106, London: SAGE.

Nordgren, K. (2017), 'Powerful Knowledge, Intercultural Learning and History Education', *Journal of Curriculum Studies*, 49 (5): 663–82.

Prediger, S., Fischer, C., Selter, C., et al. (2019), 'Combining Material- and Community-Based Implementation Strategies for Scaling up: The Case of Supporting Low-Achieving Middle School Students', *Educational Studies in Mathematics*, 102: 361–78. DOI:10.1007/s10649-018-9835-2

Prediger, S., Leuders, T. and Rösken-Winter, B. (2017), Drei-Tetraeder-Modell der gegenstandsbezogenen Professionalisierungsforschung: Fachspezifische Verknüpfung von Design und Forschung. Jahrbuch für Allgemeine Didaktik, 159–77.

Prediger, S., Roesken-Winter, B. and Leuders, T. J. (2019), 'Which Research Can Support PD Facilitators? Strategies for ContentRelated PD Research in the ThreeTetrahedron Model', *Journal of Mathematics Teacher Education*, 22: 407. DOI: 10.1007/s10857-019-09434-3

Reinfried, S., Mathis, C. and Kattmann, U. (2009), 'Das Modell der Didaktischen Rekonstruktion: Eine innovative Methode zur fachdidaktischen Erforschung und Entwicklung von Unterricht', *Beiträge zur Lehrerinnen- und Lehrerbildung*, 27 (3): 404–14.

van den Akker, J., Gravemeijer, K., McKenney, S. and Nieveen, N. (eds) (2006), *Educational Design Research*, London: Routledge.

Willbergh, I. (2016), 'Bringing Teaching Back in: The Norwegian NOU The School of the Future in Light of the Allgemeine Didaktik Theory of Wolfgang Klafki', *Nordic Journal of Pedagogy and Critique*, 2: 111–24.

Young, M. (2014), 'Powerful Knowledge as a Curriculum Principle', in M. Young and D. Lambert (eds), *Knowledge and the Future School*, 65–88, London: Bloomsbury.

Young, M. and Muller, J. (2016), *Curriculum and the Specialization of Knowledge: Studies in the Sociology of Education*, London: Routledge.

Young, M. and Mueller, J. (2019), 'Knowledge, Power and Powerful Knowledge Re-Visited', *The Curriculum Journal*, 30 (2): 196–214.

11

From a Personal to a Pedagogically Powerful Understanding of School Mathematics

Cosette Crisan

and, since he was scarcely able, unaided, to discern any connection between this task and his university mathematics, he soon fell in with the time honoured way of teaching, and his university studies remained only a more or less pleasant memory which had no influence upon his teaching.

(Klein 1932: 1)

Introduction

What kind of knowledge do teachers need for teaching school mathematics? And how can teachers be supported to tap into such knowledge in ways that empower them pedagogically, with the aim of understanding and supporting their students' thinking and learning of mathematics?

The study of teachers' knowledge of the subject matter they are expected to teach and its relationship to the quality of classroom instruction has been a fruitful area of research since Lee Shulman first launched a call for researching the different components of a professional knowledge base for teaching (Shulman 1986). Ever since, in their efforts to conceptualize mathematics teachers' professional knowledge base for teaching, researchers have put forward various alternatives for conceptualizing teachers' knowledge, each trying to better describe and gain a deeper understanding of the different components (e.g. Kunter and Baumbert 2013; Davis and Simmt 2006; Ma 2010; Rowland et al. 2009; Schoenfeld and Kilpatrick 2008). Such research was and is still needed in order to understand how to support teachers to build on their own personal understanding of the subject they chose to teach, and develop a pedagogically powerful understanding of the subject with the aim of reaching to students and supporting their learning of the subject.

This chapter contributes to the ongoing discussion on mathematics knowledge for teaching by investigating the case of teachers' knowledge about functions. The claims are substantiated by a report on a professional development workshop, which draws on the analysis of how practising teachers' own understanding of functions becomes more sophisticated and nuanced as they are supported to connect to more advanced knowledge about this mathematics concept. Such new learning also empowers them pedagogically to appreciate better the challenges their students encounter along the way towards developing an understanding of this mathematics idea of high epistemic quality. This mathematics-specific case study contributes thus to the KOSS programme (see Chapter 1), by attempting to characterize the nature of teachers' powerful professional knowledge.

Overview of the Chapter

I begin by first considering some of the most influential frameworks describing mathematics teachers' knowledge for teaching. I present an overview of researchers' attempts to describe this body of knowledge, focusing in more depth on Subject Content Knowledge (SCK), Horizon Content Knowledge (HCK) and the more recent and hence less researched Advanced Mathematics Knowledge (AMK).

I then describe how the literature I reviewed informed my design of a professional development workshop aimed at supporting practising teachers connect with their more advanced knowledge of a specific mathematics topic (function). After introducing the empirical study, I analyse the data I collected while the participating teachers engaged with one specific activity in the workshop. In the concluding section, I offer some views, which could serve as a starting point for a more advanced discussion on how teacher education could support teachers develop pedagogically powerful knowledge of the school subject they teach.

Review of the Literature

Teachers' Knowledge for Teaching: Some Theoretical Insights

The study of teachers' knowledge of subject matter and its relationship to the quality of classroom instruction has grown substantially since Lee Shulman launched a call for researching the components of teachers' professional knowledge base for teaching (Shulman 1986). While there is still no easy agreement among the mathematics education community about the relationship between these components, research has thrived in efforts to conceptualize related issues for mathematics teachers.

One such successful effort is the mathematics specific 'egg' framework advanced by Ball et al. (2008), which builds on and refines Shulman's (1986) initial categorization of types of knowledge of a teacher of any subject, namely, subject-matter knowledge and pedagogical content knowledge (PCK). Their Mathematics Knowledge for Teaching (MKT) framework lays the foundation for a practice-derived theory for mathematical knowledge for teaching. The authors divided Shulman's second category of PCK into two other subdomains, Knowledge of Content and Students and Knowledge of Content and Teaching, while Shulman's third category of Curricular Knowledge (CK) was also specified under PCK as Knowledge of Content and Curriculum.

The importance of subject knowledge (SK) has been well documented and its deficit linked, for example, to less effective teaching (Bennet and Turner Bisset 1993; Simon and Brown 1996) and overreliance on commercial schemes (Millett and Johnson 1996). Ball and colleagues (2008) went further and divided Shulman's category of subject-matter knowledge into three subdomains: Common Content Knowledge (CCK), Specialized Content Knowledge (SCK) and HCK, which I briefly describe in this chapter, as relevant to this chapter.

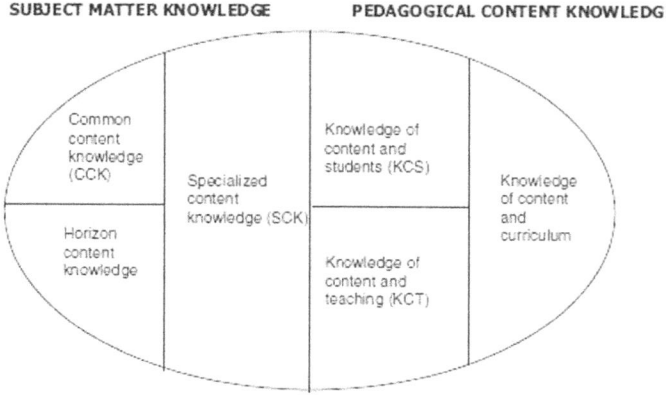

Figure 11.1 Domains of mathematical knowledge for teaching (Ball et al. 2008: 403).

Specialized Content Knowledge

SCK encompasses knowledge of mathematics needed by teachers, but not necessarily used by others, such as knowledge of a particular mathematical model or representations useful for teaching a certain concept. For instance, while engineers need to know the 'rule' about the product of two negative numbers being a positive number, in their day-to-day jobs they do not need to justify why this rule works. In other words, engineers' knowledge is CCK and used in ways that correspond with how it is used in settings other than teaching; they do not necessarily know the mathematical reasoning behind this rule, nor do they need to know how to explain why it works. Such knowledge is SCK, argued to be an intrinsic part of the foundation for a teacher's everyday classroom teaching.

In my experience as a teacher educator, irrespective of their mathematical background, prospective teachers frequently recall rules (e.g. *minus and minus makes plus*), methods (e.g. the balance method for solving equations: *whatever you do to one side, you should also do to the other side*), acronyms (e.g. *SOHCAHTOA*) that they acquired as learners of mathematics themselves, without always being able to give a mathematically sound justification of why the rule or method works, and just as importantly if it always works. In teacher education courses, recalling such rules is the starting point for prospective teachers' development of their SCK, albeit limited to a few topics. Prospective teachers and practising teachers then continue to broaden their SCK themselves over time, by exploring ways to represent all mathematical ideas, examine alternative representations, provide mathematical explanations of rules and procedures, evaluating unconventional student methods and so on, with the aims to reach to students and support their learning (see Zembat 2013, for a comprehensive list of everyday tasks mathematics teachers need to deal with regularly which require SCK).

Gericke et al. (2018) draw attention to how the 'transformation' of knowledge impacts the epistemic quality made available to students in the classroom. What will students learn? How will teachers transform their understanding of mathematics for teaching purposes? Which representations, explanations, instructional resources will they use and how will they analyse and evaluate students' responses and errors? What will be the epistemic values promoted through teachers' SCK?

This raises the question of the quality of teachers' SCK. Ball et al. (2005: 378) describe SCK as a 'bridge' that enables the teacher 'to accurately represent mathematical ideas, provide mathematical explanations of common rules and procedures, and examine and understand unusual solution methods to problems'. Hudson et al. (2015) argue that there is a need to address the *epistemic quality* of what students come to know, make sense of and be able to do in school mathematics, with the aim of maximizing the chances that all students will have *epistemic access* (Morrow 2008) to school mathematics of high epistemic quality. Hudson (2018) advises that an overemphasis on practice and memorization promotes a fragmented view of the subject and standard procedures reduced simply to rule following is likely to result in students learning a mathematics content of *low epistemic quality*. While some memorization of rules, methods, metaphors, rhymes and so on will always happen in mathematics classrooms (as some do help pupils remember 'how to do it'), teachers, and students for that matter, should also have an awareness of limitations of the validity and applicability of such rules. It is thus important that teachers scrutinize and evaluate instructional materials, and/or design or choose and use appropriate representations, with an awareness of the limitations and potential each such representation brings to the learning process. But how can teachers be supported to develop SCK that supports students' access to school mathematics of *high epistemic quality*, as encapsulated in the National Curriculum (DfE 2013) aims for all pupils, namely: to develop deep conceptual fluency, accompanied by mathematical reasoning and problem-solving?

Bass and Ball (2004) advised that unlike the work of research mathematicians which could be described in terms of 'compressing' information into increasingly concise and powerful formulations, 'the work of teachers is more often just the opposite: teachers must be adept at prying apart concepts, making sense of the analogies, metaphors, images, and logical constructs that give shape to a mathematical construct' (Davis and Simmt 2006: 300). Research evidence has strongly indicated that if teachers' SCK is not built on a conceptually sound understanding of the underlying mathematics, teachers will fall short of providing their students with high epistemic quality mathematics education, consisting of learning experiences that promote conceptual understanding (e.g. see Putnam, Heaton, Prawat and Remillard 1992 for the case for geometry).

To exemplify the aforementioned, let us consider the balance method, known as 'Whatever you do to one side, you should also do to the other side', which is often heard in mathematics lessons when teachers teach about solving equations. A visual representation of an old-fashioned scale or a seesaw are often invoked to justify why this rule works. And most of the time, the rule works! It works when the four basic operations of addition, subtraction, multiplication and division by a number other than zero are applied to both sides of an equation, but it does not work, for example, if one attempts to balance the given equation by squaring both its sides, as more solutions are yielded than those of the equation to be solved in the first place. With such awareness, teachers will caution students that the balance method has its own limitations and will not always work. These teachers will be more likely to re-phrase the rule in a more helpful manner, where the 'whatever you do' is described precisely in terms of the specific mathematical operations that are permitted if this method were to work, and hence explicitly draw students' attention to the shortcomings of this rule. This type of knowledge is described by Ball and colleagues as HCK.

Horizon Content Knowledge

According to Ball et al. (2008: 1, 403), teachers should tap into their HCK, a kind of mathematical '"peripheral vision" needed in teaching, a view of the larger mathematical landscape that teaching requires', including 'the vision useful in seeing connections to much later mathematical ideas'.

Wasserman and Stockton (2013) proposed a helpful division of HCK into: a 'curricular mathematical horizon' (knowing what mathematics is to come in the next few grades) and an 'advanced mathematical horizon' (knowing connections to higher-level mathematical ideas). Advanced mathematical horizon described as such seems to resonate with Jakobsen et al.'s (2012) interpretation of HCK, namely, that HCK is about 'being familiar with "advanced" mathematics, but in a way that supports hearing, seeing, sensing, and doing for teaching' (Jakobsen et al. 2012: 4640). Researchers thus argue that HCK relates to the engagement of advanced content in terms of its relevance to teaching and learning, how the content being taught is situated in and connected to the broader mathematical knowledge landscape, going beyond that of school mathematics.

Advanced Mathematics Knowledge

The theoretical and empirical work on HCK led researchers' interest to consider a new component of the knowledge base for teaching, namely AMK. While engaging with the MKT framework, Zaskis and Mamolo (2011) proposed to view HCK through the notion of viewing elementary (school) mathematics from an advanced standpoint, thus positioning advanced mathematical knowledge (AMK) as an important aspect of the MKT. The notion of HCK is given by Zazkis and Mamolo in terms of application of the notion of 'advanced mathematical knowledge', which they define as 'knowledge of the subject matter acquired during undergraduate studies at colleges or universities' (Zazkis and Leikin 2010: 264).

Wasserman (2016), and later Stockon and Wasserman (2017), narrowed down the description of AMK to knowledge outside the typical scope of what a school mathematics teacher would likely teach, in that AMK is relevant, the advanced mathematical ideas are connected to the content of school mathematics, but also that these forms of knowledge of advanced mathematics are in some way productive for the teaching of school mathematics content. For example, Wasserman (2016) discusses how knowledge of *groups* might influence instruction about solving simple linear equations. As a mathematics topic, *groups* could be classified as an advanced mathematics topic, as it is usually studied at undergraduate, and not school, level. But how about other advanced mathematics topics, such as, for example, non-differentiable geometry? Is this mathematics knowledge relevant or connected to school mathematics or just too distant an area, thus less relevant and less connected to school mathematics and hence not needed by teachers teaching school mathematics? The authors argue that it is this HCK which enables teachers to see more, and suggest that AMK is necessary, but not just *any* advanced mathematics knowledge. A provocation was then thrown to the mathematics education researchers: what AMK outside school mathematics has a bearing on school mathematics?

Teachers' Perception of How Teaching Is Affected by One's Own Advanced Mathematics Knowledge

The fifty-two practising secondary school teachers in Zazkis and Leikin's (2010) study, teaching mathematics in grades 8–12, including algebra, geometry and calculus, agreed that AMK was needed for: personal confidence, for ability to make connections, to respond to pupils' questions, language, aesthetic, precision, proof, elegance of solution, understanding vs. procedural fluency, or connection to history. However, none of the teachers interviewed were able to articulate (clearly or at all) specific examples of advanced mathematics content they had ever used in their teaching or to provide an example of instances where they made explicit connections between university mathematics and concrete pedagogical actions.

Similarly, based on the findings of their survey of future mathematics teachers from Germany, Hong Kong, China (Hangzhou) and South Korea nearing the end of their university studies, Buchholtz et al. (2013) found that the future teachers (including those from top mathematics performing countries or regions) often seem unable to link school and university knowledge systematically. The authors suggested that 'prospective teachers should have adaptable mathematical knowledge: a knowledge that comprises school mathematics, but goes beyond it and relates it to the underlying advanced academic mathematics, which according to Klein (1932) we call the 'knowledge of elementary mathematics from an advanced standpoint' (Buchholtz et al. 2013: 108).

We seem to have come back full circle to the quote at the start of this chapter, when back in 1932 Klein warned that since teachers were unable to see any connection between teaching school mathematics and the more advanced mathematics they studied at university, they 'fell in with the time honoured way of teaching', tapping into the 'same old' ways of teaching mathematics, thus developing a SCK that held little pedagogic potential for supporting the learning of high epistemic school mathematics knowledge. In his work, Klein refers to the 'double discontinuity' for teachers in their education. The first discontinuity concerns the well-known problems of transition which students face as they enter university, while the second discontinuity is the disconnect for these future teachers in returning back to school mathematics, where university mathematics appeared to be unrelated to the tasks of teaching. While both discontinuities still exist, it is this second discontinuity that is of particular interest in this chapter, namely exploring how knowing advanced mathematics might influence the teaching of school mathematics.

The literature reviewed in this chapter clearly indicates that good teaching requires more than knowledge of the content to be taught. Teachers should understand the processes by which a particular mathematical idea develops as students progress through different levels of school education, and how an elementary school mathematics idea is drawn to completion at advanced levels of mathematics. It is with this understanding that teachers will be better prepared to set students along a powerful mathematical development path (powerful because it helps them develop high epistemic mathematics knowledge, based on a conceptual understanding rather than memorizing facts and rules about the concept), by addressing the obstacles and opportunities that appear most frequently along the way towards an understanding of the idea or concept being taught. To achieve this, Watson and Harel (2013) also propose that teachers should possess personal mathematical knowledge significantly beyond the level at which they are teaching, although the authors themselves admit that the 'question of how formally acquired advanced knowledge becomes tacit and continuously available in teaching remains' (Watson and Harel 2013: 166). This question has remained of interest to researchers, with little progress to date towards understanding the relationship between advanced subject knowledge and subject knowledge for teaching.

The Study

In the following, I present an empirical study intended to gain an insight into this under-developed area of research.

The Context of the Study

Although prior research has offered some useful descriptions of the advanced mathematics knowledge relevant to teaching school mathematics, and some useful insight into how teachers could be supported in drawing on this knowledge in their teaching, most extant research concerned with advanced mathematics knowledge gives a picture of developments taking place outside England. In contrast to the pre-service teachers in the studies reviewed, most of whom train to become teachers during their undergraduate studies where they study advanced mathematics courses alongside their teacher preparation, the pre-service teachers in England, complete their training immediately, or some years after they complete their undergraduate studies. Pre-service teachers who enrol in a one-year postgraduate course would have studied some form of advanced mathematics as part of their undergraduate studies, but usually with no links or reference to school-level mathematics or its teaching. Moreover, in England, not all pre-service teachers would have studied advanced mathematics in the sense of formal, academic mathematics beyond the school curriculum.

Based on this understanding, I now describe how I approached the design of a professional development course to support teachers in connecting advanced mathematics knowledge/formally acquired advanced knowledge/academic mathematics knowledge/more advanced and relevant mathematics knowledge/ to their teaching of school mathematics concepts/ideas/topics. Here I have deliberately used the different terminologies encountered in the literature reviewed, as yet another description of this type of knowledge suited to the current study and the England, UK context would further complicate matters. Instead, I come back to such a description in the discussion section of this chapter.

In England, the UK, the requirements of the National Curriculum covers what subjects are taught and the standards children should reach in each subject. The New National Curriculum in mathematics (2015) includes *harder* subject material, such as more formulae to learn, set theory, iteration and functions. In the school mathematics curriculum in England, the idea of functions appears in different guises; common ways of representing functions include tables of values, graphs, algebraic representation, words and problem situations. It is important to note here that the school mathematics curriculum in England has had an informal approach to functions, and as such a formal treatment of functions is not encountered by students unless they choose to study more advanced mathematics courses beyond the age of seventeen. At the pre-university level, students encounter many more types of functions beyond linear and quadratic functions, and the New National curriculum stipulates that the more formal definition of functions and their features previously taught at pre-university level (seventeen- to eighteen-year-olds) are now being introduced at lower levels of school education. Students are also expected to learn about more advanced knowledge about functions such as: domain, range, one-to-one function, inverse function and composition of functions, including the formal definition of a function. The formal definition in school mathematics is consistent with the formal (Dirichlet-Bourbaki) definition, namely: f is a function from one set to another, say **A** to **B**, both sets of real numbers. The main requirement of this modern definition of the function concept is univalence, which requires that for each element in set **A**, called the domain of the function, there is associated only one element of **B**, called the range of the function. The introduction of the New National Curriculum saw a flourishing of professional development courses for teachers to gain familiarity with and confidence with the *harder* topics they were now expected to teach.

The Professional Development Workshop: Design Consideration

A workshop was thus designed aimed at supporting practising teachers, with experience of teaching mathematics to eleven- to sixteen-year-old students, develop and extend their knowledge for teaching about *functions*. Just as in Stockon and Wasserman (2017), in this study, the designer of the workshop activities is the researcher herself (also the author of this chapter), a mathematician and a mathematics teacher educator with considerable experience of teaching mathematics at undergraduate level, as well as the secondary school level of education in England, UK (non-advanced level: eleven- to sixteen-year-olds, but also advanced level: seventeen- to eighteen-year-olds), and also a mathematics educator with considerable experience in initial teacher education.

Wasserman et al.'s (2017) 'Building up from and Stepping down' approach to teaching undergraduate-level mathematics to pre-service teachers was adopted and adapted in designing this workshop, in that the teachers did both the *building up* and the *stepping down to practice*. Indeed, engaging teachers in mathematical thinking by working on classroom-close mathematics-related tasks that are situated in teaching practice, and reflecting on these experiences, is common to many professional learning programmes (Watson and Mason 2007; Biza et al. 2007). As such, the tasks presented to teachers were *building up from practice* by posing mathematics-focused questions that would lead on the teachers needing to connect with more advanced knowledge about functions, while the *stepping-down to practice* activities would require teachers to react to fictional pupils' scenarios, designed to encourage pedagogical consideration of the new learning.

The Participants

The workshop was attended by eight practising mathematics teachers. Data from the initial questionnaire sent to them before the workshop showed that all teachers had gained their qualified teacher status as a result of studying a one-year initial teacher education course, after graduating from university. Six teachers (T1, T2, T3, T4, four females; and T5, T6, two males) majored in mathematics, one had an engineering background (T7 male), while another teacher had an economics background (T8 male) and introduced himself as a non-specialist mathematics teacher. The participants were practising mathematics teachers, with teaching experiences varying between one and four years of teaching eleven- to sixteen-year-old students.

When asked about the reasons for choosing to attend this workshop, the teachers mentioned their familiarity with the 'usual representations of functions' in school mathematics, such as tables of values, graphs and equations of linear and quadratic functions, but expressed concerns about the need to learn about more advanced knowledge about functions given the requirements of this *harder* topic in the New National curriculum.

Research Question

In line with KOSS programme interest in characterizing the nature of teachers' powerful professional knowledge, the research carried out alongside this workshop sought to investigate whether and how participating in a professional development workshop designed to support practising teachers connect with advanced knowledge of function had empowered them pedagogically in ways productive for the teaching and learning of these concepts at all levels of school mathematics education.

Data Sources and Analysis

This study used a qualitative design. Prior to commencing the programme, participants completed an initial questionnaire. Data from the initial questionnaire provided information about the participants' teaching qualifications, numbers of years of teaching experience and school levels taught.

During delivery of the workshop, textual data were collected through field notes that detailed some of the group interactions, while photos were taken of individual teachers' notes (e.g. their mathematical work and their 'reactions' to the pupils' scenarios). Post-session reflective written notes were solicited and collected after the end of the session. The teachers were asked to reflect on and write about the activities in relation to their own learning, their pupils' mathematical learning, and their teaching about functions in the future, as a result of the learning during the workshop.

In this chapter, the data collected following the teachers' involvement with the very first activity of the workshop are analysed. The analysis uses descriptions of the dimensions of the professional knowledge base for teaching as reviewed in this chapter, in particular SCK, HCK, AMK, with a view to allowing for an insight to be gained into how teachers' engagement with the tasks benefitted them both conceptually and pedagogically.

Results

The first activity the participants were given required them to sketch graphs of four functions. The four functions varied in that they had different domains of definition, namely: the whole set of real numbers; an open interval; a union of open and closed intervals; and a discrete set of integer numbers, but they all shared the same function rule (equation), namely $f(x) = x^2$. The eight practising teachers worked in pairs, and each pair was asked to sketch the graph of one of these four functions.

When sharing their graphs and approaches to sketching the graphs, all pairs reported that they straightaway drew *the parabola*, which is in fact the graphical representation of *the quadratic function* $y = x^2$, whose domain of definition is the set of all x real numbers, hence a function distinct from those the teachers had been asked to sketch. In the midst of explaining their approaches to this activity, three teachers turned their attention to the given domains of definitions of the functions assigned to them, raising some confusion about the significance of domains to the graph-sketching activity.

In this activity, the practising teachers displayed the same misconceptions about functions as the well-documented students' misconceptions, namely, that they usually call upon one part-representation of functions, in this case, its equation or function rule (Markovits et al. 1986), namely $(x) = x^2$. The practising teachers also focused on the function rule, at first ignoring the given domains of definition. This explains why all teachers ended up with the same graphical representation for the four different functions, more precisely, that of a smooth curve in the shape of a parabola.

Teachers Reaching for More Advanced Knowledge about Functions

When the graphs produced were shared with the whole group, the teachers became aware of the similarities (the same function rule), but also the differences (the different domains of definition) among their functions. They realized they had been assigned different functions to sketch, and so their graphs could not have looked the same. This realization led to a discussion about the 'full description' or definition of a function, and as a result the teachers were then able to sketch the appropriate graphs to the given functions, as in Figure 11.2.

In the school mathematics curriculum in England for eleven- to sixteen-year-olds, there is an implicit hidden assumption that the domain of any 'school mathematics' function is the whole set of real numbers. This assumption means that most of the 'school mathematics' functions are 'well behaved', with continuous graphs, and the usual approach to sketching such graphs as encountered by students in textbooks or in their teachers' explanations is that of choosing a few real number values for the independent variable x in the table of values, usually consisting of 'easy integer number values' chosen to be values around zero, followed by calculation of the values of the dependent variable, and lastly plotting and neatly joining up these points either by continuous straight-line segments or by line curves.

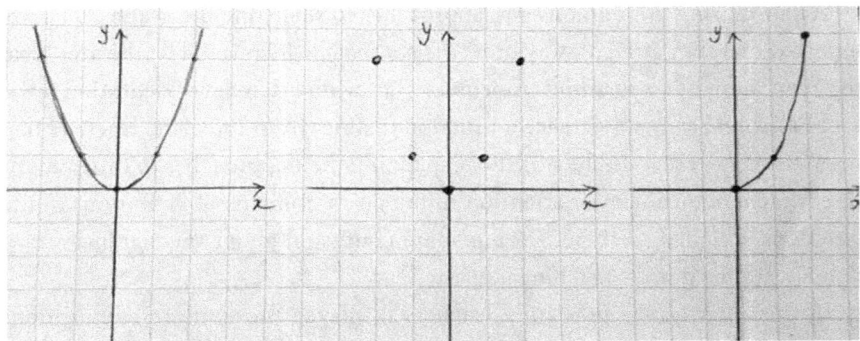

Domain is 'all real number values of x'; Domain is 'all the integer values of x'; Domain is 'all the positive real values of x'

Figure 11.2 Graphs of $f(x) = x^2$ for different domains of definitions.

During this workshop, there was clear evidence that such limited representations of functions were part of the participating teachers' SCK but, most importantly, the teachers themselves became aware of the limitations of their own SCK! Those teachers with a formal mathematics background recalled having encountered the formal definition of a function in their undergraduate studies (HCK), while the others (T7 and T8) did not seem to have any such recollection. In an attempt to define and fully describe a function, suggestions from the teachers were collected, such as domain, range and one-to-one correspondence (T1 to T6), co-domains (T3 and T6), notation conventions for composite functions (T5). Just like the first-year undergraduates in Nardi's (2001) study, these teachers' concept images of functions lacked in understanding the concept as being inextricably connected with its domain, co-domain and relationship expressed algebraically. Such a recollection enabled the practising teachers to assemble and 'put together' a definition (the formal definition), with some guidance from the course tutor. A fruitful discussion ensued about the difference between the range and co-domain of a function, and this discussion even led to recollection of other features and properties of functions, such as the relationship between functions and their inverses.

For the two teachers (T7 and T8) who had not studied formal mathematics at undergraduate level, their only recollection about functions was about using the y-notation for functions and solving problems that required differentiation or integration. Their participation in the group discussion about describing fully a function, by asking clarifications from the other teachers about features and properties mentioned meant that they too had familiarized themselves with the formal definition of a function.

Teachers' Connecting to More Advanced Mathematics Knowledge

The activity described above provided a stimulus for T1 to T6 to reach for and (partially) recall their advanced knowledge of functions, while for T7 and T8, the activity led to new learning because they had not previously encountered the formal definition of a function.

With gained awareness that functions are uniquely defined by a rule and their domains of definition, the teachers revisited the allocated functions and re-drew their graphs, correctly this time. T2, a mathematics graduate, stated that 'it did not occur to me to relate this activity with the formal definition', while T1 justified the lack of engagement with his advanced mathematics background as 'that was high-level mathematics not much used after the course'.

Teachers' Pedagogical Learning: Understanding Curriculum Progression

The teachers expressed surprise about the fact that there had never been occasions in their teaching when making explicit these features of a function was ever needed. This led to a fruitful discussion among the teachers about the quality of students' learning experiences of functions as part of the school mathematics curriculum. Indeed, at the secondary school level (in England) the formal definition of a function is not introduced to students until the more advanced levels of education (pre-university and undergraduate levels). The teachers admitted that in their planning they never even thought to consider the formal definition of a function, focusing instead on the common representations of functions across the secondary school curriculum (one-to-one or many-to-one mappings; input/output machines; relations between particular x-values and y-values; expressions to calculate the y-values from given x-values; and graphs), with the intention to build up to a fuller understanding of functions.

During the workshop, the practising teachers were encouraged to connect their newly acquired/recalled advanced knowledge about functions and relate explicitly each of these representations to the formal definition of functions. In doing so, the practising teachers came to realize that each of these representations explained particular features of the concept itself, but without being able to describe it completely! Teachers realized that overreliance on one representation, and a lack of connections between such representations make way for misconceptions while working with functions. This was strong evidence that the participating teachers had benefitted from engaging with the more advanced, formal definition of a function. Reflecting on their learning, the practising teachers thought they had benefitted conceptually. T3 reckoned that he 'became aware of the stages of building up to the definition of a function', while T1 stated that she had learned about: 'Different representations of functions – I've always seen them as disconnected representations, but they complement each other nicely towards fully understanding functions'.

Teachers' Pedagogical Learning: Supporting Pupils' Learning

In this workshop, the practising teachers shared the challenges their students encounter while working with functions and graphs. For each challenge shared, the practising teachers were encouraged to find a possible justification in the light of their new learning.

One challenge shared was pupils' perception of the graph of a linear function as a straight-line segment, which neatly joins the plotted points according to their choice of values in the table of values. In fact, this misconception was clearly 'demonstrated' by T2 herself while describing her approach to teaching about sketching graphs: 'once the few points in the table of values are plotted, they should always be joined up, with the graph extending between the lowest and highest point plotted [. . .]. The data points are needed in order to draw a smooth graph.' Following a group discussion on this approach, the practising teachers came to realize that lack of explicitness of the convenient choice of a few integer number values of x in the table leads to the students' misconception mentioned earlier. Lack of explicitness about the domain of a function, usually the whole set of real values, and its connection with drawing a 'continuous' graph was also identified by the teachers as a reason why students think of joining plotted points from the table with line segments. There was clear evidence in this episode that teachers' new learning about a function (AMK) had also supported them pedagogically in that not only their SCK was enriched by understanding why students hold specific misconceptions, but they also felt they know how to support students in addressing their misconceptions.

Discussion

This study adds to the evidence that teachers' knowledge of advanced mathematics holds the potential to transform teachers' own understanding of the school mathematics content they teach in ways that are pedagogically powerful.

The analysis of the data collected revealed that the participating teachers had benefitted from engaging with the more advanced, formal definition of a function. While all the participating teachers recognized that such a definition was not appropriate to be taught to secondary school students (unless seventeen-year-olds choose to study advanced mathematics courses), they all felt they had benefitted conceptually by gaining personal advanced knowledge about functions. The teachers' own understanding of functions became more sophisticated and nuanced as a result.

Moreover, these teachers also believed that they gained a powerful pedagogical understanding by reflecting on how their SCK benefitted from the more advanced knowledge. The pedagogical potential of their SCK was realized, as evidenced in teachers' realization of why students have certain misconceptions and of how they could support students to develop an understanding of this mathematics idea of high epistemic quality. Even if the 'methods' and 'rules' continued to be used by students, the teachers had become aware of the importance of making explicit to the students the conceptually sound grounding of the underlying mathematics.

Implications for Teacher Knowledge Development

The design of the activities in which the participants were involved in this professional development workshop was important. The mathematics activities created some tension in what the teachers knew about functions and their graphical representations and, in order to address the differences in their solutions, the need to engage with more advanced mathematics knowledge about functions was brought out into the open. With some support and guidance throughout the workshop, the teachers engaged with this knowledge in a way that saw them benefit both conceptually and pedagogically.

These teachers had SCK about various representations of functions, but their SCK was limiting as they all shared common misconceptions about their students' working with functions. 'Today's session helped me understand how I could have addressed the [pupils'] errors and how I can clarify things in the future' (T2), while another teacher shared his learning in the session: 'What I have learnt today? About advanced mathematics knowledge and its place in classroom and planning' (T5).

In responding to the question posed by Furlong and Whitty (2017) as to what may constitute the powerful professional knowledge required for teacher education, this study indicated that with support, when teachers accessed more advanced knowledge, such knowledge then became productive for their teaching and thinking about their students' learning.

This chapter thus helps situate the study of advanced mathematics in relation not only to school mathematics content but also its teaching, and it proposes that in England such support should be the remit of Initial Teacher Education (ITE) programmes (including opportunities for continuing professional development). These should look at school mathematics from an advanced standpoint, to examine school mathematics topics by engaging with advanced mathematics knowledge, where guidance is provided in terms of the relevant AMK, and how this could inform the teaching of school mathematics. If left to the teachers themselves, such links might never happen. But if support is provided, and creating links between advanced mathematics and school mathematics is modelled and practised in teacher education programmes, then such habits could be carried forward by teachers when they enter the teaching profession.

References

Ball, D. L., Hill, H. C. and Bass, H. (2005), 'Knowing Mathematics for Teaching: Who Knows Mathematics Well Enough to Teach Third Grade, And How Can We Decide?', *American Educator*, 29: 14–22.

Ball, D. L., Thames, M. H. and Phelps, G. (2008), 'Content Knowledge for Teaching: What Makes it Special?', *Journal of Teacher Education*, 59 (5): 389–407.

Bass, H. and Ball, D. L. (2004), 'A Practice-Based Theory of Mathematical Knowledge for Teaching: The Case of Mathematical Reasoning', in W. Jianpan and X. Binyan (eds), *Trends and Challenges in Mathematics Education*, 107–23, Shanghai: East China Normal University Press.

Bennet, N. and Turner-Bisset, R. (1993), 'Case Studies in Learning to Teach', in N. Bennett and C. Carre (eds), *Learning to Teach*, 165–90, London: Routledge.

Biza, I., Nardi, E. and Zachariades, T. (2007), 'Using Tasks to Explore Teacher Knowledge in Situation Specific Contexts', *Journal of Mathematics Teacher Education*, 10 (4-6): 301–09.

Buchholtz, N., Leung, F. K., Ding, L., Kaiser, G., Park, K. and Schwarz, B. (2013), 'Future Mathematics Teachers' Professional Knowledge of Elementary Mathematics from an Advanced Standpoint', *ZDM*, 45 (1): 107–20.

Davis, B. and Simmt, E. (2006), 'Mathematics-For-Teaching: An Ongoing Investigation of the Mathematics that Teachers (Need To) Know', *Educational Studies in Mathematics*, 61: 293–319.

DfE (Department for Education) (2013), *National Curriculum in England: Mathematics Programmes of Study*. https://www.gov.uk/government/publications/national-cur riculum-in-england-mathematics-programmes-of-study

Furlong, J. and Whitty, G. (2017), 'Knowledge Traditions in the Study of Education', in G. Whitty and J. Furlong (eds), *Knowledge and the Study of Education: An International Exploration*, 13–57, Oxford: Symposium Books.

Gericke, N., Hudson, B., Olin-Scheller, C. and Stolare, M. (2018), 'Powerful Knowledge, Transformations and the Need for Empirical Studies across School Subjects', *London Review of Education*, 16 (3): 428–44.

Hudson, B. (2018), 'Powerful Knowledge and Epistemic Quality in School Mathematics', *London Review of Education*, 16 (3): 384–97.

Hudson, B., Henderson, S. and Hudson, A. (2015), 'Developing Mathematical Thinking in the Primary Classroom: Liberating Students and Teachers as Learners of Mathematics', *Journal of Curriculum Studies*, 47 (3): 374–98.

Jakobsen, A., Thames, M. H. and Delaney, S. (2012, July), 'Using Practice to Define and Distinguish Horizon Content Knowledge', *12th International Congress in Mathematics Education (12th ICME)*, 4635–44.

Klein, F. (1932), *Elementary Mathematics from an Advanced Standpoint. Part 1: Arithmetic, Algebra, Analysis*, Translated from the third German edition by E. R. Hedrick and C. A. Noble, New York: Macmillan.

Kunter, M. and Baumert, J. (2013), 'The COACTIV Research Program on Teachers' Professional Competence: Summary and Discussion', in M. Kunter, J. Baumert, W. Blum, U. Klusmann, S. Krauss, and M. Neubrand (eds), *Cognitive Activation in the Mathematics Classroom and Professional Competence of Teachers*, 345–68, Boston, MA: Springer.

Ma, L. (2010), '*Knowing and Teaching Elementary Mathematics – Teachers' Understanding of Fundamental Mathematics in China and The United States*, London: Routledge.

Markovits, Z., Eylon, B. S. and Bruckheimer, M. (1986), 'Functions Today and Yesterday', *For the Learning of Mathematics*, 6 (2): 18–28.

Millett, A. and Johnson, D. C. (1996), 'Solving Teachers' Problems? The Role of the Commercial Mathematics Scheme', *Implementing the Mathematics National Curriculum: Policy, Politics and Practice. New BERA Dialogues Series*, 1: 54–70.

Morrow, W. (2008), *Bounds of Democracy: Epistemological Access in Higher Education*, Pretoria: HSRC Press.

Nardi, E. (2001), 'Domain, Co-Domain and Relationship: Three Equally Important Aspects of a Concept Image of Function', *Proceedings of the Conference of the British Society of Research into the Learning of Mathematics*, 21 (1): 49–54.

Putnam, R. T., Heaton, R. M., Prawat, R. S. and Remillard, J. (1992), 'Teaching Mathematics for Understanding: Discussing Case Studies of Four Fifth-grade Teachers', *The Elementary School Journal*, 93 (2): 213–28.

Rowland, T., Turner, F., Thwaites, A. and Huckstep, P. (2009), 'Transformation: Using Examples in Mathematics Teaching', in *Developing Primary Mathematics Teaching: Reflecting on Practice with the Knowledge Quartet*, 67–100, SAGE Publications Ltd, https://www.doi.org/10.4135/9781446279571.n4

Schoenfeld, A. H. and Kilpatrick, J. (2008), 'Toward a Theory of Proficiency in Teaching Mathematics', in D. Tirosh and T. Wood (eds), *International Handbook of Mathematics Teacher Education, Volume 2: Tools and Processes in Mathematics Teacher Education*, 321–54, Rotterdam: Sense Publishers.

Shulman, L. S. (1986), 'Those Who Understand: Knowledge Growth in Teaching', *Educational Researcher*, 15 (2): 4–14.

Simon, S. and Brown, M. (1996), 'Teacher Beliefs and Practices in Primary Mathematics', *The PME Conference*, Valencia, Spain.

Stockton, J. C. and Wasserman, N. (2017), 'Forms of Knowledge of Advanced Mathematics for Teaching', *The Mathematics Enthusiast*, 14 (1): 575–606.

Wasserman, N. H. (2016), 'Abstract Algebra for Algebra Teaching: Influencing School Mathematics Instruction', *Canadian Journal of Science, Mathematics and Technology Education*, 16 (1): 28–47.

Wasserman, N. H., Fukawa-Connelly, T., Villanueva, M., Mejia-Ramos, J. P. and Weber, K. (2017), 'Making Real Analysis Relevant to Secondary Teachers: Building Up from and Stepping Down to Practice'. *Primus*, 27 (6): 559–78.

Wasserman, N. H. and Stockton, J. (2013), 'Horizon Content Knowledge in the Work of Teaching: A Focus on Planning', *For the Learning of Mathematics*, 33 (3): 20–22.

Watson, A. and Mason, J. (2007), 'Taken-As-Shared: A Review of Common Assumptions about Mathematical Tasks in Teacher Education', *Journal of Mathematics Teacher Education*, 10 (4–6): 205–15.

Watson, A. and Harel, G. (2013), '"The Role of Teachers' Knowledge of Functions in Their Teaching: A Conceptual Approach with Illustrations from Two Cases', *Canadian Journal of Science, Mathematics and Technology Education*, 13 (2): 154–68.

Zazkis, R. and Leikin, R. (2010), 'Advanced Mathematical Knowledge in Teaching Practice: Perceptions of Secondary Mathematics Teachers', *Mathematical Thinking and Learning*, 12 (4): 263–81.

Zazkis, R. and Mamolo, A. (2011), 'Reconceptualizing Knowledge at the Mathematical Horizon', *For the Learning of Mathematics*, 31 (2): 8–13.

Zembat, I.O. (2013), 'Specialized Content Knowledge of Mathematics Teachers in UAE Context', *Proceedings of the Eighth Congress of European Research in Mathematics Education-CERME*, Vol. 8.

12

Implications of Powerful Professional Knowledge for Innovation in Teacher Education Policy and Practice

Martin Stolare, Brian Hudson, Niklas Gericke
and Christina Olin-Scheller

Introduction

In the introductory chapter of this book, the question asked was: *How can the nature of teachers' powerful professional knowledge be characterized, and what are the implications for teacher education policy and practice?* In this closing chapter, we return to the question, which can be split into two. The first part of the question points to epistemic dimensions as it explicitly addresses teachers' professional knowledge and what can be said about the nature of that knowledge. Our response to the second part of the question focuses on the structure of teacher education, and how it should be organized, representing an innovation that enables the development of powerful professional knowledge.

The term 'powerful professional knowledge' was first used by Furlong and Whitty (2017) and, as educational sociologists, their framing of the concept is naturally more general. An ambition in this book is, therefore, to pick up where Furlong and Whitty left off. This has been done by relating the concept of powerful professional knowledge to different subjects and national school contexts. However, before we go any further and delve into the different chapters, there are reasons to return to Furlong and Whitty's question about the nature of powerful professional knowledge, which we referred to in the first chapter:

> How can disciplinary knowledge and other external knowledges be brought together with professionals' reflective practice and practical theorizing in professional arenas to produce really powerful professional knowledge and learning? (Furlong and Whitty 2017: 49)

Furlong and Whitty believe that different forms of knowledge must be combined, which should no doubt be recognized as an epistemological difficulty. An aspect of the challenge is to integrate knowledge that has its background in different knowledge traditions. Second, powerful professional knowledge is a form of professional knowledge in the sense that theoretical knowledge is linked to a reflective approach to practice. Third, and here lies the real challenge, what of this professional knowledge is powerful along social realism lines? As we understand it, this is the core of their question. What is really meant by 'powerful'? Is there professional knowledge constructed in a specific social context that can be detached from that context? Consequently, the question Furlong and Whitty ask becomes far more qualified.

In the introductory chapter, we proposed that one way to address this issue is to link to the didactics tradition, implicitly portraying that as an innovation of teacher education in countries in which the perspectives of the didactics do not yet have a prominent role. It was argued that it is possible to recognize how theory and practice can be integrated through the relational perspective that permeates the didactics. Moreover, we consider that the didactics tradition might even give direction to how powerful professional knowledge can be generated. In this concluding chapter, this argumentation will be further developed in an analysis of the book's various chapters. Our analytical questions will then be: How is the issue of teachers' knowledge base discussed, and to what extent is it spoken of as powerful? How should teacher education be organized to place powerful professional knowledge at the centre?

Teachers' Knowledge Base and Powerful Professional Knowledge

Capturing Teachers' Knowledge Base

With his paradigm-generating articles, Lee Shulman turned his attention to the structure of teachers' knowledge base (Shulman 1986, 1987). He argued that it is not enough for teachers to have in-depth content knowledge in combination with pedagogical knowledge. There were also other essential parts of teachers' knowledge base, not least what Shulman came to call pedagogical content knowledge (PCK). This concept emphasizes the transformation processes as it captures the teacher's aspiration and ability to connect the students with the content, making it possible for them to learn. PCK emerges as a sort of core knowledge for the teacher or the glue that makes the other parts of teachers' knowledge base stick together.

There is obviously a strength in the PCK approach and the model of teachers' knowledge base for which Shulman laid the foundation. The model's impact has been significant. This is also apparent in various chapters of this book where the PCK approach implicitly, yet also explicitly, appears as a point of reference. The latter is the case in Chapter 8 by Hudson (this volume), who presents a figure (Figure 12.1) in which the central concepts of the PCK approach are placed in relation to the basic model within the didactic tradition, that is, the didactic triangle.

Corresponding concepts have not been developed in English within the didactic tradition, meaning that, when researchers rooted in the didactic tradition communicate in English, they have turned to the PCK terminology (e.g. Kattman et al. 1997; Duit et al. 2012). As a result, the integrative dynamic approach that permeates the didactic tradition has faded into the background. A very significant starting point in the didactic tradition is to ask the didactic questions such as: *why, what, how, for whom,* and *when* – and these questions must be handled in relation to each other. The didactic triangle also indicates a more extensive objective than the PCK approach. It is the case that the didactical triangle enables emphasis on the teacher's role while focusing on planning and teaching; yet, the triangle can also be rotated so as to place either the content or the student in the foreground.

The relationship between the Anglo-Saxon curriculum tradition, within which the PCK approach has been developed, and the European continental didactic tradition has long been and remains a focus in ongoing dialogue (Qvortrup et al. 2021; Deng 2020; Gundem and Hopmann 1998). One way to

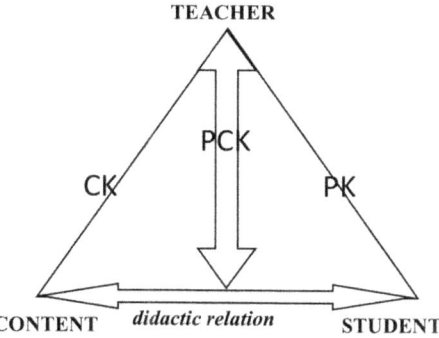

Figure 12.1 Mapping Shulman's categories onto the didactic triad (Hudson, this volume).

explain the differences between the two traditions has been to stress how they have developed in different educational contexts. Not least, the continental European idea of a Lehrplan, providing a relatively high degree of freedom for the exercise of teacher agency, has been highlighted as a significant aspect of background for the perspectives developed in the didactic tradition (Westbury 2000). While discussing what separates the two traditions, it is vital to notice that the PCK approach has developed since Shulman first launched it in the mid-1980s, with an outcome being the curriculum tradition has come closer to didactical perspectives on teaching and learning (Berry et al. 2015).

This book includes researchers who have their roots in both traditions. In several chapters, attempts are made to link underlying ideas from both the curriculum and didactics traditions to each other. In this sense, the book becomes part of the exchange between the two traditions. One example of this is Chapter 5 in which Stones and Fraser-Pearce (this volume) address religious education in English secondary school, where the starting point is taken from Wolfgang Klafki's theory of categorial *Bildung*. As shown earlier, in Chapter 8 Hudson places the curriculum-generated PCK approach in a didactic context by underscoring the similarities between the didactic tradition and the perspective of the teacher as a curriculum maker. This is a framework that has been developed in Anglo-American curriculum research (Lambert and Biddulph 2015), which describes curriculum-making as taking on a 'trinity of educational practice' that involves subject, child and teacher. Further, in Chapter 4 Standish and Mitchell (this volume) relate to the framework of teachers as curriculum makers. This framework is close to a didactic perspective. A common ground is an emphasis on the three-part dynamic interaction (content–student–teacher) and its importance for teaching and learning processes. In Chapter 8, Hudson emphasizes the relationship between the didactics tradition and the PCK approach in the final discussion by arguing that the concept of PCK 'can be seen as the professional knowledge required by teachers in guiding the didactic relation' (Hudson, this volume).

Possible explanations of the role the PCK approach has come to play in the didactic tradition and vice versa are that the two traditions' perspectives might be converging and there is heuristic strength in the PCK approach, while the didactics tradition lacks corresponding terminology in English (Kansanen 2009).

The following sections discuss the chapters in the book by drawing on Figure 12.1, primarily highlighting two dimensions of the model. One concerns the teachers' content knowledge, and the other is the didactical relationship, which in the model by Hudson (this volume) is linked to PCK. By focusing on both dimensions, the aim is to illuminate the character of powerful professional knowledge in the different chapters.

Teachers' Content Knowledge as Subject-Specific Educational Content Knowledge

By using the phrase 'Bringing Knowledge Back In', Young and others, who developed the concept of powerful knowledge, have succeeded in reframing the focus of curriculum research and once again making questions about knowledge and content central. From this point of view, it seems relevant to focus on teachers' content knowledge and to problematize it.

Based on their project dealing with the discipline of English and teacher education for teachers of English in Australia, in Chapter 6 McLean Davies et al. (this volume) problematize the concept of powerful knowledge. They argue it is crucial for teachers and student teachers to gain a deeper understanding of their discipline (here English as L1). More specifically, they make the case that student teachers not only should develop a notion of the declarative aspects of the discipline (knowing that). They should also gain knowledge and insight into the knowledge production tradition of the discipline (knowing how), and not least to relate the different forms of knowledge to each other. The idea they express – that teachers need to have deep and well-developed content knowledge – is not unexpected in a book whose theme is knowledge and where the teacher's professional platform is discussed. It might even be regarded as a truism, with similar views being expressed in all chapters. As another example; in Chapter 4, in which Standish and Mitchell discuss teacher education for teachers of geography in England, they point to the importance that student teachers acquire an understanding of the discipline and its (different) traditions. It might be said that they wish the future geography teachers to achieve a meta-perspective on the discipline and the school subject.

The importance of having a disciplinary meta-perspective is a central theme in Chapter 5 by Stones and Fraser-Pearce (this volume). Referring to religious education in English secondary school, they refer to the challenges teachers experience while moving between different knowledge traditions. This is also well in line with how Furlong and Whitty discuss the nature of powerful professional knowledge, who stress the idea of linking different epistemological traditions in their framing of the concept. However, in Stones and Fraser-Pearce (this volume) it is not so much between the disciplines of the school subjects and a broader field of education. What they instead emphasize is the challenge that may exist in a single school subject. Like many other school subjects, religious education is not exclusively linked to a single discipline. In this chapter, they launch the concept of epistemic literacy, pointing to an ability that all in-service teachers ought to have and that student teachers should develop. By epistemic literacy, they mean:

> If students and teachers are to avoid epistemological misconceptions and develop insights into specific knowledge forms presented in Religious Education (RE) in England's secondary school curriculum, we argue that they should be given opportunities to develop epistemic literacy to support navigation of the challenging and epistemologically complex questions that exist in the interfaces between subject disciplines. (Stones and Fraser-Pearce, this volume: 87)

Thus, with the concept of epistemic literacy they stress the centrality of the knowledge dimension in education in general and particularly so in teachers' daily practice. Epistemic literacy is seen as an essential dimension of powerful professional knowledge. They argue that a goal in teacher education should be that the student teachers have achieved epistemic literacy themselves and know how to integrate the concept into their future teaching.

In their discussion of what powerful knowledge might be for Australian English teachers and how that powerful knowledge can become part of teacher education, McLean Davies et al (this volume). clarify how essential it is that powerful knowledge is framed relative to educational practice. This suggests that teachers' content knowledge should have a particular quality, something touched upon in more than one chapter and hence a recurring theme in the book. For example, in Chapter 11 Crisan (this volume) explicitly focuses on secondary teachers' content knowledge in mathematics education. Making the PCK approach her point of reference, she shows how necessary it is that mathematics teachers possess knowledge in mathematics that differs from other professional groups for which mathematical knowledge also forms part of the knowledge base. The term used for this content knowledge that is special to teachers is Specialized Content Knowledge (SCK) and attributed to the work of Ball et al. (2008).

> Specialized Content Knowledge SCK encompasses knowledge of mathematics needed by teachers, but not necessarily used by others, such as knowledge of a particular mathematical model or representations useful for teaching a certain concept. (Crisan, this volume: 208.)

Crisan convincingly argues that teachers ought to have in-depth disciplinary content knowledge since that kind of high-quality knowledge can lead to a much-needed reflective relation to the specialized subject knowledge of the school subject. She connects content knowledge and the assignment as a mathematics teacher, stressing that it is not enough for teachers to have a general understanding of mathematics. The teachers' content knowledge must include (see the previous quote) aspects of content knowledge, enabling them to design situations in which students can learn. Crisan's reasoning resembles what is articulated in Chapter 10 by Stolare, Bladh and Kristiansson, this volume, in which they use the model of *didaktical* reconstruction to analyse teachers talking about their teaching on migration in upper secondary school. Based on the model, they declare that teachers need to possess deep disciplinary specialized knowledge, understanding the basic structure of the content, since that will allow them to address the basic themes and recognize the obstacles students may encounter in their learning process.

The concept of SCK has grown out of the PCK approach. Of particular interest here, where the relationship between curriculum and didactics is an underlying theme, is that SCK might provide an opening for the 'didacticization' of PCK. As SCK is defined, it is about content knowledge; there is no doubt about this. Yet, it is an idea of content knowledge defined in relation to the teachers' educational and didactical mission. It is Subject-Specific Educational Content Knowledge (SSECK) if one is to allow the didactic terminology to characterize the concept. What it means is that teachers' content knowledge has a distinct integrated didactic character. The PCK concept emphasizes the *how* question, while the selection of teaching content, and the relation between discipline and subject, tends to fall into the background (Kansanen 2009). In the tradition of didactics, the *what* question is more central, relating to teachers' subject conceptions; the *what* question is closely connected to other didactic questions like *why?*, *how?* and *for whom?* By focusing on SSECK, the importance of perceiving the teacher's content knowledge from a relational and integrative perspective is stressed but without losing sight of the broader educational goals. Based on Crisan and Stolare et al., SSECK might be expressed as an insight into the basic knowledge structure of the discipline and the school subject, and in reflected experiences of what it really means to acquire the specific knowledge. This experience could act as a starting point and a guide for the process of planning and executing teaching.

Accordingly, well-developed content knowledge appears to be a necessary part of teachers' knowledge base. It also seems that a reflective view on the discipline and its knowledge traditions, in which the teacher has acquired an understanding of the discipline's various forms of knowledge and the inner structure, is essential. One way of framing powerful professional knowledge is thus to understand it as in-depth and reflected practice-relevant content knowledge, which with a tradition-breaking ambition may be called SSECK.

Teachers' Reflective Practice and Practical Theorizing

Another prominent theme in the book is the relationship between theory and practice, that is, that a specific feature of teachers' knowledge base is the ability to relate theory to practice and vice versa.

One example of the need to relate to practice is discussed by Standish and Mitchell in Chapter 4. Based on the previously referenced model of the teacher as a curriculum maker, they describe teachers' knowledge as practical knowledge, or, as they put it: practical wisdom. The latter reflects the expression Lee Shulman also used to describe the character of the teacher's knowledge (Shulman 2007). Further, Standish and Mitchell describe their goal with geography teacher education to enable the student teachers to develop phronesis.

> The teacher has to develop good judgement with respect to planning, teaching and assessing learning, and they need to embody and model the academic values inherent to the profession. Hence, we believe in the *practical competence* and wisdom of teachers being connected to a theoretical body of knowledge about education and geography education specifically: the secondary geography ITE curriculum (Table 4.1). (Standish and Mitchell, this volume: 65)

From the previous quotation, teachers' knowledge emerges as 'förtrogenhetskunskap' (in Swedish), generally directly translated as 'familiarity knowledge' that is established in teacher education through collaboration and the integration of practical and theoretical elements. This might be considered a form of 'knowledge by acquaintance' (Winch 2013) gained through the direct experience of the professional practice of teaching. In this way, Standish and Mitchell can be seen to assign a form of *Bildung* as a mission for teacher education. It is an education that should relate student teachers to the reservoir of practical and theoretical knowledge, at the same time as it is an education which, by highlighting the basic values involved in what it means to be a teacher, can also help the individual student teacher grow.

The relationship between theory and practice is a central question in history teacher education in Finland, states Puustinen (this volume) in Chapter 3. He points to the historical tension between theory and practice in teacher education. Based on Weniger (1957), Puustinen speaks of this tension in terms of 'the tyranny of theory and the tyranny of experience' (Puustinen, this volume: 47). He believes it has been hard to balance the two: theory and practice. Teachers must deal with different knowledge traditions, and the challenges they face in doing so become transparent in Chapter 9. In this chapter, Randahl and Kristiansson (this volume) analyse professional conversations between Swedish social studies teachers and researchers and underscore teachers' difficulties in relating teaching to practice. The teachers struggle to link their experience-based knowledge to specialized knowledge but also to adopt a meta-perspective on the practice of teaching. The teachers in their study simply find it challenging to combine theory and practice. This problem is a challenge for both in-service teachers and student teachers. One suspects that this might be why Furlong and Whitty stress the need to be able to deal with different knowledge traditions as a central aspect of powerful professional knowledge for teachers. Puustinen captures this complexity well:

> As a consequence, the teacher should be able to theorize and reflect on schooling and learning situations with disciplinary concepts that are drawn both from educational science and the background discipline(s) of the teaching subject. This is not an easy task for student teachers, for working teachers, nor for teacher education systems. (Puustinen, this volume: 46)

The organization of teacher education is hence a central issue for linking theory and practice, and this is addressed by Iversen Kulbrandstad and Kulbrandstad (this volume) in Chapter 2. In their historical account, they describe the academicization of the Norwegian teacher education system. The background to this development over the last decade has been the belief that in-depth theoretical studies will add to the student teachers' development of tools to analyse and reflect on the educational practice. To make this possible, it has been decided that a professional perspective should permeate all of teacher education. Therefore, when the student teachers of Norwegian study the discipline linked to their school subject, they do that with an educational focus, knowing they will be teaching the subject in the future. Consequently, subject didactics is an integral part of teacher education in Norway (also in Sweden). The creation of special disciplinary-based teacher education subjects in which practice and theory are linked together reflects the discussion that Crisan had about SCK and what we have referred to as *Subject-Specific Educational Content Knowledge*.

How Can Teachers' Powerful Professional Knowledge Be Characterized?

In the analysis of the various chapters, the ambition has been to find common features and themes, three of which have so far been identified. First, the tendency to implicitly, but also explicitly, relate to the conceptual framework developed in the PCK approach. A second theme has been the quality of teachers' content knowledge stressing that teachers need a well-developed disciplinary understanding of the discipline or disciplines linked to the school subject. The third dimension refers to the fact that teachers must be able to navigate between different knowledge traditions, concretely expressed in the relationship between theory and practice. In this section, we focus more directly on the concept of powerful professional knowledge and how it is discussed throughout the book. Still, it should be stressed that the term is not used explicitly in every chapter.

> Teacher education subjects might contribute to student teachers' development of powerful professional knowledge by presenting a knowledge base built on different theories, making the students reflect on practice with help of theories, and by focusing on the importance of choice of content for quality teaching. (Iversen Kulbrandstad and Lars Kulbrandstad, this volume: 27)

The previous quote recognizes this an opportunity to organize teacher education such that it supports the development of powerful professional knowledge among student teachers. The starting point of Iversen Kulbrandstad and Lars Kulbrandstad is that theory and practice must be combined in teacher education. Creating structural conditions is crucial if student teachers are to develop powerful professional knowledge. By teacher education subjects, it is meant, as referred to earlier, that the entire education should have a professional perspective, including those parts where the student teachers focus on the academic discipline(s). Puustinen agrees with their position in that he also points to the importance of teacher education being organized so that student teachers can handle theory and practice relative to each other as a prerequisite for developing powerful professional knowledge. In line with this, Standish and Mitchell frame powerful professional knowledge as a form of theory-based practical knowledge:

> A strong notion of subject discipline and education as potentially transformative and how this can be applied in practical planning, teaching, assessment

and evaluation, is a way that powerful professional knowledge (PPK) can be characterized. (Standish and Mitchell, this volume: 81)

In their discussion, Stones and Fraser-Pearce in Chapter 5 turn to meta-knowledge as a core dimension of powerful professional knowledge. By developing epistemic literacy, teachers should be able to handle different knowledge traditions, within and between disciplines, yet also between theory and practice. As they believe the development of epistemic literacy is crucial, they argue for the organization of teacher education that enables student teachers to develop this ability. Further, in Chapter 7 Juuti and Gericke (this volume) highlight teachers' ability to handle different disciplines, in their case while planning a course in circular economy, while in Chapter 11 Crisan recognizes, as noted earlier, the unique potential held by content knowledge. Crisan understands in-depth content knowledge as the key to developing powerful professional knowledge.

The reasoning of Stolare et al. in Chapter 10 is well in line with the other chapters. They argue that a central aspect is the teacher's understanding of the discipline, linked to the selection and organizing of the content knowledge, which must be placed in the context of practice. Powerful professional knowledge is described in terms of knowings:

> The relational perspective permeating the *didaktik* tradition gives an idea of how to think about powerful professional knowledge. Rather than being understood as knowledge of specific disciplinary content, it could be described as a 'knowing' (Carlgren 2020). A subject-specific 'knowing', somewhat simplified, can be described as the ability to create learning environments based on a dialectical relationship between the clarification of specialized knowledge and an understanding of the pupils' relationship to the potential subject matter. (Stolare, Bladh and Kristiansson, this volume: 201)

The interplay between theory and practice also appears in Stolare et al. as a dominant aspect. Their reasoning may be related to Standish and Mitchell, who stress that powerful professional knowledge should be perceived as an ability to act in practice, as an expression of phronesis.

Finally, a similar way of addressing powerful professional knowledge is expressed by Hudson in Chapter 8. Powerful professional knowledge is framed as something the teacher does to establish a practice for teaching and learning a specific content. Four dimensions in the teacher's practice are identified from a study of teachers as curriculum makers in school mathematics that could signify powerful professional knowledge. These four dimensions are related to both the didactic triangle and the PCK approach (Figure 12.2).

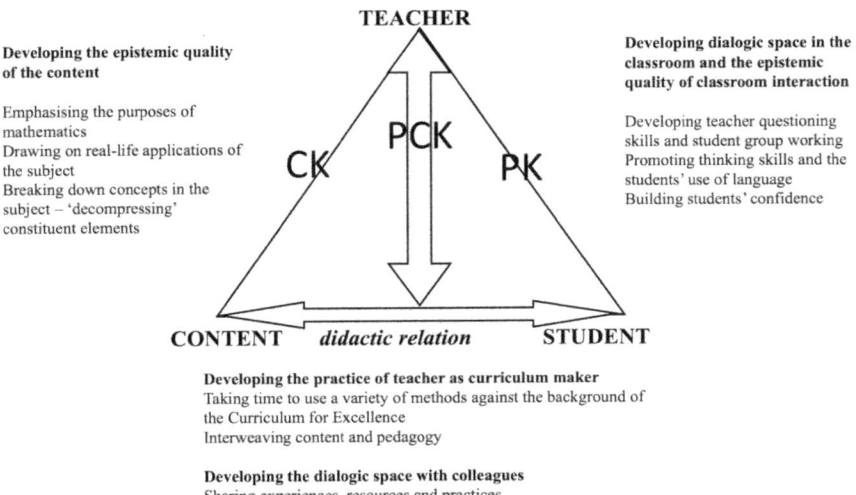

Figure 12.2 Mapping the emerging themes onto Shulman's categories and the didactic triad (Hudson this volume).

By characterizing powerful professional knowledge in terms of four dimensions, Hudson delimits the concept and fleshes it out more substantially.

What then can be said about teachers' knowledge base and, more precisely, the concept of powerful professional knowledge based on the contributions in this book? A common feature is the role given to a subject didactic perspective in the sense that powerful professional knowledge is founded on the teacher's reflective relationship to the school subject they are teaching. This makes it a matter of having understanding and insight into the knowledge traditions of the discipline, as the place and function of the various forms of disciplinary knowledge. At the same time, powerful professional knowledge requires knowledge of the processes that influence the students' conditions for learning. This is based on the view that powerful professional knowledge is generated in connection to practice. In this sense, the awareness of practice always forms part of a subject didactic approach (Kansanen 2009).

Conclusion

The approach in this book project has been one of comparative subject didactics. By gathering researchers from different countries representing a variety of school subjects, the hope was to paint a nuanced picture of the powerful professional knowledge concept and its role in teacher education. We believe we have been successful in this sense and that certain themes act to unite the chapters, while shared views are expressed across countries and subjects. Hence, in concluding this chapter we again consider the research question that has been our point of departure: *How can the nature of teachers' powerful professional knowledge be characterized, and what are the implications for teacher education policy and practice?* In particular, we focus on the implications for innovation in teacher education policy and practice.

As discussed in the introduction to this final chapter, Furlong and Whitty provide a way to frame the concept of powerful professional knowledge. They thereby answer the previous question or at least put forward an idea of where the answer may be sought. The goal is to identify a knowledge base for teachers that can be declared to be powerful; still, what is really meant by this term *powerful*?

One can address the *powerful* aspect by pointing out the opportunities for agency the knowledge might enable and discussing what it may represent in terms of content (Maude 2018). This is also how the concept is discussed in most chapters in this book. Yet, it is also possible to characterize powerful professional knowledge differently, focusing not so much on what it tangibly represents or how it empowers the teachers and to instead approach the concept from the perspective of social realism (Young 2008; Moore 2013).

The powerful knowledge approach is based on the notion of knowledge boundaries discussed in Chapter 1 (Stolare et al., this volume). Powerful knowledge is specialized and not the same as the everyday knowledge pupils bring to school (Young 2013). Unlike everyday knowledge, specialized knowledge is not embedded in the context in which it has been generated. This knowledge is powerful because it is useable in several different social contexts. Accordingly, one response to the question of how powerful professional knowledge may be characterized can then be related to the question: is it possible to embed in different social contexts? This is, however, not a particularly constructive concrete response in the sense of what powerful professional knowledge is or can be, nor does it guide processes of content selection. Yet what it does say something about is the nature of the knowledge that educational research can contribute to practice.

Addressing the relationship between the specific and the general entails a considerable challenge in teacher education and in building teachers' knowledge base. Rephrased: it is not easy to establish a knowledge base that responds to the need for establishing general understandings without ending up so far from the practice that its relevance is lost.

One strategy for developing powerful professional knowledge to a level where theory and practice fertilize each other involves drawing on the work of Klafki and his idea of the 'exemplary'. In the teacher education context, this means that specific teaching examples are used to represent more general didactical issues (Klafki 1985/2001). This would also be in line with didactics, and the integration of theory and practice (Vollmer 2014). Learning from a concrete example, how to separate the general from the specific, and thereby handling the question of the scope of knowledge in a planning and teaching process, is what student teachers would do during their education. Thus, as part of the process of developing powerful professional knowledge, subject didactics represents theory-building opportunities on a middle-range level as exemplified by Klafki's discussion about lesson preparation:

> Preparing lessons is one of those tasks of the teacher in which the basic pedagogical problems of the school converge. It is the place where the interactive relationship between theory and practice fundamental to all education, the interplay between experience and reflection, must be concretized in the form of reflected decisions for planning instruction and learning. (Klafki 1995: 15)

Reflecting on Crisan's discussion in Chapter 11 on specialized content knowledge, we have launched the concept of SSECK. With SSECK, we wish to stress how the didactic dimension should be understood as an integral and inseparable part of teachers' content knowledge. This means the concept of SSECK should be seen as an attempt to 'didacticize' the PCK approach. The point is to recognize that teachers' subject knowledge must be of a special nature and that there is an inherent didactic understanding in this knowledge. We see an opportunity in the concept of SSECK and its didactic connotation. It signals that teachers must show agency when it comes to the didactic questions of *what* and not forgetting *why*; they need to be active in selecting the content. Teachers must also dive deep into their content knowledge, in the form of concepts, models and contexts, that connect to the chosen teaching content. Teachers have to think about what it actually means to know what the students should learn in order to register this knowledge when expressed by the students. The teaching practice and the experience of that are vital aspects of the teachers' SSECK. Understanding SSECK as anchored in educational practice experiences makes it plausible to link SSECK to what might be called 'familiarity knowledge'. Teachers develop knowledge that allows them to evaluate and decide how to act in a specific situation. In teacher education –

ITE as well as CPD – 'familiarity knowledge' can be connected to the notion of *Bildung*, meaning that teachers' knowledge base consists of an almost embodied specific understanding of the subject and its linked discipline(s), enabling them to transform the content knowledge and having the methods to do so. Teachers' selection and transformation of content are made in relation to an experience of practice that helps them momentarily adapt to the specific teaching situation (Ongstad 2006).

Until this point, we have focused on teachers' knowledge base and powerful professional knowledge, but what impact would a stronger emphasis on subject didactics (Vollmer 2021) have on the organization of teacher education, both ITE and CPD? In the introductory chapter, we discussed the possibilities of establishing subject didactics within teacher education as a field of knowledge with boundaries, as an applied discipline (Muller 2009) that has features reminiscent of singulars. Subject didactics would thus be the basis for the region of professional knowledge in education (Bernstein 2000; Hordern 2016). This argument is supported by the various studies presented in this book, most prominently by Iversen Kulbrandstad and Lars Kulbrandstad in Chapter 2).

The inherent nature of subject didactics in connecting theoretical perspectives and doing so relative to a teaching practice corresponds well with Furlong and Whitty's reasoning while setting up the framework for powerful professional knowledge. It also corresponds well with the way in which Barret and Hordern (2021) discuss the possibilities of establishing a foundation for teacher education that can be an expression of powerful professional knowledge. In vocational education like teacher education, the relationship between theory and practice is key (Wheelahan 2015). Hence, strong arguments exist for making subject didactics the central field of knowledge within teachers' education. The subject didactic perspective from which teaching, seen in the contextual knowledge–teacher–student interaction, also characterizes the teachers' disciplinary studies and responds precisely to the desirability of developing teachers' strong Subject-Specific Educational Content Knowledge. However, to enable teachers to develop the type of knowledge where practice and theory are interwoven, higher education must still play a vital role in teacher education. The trend towards decoupling teacher education from university teacher education institutions evident in countries like England, the United States and Australia is a cause for concern. It is hard to see how this development can contribute to developing a knowledge base founded on what may be characterized as powerful professional knowledge.

References

Ball, D., Thames, M. H. and Phelps, G. (2008), 'Content Knowledge for Teaching: What Makes It Special?', *Journal of Teacher Education*, 59 (5): 389–407.

Barret, B. and Hordern, J. (2021), 'Rethinking the Foundations: Towards Powerful Professional Knowledge in Teacher Education in the USA and England', *Journal of Curriculum Studies*, 53 (2): 153–65. DOI: 10.1080/00220272.2021.1887359.

Bernstein, B. (2000[1996]), *Pedagogy, Symbolic Control and Identity: Theory, Research, Critique* (Rev. ed), Lanham, MD: Rowman and Littlefield Publishers.

Berry, A., Friedrichsen, P. and Loughran, J. (2015), *Re-examining Pedagogical Content Knowledge in Science Education*, New York: Routledge.

Carlgren, I. (2020), 'Powerful Knowns and Powerful Knowings', *Journal of Curriculum Studies*, 52 (3): 323–36. DOI: 10.1080/00220272.2020.1717634

Deng, Z. (2020), *Knowledge, Content, Curriculum and Didaktik*, Abingdon: Taylor and Francis.

Duit, R., Gropengießer, H., Kattmann, U., Komorek, M. and Parchmann, I. (2012), 'The Model of Educational Reconstruction – a Framework for Improving Teaching and Learning Science', in D. Jorde and J. Dillon (eds), *Science Education Research and Practice in Europe: Cultural Perspectives in Science Education*, Vol. 5, 13–37, Rotterdam: SensePublishers.

Furlong, J. and Whitty, G. (2017), 'Knowledge Traditions in the Study of Education', in G. Whitty and J. Furlong (eds), *Knowledge and the Study of Education: An International Exploration*, 13–57, Oxford: Symposium Books.

Gundem, B. B. and Hopmann, S. (eds) (1998), *Didaktik and/or Curriculum: An International Dialogue*, New York: Perter Lang.

Hordern, J. (2016), 'Regions and their Relations: Sustaining Authoritative Professional Knowledge', *Journal of Education and Work*, 29 (4): 427–49. DOI: 10.1080/13639080.2014.958653

Kansanen, P. (2009), 'Subject-matter Didactics as a Central Knowledge Base for Teachers, Or Should It Be Called Pedagogical Content Knowledge?', *Pedagogy, Culture and Society*, 17 (1): 29–39. DOI: 10.1080/14681360902742845

Kattmann, U., Duit, R., Gropengießer, H. and Komorek, M. (1997), 'Das Modell der didaktischen Rekonstruktion – Ein Rahmen für naturwissenschaftsdidaktische Forschung und Entwicklung', *Zeitschrift für Didaktik der Naturwissenschaften*, 3 (3): 3–18.

Klafki, W. (1985/2001), *Dannelseteori och Didaktik – Nye studier*, Aarhus: Klim.

Klafki, W. (1995), 'Didactic Analysis as the Core of Preparation of Instruction [Didaktische Analyse als Kern der Unterrichtsvorbereitung]', *Journal of Curriculum Studies*, 27 (1): 13–30. DOI: 10.1080/0022027950270103

Lambert, D. and Biddulph, M. (2015), 'The Dialogic Space Offered by Curriculum-Making in the Process of Learning to Teach, and the Creation of a Progressive

Knowledge-Led Curriculum', *Asia-Pacific Journal of Teacher Education*, 43 (3): 210–24.

Maude, A. (2018), 'Geography and Powerful Knowledge: A Contribution to the Debate', *International Research in Geographical and Environmental Education*, 27 (2): 179–90. DOI: 10.1080/10382046.2017.1320899

Moore, R. (2013), 'Social Realism and the Problem of the Problem of Knowledge in the Sociology of Education', *British Journal of Sociology of Education*, 34 (3): 333–53. DOI: 10.1080/01425692.2012.714251

Muller, J. (2009), 'Forms of Knowledge and Curriculum Coherence', *Journal of Education and Work*, 22 (3): 205–26. DOI: 10.1080/13639080902957905

Ongstad, S. (ed.) (2006), *Fag og didaktikk i læerutdanning: Kunnskap i grenseland*, Oslo: Universitetsforlaget.

Qvortrup, A., Krogh, E. and Ting Graf, S. (2021), *Didaktik and Curriculum in Ongoing Dialogue*, London: Routledge.

Shulman, L. S. (1986), 'Those Who Understand: Knowledge Growth in Teaching', *Educational Researcher*, 15 (2): 4–14.

Shulman, L. S. (1987), 'Knowledge and Teaching: Foundations of a New Reform', *Harvard Educational Review*, 57 (1): 1–22.

Shulman, L. S. (2007), 'Practical Wisdom in the Service of Professional Practice', *Educational Researcher*, 36 (9): 560–3.

Young, M. (2013), 'Overcoming the Crisis in Curriculum Theory: A Knowledge-based Approach', *Journal of Curriculum Studies*, 45 (2): 101–18.

Young, M. (2008), *Bringing Knowledge Back in: From Social Constructivism to Social Realism in the Sociology of Education*, Abingdon, Oxon: Routledge.

Vollmer, H. (2014), 'Fachdidaktik and the Development of a Generalized Subject Didactics in Germany', *Education and didactique*, 8 (1): 23–34. DOI: 10.4000/educationdidactique.1861

Vollmer, H. (2021), 'Powerful Educational knowledge through Subject Didactics and General Subject Didactics: Recent Developments in German-speaking Countries', *Journal of Curriculum Studies*, 53 (2): 229–46. DOI: 10.1080/00220272.2021.1887363

Weniger, E. (1957), 'Theorie und Praxis in der Erziehung' [Theory and practice in education], in E. Weniger (ed.), *Die eigenständigkeit der erziehung in theorie und praxis* [*The Independence of Education in Theory and Practice*], 7–22, Weinheim: Beltz.

Westbury, I. (2000), 'Teaching as a Reflective Practice: What Might Didaktik Teach Curriculum?', in I. Westbury, S. Hopmann and K. Riquarts (eds), *Teaching as a Reflective Practice: The German Didaktik tradition*, 15–40, London: Routledge.

Wheelahan, L. (2015), 'Not Just Skills: What a Focus on Knowledge Means for Vocational Education', *Journal of Curriculum Studies*, 47 (6): 750–62. DOI: 10.1080/00220272.2015.1089942

Winch, C. (2013), 'Curriculum Design and Epistemic Ascent', *Journal of Philosophy of Education*, 47 (1): 128–46.

Index

academization   51, 52, 53
access, epistemic   91, 98, 146, 162, 163, 209
  categorial *Bildung*   93, 96
accountability   3, 14, 64
action research   145, 153–4, 157–8, 159, 163
advanced mathematics knowledge (AMK)   210–11, 212, 213, 219, 221, 222
advisory staff (LEA)   145, 146, 153
agency   70, 118, 228, 237, 238
'aha' moments   104, 193, 196, 197, 200
aims, broader educational   17, 77, 99–100, 231
aims, educational   67–8, 69, 77, 81, 100
analytical frameworks   56, 181
analytical tools   57, 168, 174, 181–2
  didactic triad   148
  semantic plane   170, 171, 175, 180
Anglo-Saxon curriculum tradition   185, 227
artefacts, teaching   186, 188, 189, 196, 197, 198–9
assessment frameworks   74, 152
assessment of learning   14, 31, 54, 66, 81, 153
assumptions   89, 90, 96, 116, 121, 217
  curriculum thinking   64
attitudes   97, 120, 156, 158, 159, 164. *See also* motivation, student
Australia   110, 113, 114–15, 120, 229, 230
  national curriculum   14
authenticity   130, 135, 136, 137, 140
autonomy   11, 56, 93, 96, 103, 118. *See also* judgement, professional

backgrounds
  of students   33, 96
  of teachers   103, 208, 215, 218, 219
balance (between)   77, 81, 156, 201, 210. *See also* tensions
  Curriculum Making Model   70
  curriculum thinking   82, 148

subject and pedagogy   46, 69
theory and practice   25, 52, 58, 233
Ball, D.   161, 207, 208, 209, 210, 230
beliefs   67, 89, 94–5, 96, 147, 164
  fallible knowledge   10
  multidisciplinary approaches   50
benefits, research   157, 216, 220, 221. *See also* unintended consequences
Bennetts, T.   74, 80
Bernstein, B.   8, 11, 12, 152, 181, 239
  pedagogic devices   167, 179
bias   101, 102, 103–4
Biddulph, M.   147, 148, 150, 155, 157, 160
'Big Questions'   88, 93–6
Bildung (description)   92. *See also* categorial *Bildung*; formal *Bildung*; material *Bildung*
Bildung-informed *didaktik*   88, 91, 103
Billingsley, B.   94, 95
blended learning   146, 153, 163
boundaries   5, 13, 64, 91, 137
  singulars   12, 14, 239
  social realism   15, 237
bridging   12, 181, 208
Brundtland, G.   128
building blocks   191, 200
building up   215, 220
Bullock Report, A Language for Life   112

canonical knowledge   26, 117–18
capabilities. *See also* competencies; transformative potential
  approach   97, 102
  of students   26, 68, 70, 98, 130, 140
  of student teachers   201
  of teachers   56, 152
capitalism, late   64, 65
case studies   46, 53, 75, 78–9, 88, 206
categorial *Bildung*   91, 96, 97, 190, 201, 228
  formal *Bildung*   92, 93, 187
  material *Bildung*   92, 93, 187

Index

Catling, S. and Martin, F., *Contesting Powerful Knowledge* 6, 7, 10, 93
Chevallard, Y. 8, 9, 147
circle. *See* research-development-circle (RD-circle)
circular economy (core idea) 130. *See also* resource-efficient economies; sustainable development
citizens, future 2, 68, 135, 193
classroom interaction 155-7, 161, 163
classroom practices 49, 53, 63, 152, 181
coding data 154, 175
colleague(s). *See also* peer discussion
  collaboration 31, 55, 57, 58
  comparison 37
  dialogic space with 155, 157, 162, 163
commitment 101, 102, 103, 114, 140, 188
  and trust 139, 160
community-rooted views 17, 200
competencies
  students 6, 45, 133
  student teachers 27, 32, 37, 50, 65, 232
  teachers 14, 33, 36, 149
competition 64, 95, 129, 139
concept map 76, 78, 80
conceptual frameworks 2, 87, 93, 95, 100, 234
conditions for development 14, 114, 186, 188, 234, 236
confidence 33, 156, 159, 160, 163, 214
'conflict model' (religion and science) 94, 99
content, choice of 26, 27, 35-6, 88, 101, 234
  migration 169
context-independency 57, 68, 72, 133, 172
  meta-theoretical thinking 47-8, 56
contextual knowledge 73, 78, 79, 135, 239
continuing professional development (CPD) 2, 3, 101, 164, 222, 239
cumulative knowledge building 167, 180, 181
Curriculum for Excellence 145, 153, 157, 158, 159, 162
curriculum makers, students as 159

Curriculum Making Model 70, 71, 81
curriculum planning 63, 67-72, 75-81, 187
curriculum principle 26, 185, 187, 202
curriculum theory 64-5, 75
curriculum thinking 64, 65, 69, 82, 148, 187

decision-making 56, 88, 90, 103, 113, 133
  participative 131
  process 130
'decompression' 161
deconstructing
  knowledge 102, 161, 191, 196
  pedagogical transformations 91
  sources 99, 118
decontextualized educational knowledge 52-3, 56, 152
dematerialization 131
Deng, Z. 7, 92, 130, 140, 187, 202
Derry, Jan 69-70, 78
Developing Mathematical Thinking in the Primary Classroom (DMTPC) 145, 152, 153
development, conditions for 14, 114, 186, 188, 234, 236
dialectical relationship 64, 97, 201, 235
dialogic space 148, 150, 151, 155-7, 161
  with colleagues 155, 157, 162, 163
dichotomist thinking 6, 7, 47, 56
didactical analysis 27, 186, 190, 191, 192
didactic questions 187, 191, 227, 238
  'how' questions 8, 231
  'what' questions 9, 231
didactic relation 8, 76, 148, 149, 160, 176
  pedagogical content knowledge (PCK) 161, 162
didactic transposition 9, 187
didactic triad 148, 150, 163, 236
  didactic relation 149, 160, 161, 227
didactic triangle 7, 80, 81, 100, 189, 235
  didactic questions 8, 9, 187, 191
  didactic relation 71
didaktical reconstruction 185, 190-2, 196, 200, 202, 231. *See also* model of *didaktical* reconstruction
disciplinary approaches 47, 91, 104. *See also* multidisciplinary
disciplinary history 46, 49, 55

disciplinary lenses   99
disciplinary perspective   130, 133. *See also* multidisciplinary
disciplinary traditions   11, 81, 127, 141
disciplines, background   46, 57, 59, 233
disciplines, traditional academic   24, 25, 34, 38
Dixon, John   114, 117, 119, 120, 123
domains of knowledge   68, 207
Durkheim, E.   68, 91, 93, 99

economic growth   127, 128, 129, 136, 139
economic sustainability   127, 128, 131
economies, resource-efficient   129, 139
economy, the   128, 129, 132
educational design   169, 186, 188
educational design research (EDR)   169
educational science   46, 57, 233
education for sustainable development (ESD)   128, 129, 130
elementarization   191, 195, 196, 198
emerging themes   17, 114, 159, 160, 163, 236
empathy   33, 36, 90, 103, 104, 117
empirical data   145, 154, 174
England   17, 88–91, 113, 213–14, 219, 229
 advanced mathematics knowledge (AMK)   222
 Bullock Report   112
 higher education   11
 misconceptions   87, 217, 230
 national curriculum   74, 209, 214, 215
 qualified teacher status   101
 reforms   89, 92
 teacher education institutions (TEIs)   239
entitlement, student   1, 26, 89, 90, 91
environment, learning   146, 153, 160, 163, 201, 235
epistemic access. *See* access, epistemic
epistemic ascent   9, 71, 147, 150
epistemic capacity   10, 147
epistemic literacy, concept of   97–8
epistemic quality, evolution of   9–10
'epoch-typical key problems'   92, 101
equations   208, 209, 210, 211, 216, 217
Ertsas and Irgens, *Professional Theorizing*   47, 48, 56, 57, 58

ethics   89, 92, 98, 103
European Green Deal framework (EU)   128–9
everyday experience, beyond   79, 91, 93, 167, 168, 169
 powerful knowledge (introduction)   26
experience, tyranny of. *See* tyranny of experience
expertise   28, 57, 93, 138, 169
 subject   9, 46, 51, 101, 147, 150
expert knowledge   88, 91, 97, 98, 104
'explanatory space'   95

fallible knowledge   5, 6, 10, 70, 146, 147
'familiarity knowledge'   232, 238, 239
fear of being wrong   160, 163
Finland   46, 49–55, 56–7, 58, 127, 233
 master's level   37
 multidisciplinary approaches   133
 national curriculum   16, 54, 55, 140
 observation studies   48
Finnish national core curriculum   16, 54, 55
formal *Bildung*   92, 93, 101, 187, 188
French didactics   9
Furlong, J.   151, 201, 225, 229, 233, 239
 advanced mathematics knowledge (AMK)   222
 integrated knowledge traditions   97
 powerful professional knowledge (PPK) focus   11, 12, 14
 social context   226, 237
 transformation processes   134
future citizens   2, 68, 135, 193
futures, curriculum   5–7, 52

Gaffield, Chad   45, 59
generalization   26, 68, 170, 172, 175
general pedagogical knowledge (GPK)   152
generations   26, 47, 69, 127
Geographical Association   70, 71, 74
geography's epistemology   72–5, 81. *See also* 'thinking geographically'
German traditions
 Bildung (description)   92
 didactics   2, 12, 25, 87, 152, 185
Global Migration: The Basics   192

Gottlieb and Wineberg, *Between Veritas and Communitas* 96, 102, 104 n.2
Green, B. 112–13
Green Deal. *See* European Green Deal framework (EU)
Grimen, H. 24, 25, 37

habitual practices 47, 48, 59, 71, 222
Hannam, P. 95, 97, 98
Hawken, P. 131, 133, 134
higher education 11, 23, 35, 51, 239. *See also* master's; university-based teacher education
historical development of teacher education 47, 50, 53, 55
historical thinking 45, 46, 49, 53, 54, 58
history instruction 46, 49, 53–5
Hordern, J. 11–12, 14, 46, 151, 160, 239
horizon content knowledge (HCK) 206, 207, 210, 218
'how' questions 8, 231
how to teach
 circular economy (core idea) 135–9
 history 15
 migration 170, 172, 179, 188
 Norwegian 64
 and what to teach 7, 26, 34, 130
humanities 72, 109, 110

identity 33, 89, 96, 112, 176, 195
 and epistemology 104 n.2
 of subjects 65, 103
 of teachers 65, 148
identity, undermined 11, 97
impact on learning 96, 112
 mathematical thinking 145, 154, 155–6, 158, 159
inclusive education 6, 98, 103, 138, 146, 162
in-depth study 38, 226, 231, 232, 233, 235
institutional
 change 100
 context 110, 115, 128, 197
 experiences 115
 perspectives 28, 89, 197
institutionalization of subject didactics 14
institutions, teacher education. *See* teacher education institutions (TEIs)

integrated knowledge traditions 97
interdisciplinary approaches 4, 10, 31, 99
international student assessments 1, 14
interpretative subjects 46, 49, 55
interviews 94, 111, 138, 211
 interpretative subjects 46, 49, 55
 literary canon 117, 118
 post-trial 145, 154, 155–9
 powerful disciplinary knowledge (PDK) 38
 reforms 37
 teachers, novice 115, 119, 121

judgement, professional 35, 65, 68, 81, 135, 232. *See also* reflective practice
trust 24

Kansanen, P. 2, 14, 148, 228, 231, 236
Kattmann, U. 185, 190, 191, 227
Klafki, Wolfgang 9, 26, 87, 148, 191, 238
 artefacts, teaching 189
 categorial *Bildung* 93, 97, 187, 190, 201, 228
 didactic triangle 100
 'epoch-typical key problems' 92
Klein, F. 209, 212
'knower' 52, 101
Knowledge and Quality Across School Subjects and Teacher Education (KOSS) Network 63, 110, 127
knowledge building
 analysis 170–2, 173, 174, 175
 conversation 151
 cumulative 167, 180, 181
 'decompression' 161
 process 168
knowledge by acquaintance 9–10, 147, 232
knowledge form(s) 8, 66, 68, 97, 110, 232. *See also* meta-knowledge
 advanced mathematics knowledge (AMK) 211
 'Big Questions' 88, 94, 95
 boundaries 5
 categorization 207
 connections 15, 46, 48, 151, 226, 229
 entitlement, students' 91
 Geographical Association 74
 misconceptions 87, 230

knowledge how. See also procedural knowledge
  epistemic ascent   9, 150
  epistemic capacity   10, 147
  and *knowledge that*   120, 229
  pedagogical content knowledge (PCK)   162
  pedagogical knowledge (PK)   161
  tertiary education   121–2
knowledge-led curriculum   91, 148, 150
knowledge production   5, 56, 59, 121, 122, 229
knowledge structure   59, 73, 231
knowledge that. See also propositional knowledge
  epistemic ascent   9, 147, 150
  epistemic capacity   10
  and *knowledge how*   120, 229
  tertiary education   121–2
Korhonen, J.   129, 131, 132, 133, 137, 140
KOSS Network (Knowledge and Quality Across School Subjects and Teacher Education) Network   63, 110, 127

Lambert, David   147, 148, 150, 155, 157, 160
learning environment   146, 153, 163, 201, 235
lecturing   48, 53, 54
legitimacy   6, 11, 25, 48, 56
legitimation code theory (LCT)   16, 167, 170
Lehrplan (teacher agency)   228
lenses   7, 90, 93, 99, 100, 119
  theoretical frameworks   154
lesson observation   46, 48, 49, 155–6
lesson plans. *See* plans, teaching
light bulb moments. *See* 'aha' moments
linguistics   23, 31, 34, 35–6, 111, 180
literacy, case for epistemic   97–101
literary canon   117–18. *See also* canonical knowledge
literary knowledge, investigating   114–15
LNU (national association for the teaching of Norwegian)   35
Local Education Authority (LEA)   145, 146, 153
logic   11, 14, 81, 136, 193, 209
longitudinal research   16, 110, 114, 115

master's. *See also* postgraduate education
  level   29, 37, 38, 50, 51, 56
  programme   23, 31, 33, 35, 37, 38
  reform   24, 38
  thesis   29, 37, 38, 49
material *Bildung*   92, 93, 101, 187, 188
mathematical content knowledge (MCK)   152
mathematical fundamentalism   146
mathematical pedagogical content knowledge (MPCK)   152
mathematical thinking   27, 153–4, 159, 160, 215. *See also Developing Mathematical Thinking in the Primary Classroom* (DMTPC)
Mathematics Knowledge for Teaching (MKT)   207, 210
Maton, K.   167, 168, 170, 172
Medway, P.   111, 112, 113
'membership'   96
memorization
  access, epistemic   209
  of facts   45, 58, 91, 212
  lecturing   48–9
  tyranny of experience   53, 56
mentoring   53, 58, 102
meta-knowledge   97, 235
meta-theoretical thinking   47, 48, 56
migration (choice of content)   169
Ministry of Education (Norway)   24, 27, 28, 31, 39–40
misconceptions   87, 194, 217, 220, 221, 230
model of *didaktical* reconstruction   186, 187, 190–2, 193, 199, 200–1
  elementarization   196
moderation   168, 170, 173, 176, 181
moral development   72, 89, 90, 92, 93
Morgan, J.   6, 64, 68
motivation, student   137, 155, 156–7, 159, 168
Muller, J.   14, 57, 109, 151, 186
  curriculum futures   5–6, 7, 52
  'power,' meaning of   26, 187
multidisciplinary
  approaches   50, 89, 133, 136, 139, 140
  practices   24, 140
  subjects   34, 59, 129

national association for the teaching of Norwegian (LNU) 35
national curriculum
  Australia 14
  England 74, 209, 214, 215
  Finland 16, 54, 55, 140
natural resources 127, 128, 129, 130, 136
nature of knowledge 101, 103, 122, 225, 237
  categorial *Bildung* 87, 93
  epistemic switching 96
Nordic traditions 2, 87, 92, 187
Norway 29, 30, 36, 38, 223, 233
  Ministry of Education 24, 27, 28, 31, 39–40
  practical syntheses 25, 37
  reforms 23–4, 28–33, 34, 37
Norwegian (subject) 23, 24, 28, 30–3, 34–8

observation
  lesson 46, 48, 49, 155–6
  student 159
  studies 45, 48, 49, 54, 55
Ongstad, S. 8, 36, 239
online environment 92, 146, 153, 157, 163
ontology 90, 94, 95
'open collective cycle' (OCC) 146, 153, 163
open-ended enquiry 48, 52, 137
organization of teacher education 2, 5, 10, 11, 235, 239
  academicization 233
Our Common Future 128

parent disciplines 12, 87, 90, 100
participative decision-making 131
partnership group (Curriculum for Excellence Development) 145, 153
pedagogical content knowledge (PCK) 17, 77, 161, 226, 234, 235–6
  Anglo-Saxon curriculum tradition 227
  Curriculum for Excellence 162
  mathematical pedagogical content knowledge (MPCK) 152

  and specialized content knowledge (SCK) 207, 230, 231
  and subject-specific educational content knowledge (SSECK) 229, 230, 231, 238
pedagogical relation 148, 149, 161
pedagogical studies 49, 52, 53, 219–20
pedagogic devices 167, 169, 179
peer discussion 153, 171, 172, 173, 175, 181
  transformation processes 168, 170, 180
performance 64, 65, 82, 193
personal practical theory (PPT) 51, 52, 57
philosophies, educational 68, 75, 76, 77, 81, 102
phronesis 65, 232, 235
physics 59, 112, 135
plans, teaching 104 n.1, 188, 191, 192, 196, 197. *See also* curriculum planning
  model of *didaktical* reconstruction 186
policy documents 128, 133, 140
policy level 9, 16, 58, 130, 133
political
  questions 69, 79, 110, 129, 140
  system 3, 51
politicians 29, 113
poor practice 47, 56. *See also* quality, low epistemic
postgraduate education 24, 38, 145, 153, 213. *See also* master's
post-trial interviews 154, 155–9, 211
potential, transformative 2, 68
'power,' meaning of 26, 187
powerful disciplinary knowledge (PDK) 63, 68, 72, 77, 81–2, 129
  curriculum thinking 69
powerful knowledge (introduction) 1, 4–7, 26
powerful literary knowledge 119–21
powerful professional knowledge (PPK) characterizing 234–6
powerful professional knowledge (PPK) conclusions 81–2
powerful professional knowledge (PPK) focus 10–15, 151–2

PowerPoint   48, 170, 172, 178
practical syntheses   24, 25, 37
practical theorizing   151, 225, 232–3
Prediger, S.   186, 189, 200, 201
prescriptive orientation   50, 52, 118
primary education   3–4, 6, 137, 163–4, 185, 202 n.2. *See also Developing Mathematical Thinking in the Primary Classroom* (DMTPC)
   access, epistemic   146, 162
   community-rooted views   17, 200
   context-independency   48
   educational design research (EDR)   188
   Norwegian (subject)   23, 28, 30, 33, 37, 38
   researchers   10
   teachers   38, 50, 186
problematization   140, 185, 187, 198, 229
problem-solving   136, 137, 138, 139, 190, 218
   equations   209, 210, 211
procedural knowledge   9, 27, 73, 76, 147, 201. *See also knowledge how*
production of knowledge   5, 56, 59, 121, 122, 229
professional development (PD)   189
professional development workshop   206, 214–15, 216, 221
professionalization   11, 29
professional judgement. *See* judgement, professional
professional learning community   146, 153, 163
professional theorizing   46, 48
profession orientation   28, 29, 33, 34, 35, 36
professors   53, 58, 115
propositional knowledge   9, 113, 116, 117, 121, 147. *See also knowledge that*
   and contextual knowledge   73
   low epistemic quality   27
prototyping   131, 138, 139, 169, 188
psychology   49, 135
publications   53, 58, 74
purpose of education   36, 67, 68, 77, 93, 109
push-and-pull factors   176, 177, 179, 197, 199

qualified teacher status   101, 215
quality, low epistemic   27, 146, 209. *See also* poor practice

'reading the world'   119, 120
real-life challenges   136, 140, 158, 161
real-world, the   73, 75, 78, 79, 137, 139
recontextualization   8, 71, 100, 102, 168, 170
   legitimation code theory (LCT)   167
   pedagogic devices   169, 179
reflective practice   15, 148, 151, 225, 232–3
reflexivity   97, 98, 103
reforms
   England   89, 92
   Finland   50, 51
   Norway   23–4, 28–33, 34, 37, 38
   Scotland   145
regional geography   74
regions (concept)   12, 152, 239
regulation   27, 28, 29, 39, 56
reliable explanations   1, 26, 68, 77
Religious Instruction (RI)   88
repacking   168, 169, 175, 176, 181
reproduction   59, 75, 118, 136, 180, 181
   legitimation code theory (LCT)   167
   and recontextualization   170, 179
research benefits   157, 216, 220, 221. *See also* unintended consequences
research-development-circle (RD-circle)
   artefacts, teaching   186, 188, 189, 196, 197, 198
   elementarization   195, 196, 198
   how to teach   172, 179, 188
   model of *didaktical* reconstruction   192, 200, 201
   overview   168–9, 193
   peer discussion   171, 172, 175, 180, 181
   semantic plane   171, 175, 180
   social realism   202
Research Group for Social Studies Education (University of Helsinki)   46
research methods   45, 51, 58. *See also* action research; interviews; observation

research questions   36, 63, 151, 186, 215–16, 237
  blended learning   146
  empirical data   154
  knowledge form(s)   88
  scope of research   4
  sustainable development   127–8
resource-efficient economies   129, 139
resources. *See* artefacts, teaching
Roberts, D.   135, 136
Rosenlund, D.   55, 57, 58

scaffolding   72, 172, 180
school-based teacher education   3, 102
scope of research   4, 68, 81, 82
Scotland   16, 145, 153
Scottish Government (2010–12)   16, 145
Scottish Survey of Literacy and Numeracy   153
scrutinization   180, 181, 209
semantic density   170–1, 175, 181
semantic gravity   170–1, 175
semantic limit   179
semantic plane   170–1, 175, 176, 180
semantic profiles   172, 175, 177, 179–80, 181
semantic relations   174
semantic shifts   170, 171, 175, 178, 181
semantic waves   168, 170, 171, 172, 175, 177–8
Shaw, M.   97, 98
Shulman, Lee   160–1, 205, 206–7, 226–7, 228, 232
  categories   161, 163, 227, 236
significant knowledge   7, 25, 110, 113, 194, 196
  assumptions   121
Simola, H.   50, 51, 52, 53
singulars   12, 14, 152, 239
Sitra (foundation)   129, 130
social context   6, 110, 115, 226, 237
social justice   77, 91, 92, 113
social realism   10, 11, 186, 202, 226, 237
  curriculum futures   6
  future citizens   2
  perspective   1, 15
social science   30, 109, 135, 138, 202
societal change   77, 100, 130
societal context   149, 150

sociologists, educational   1, 225
Spangenberg, J.   128
specialized content knowledge (SCK)   207, 208–9, 218, 230, 231, 233
  misconceptions   220, 221
special nature, knowledge of   17, 238
Stahel, W.   130–1, 132
stepping down to practice   215
structural conditions   236
structure, knowledge   59, 73, 231
student backgrounds   33, 96
students as curriculum makers   159
student teacher competencies   27, 32, 37, 50, 65, 232
subject didactics, development of   12–15
subject didactics, strengthening   2, 24, 29
subject expertise   9, 46, 51, 101, 147, 150
subject-specific educational content knowledge (SSECK)   17, 164, 229–32, 238
substantive knowledge   45, 53, 54, 55, 56
Sunday School Movement   88
sustainable development   127, 128, 131, 132, 139, 146
Sweden   167, 176, 177, 194, 195, 233
  subject didactics, development of   12–14
  substantive knowledge   55
  sustainable development   127
switching, epistemic   96, 98, 102
systematicity   69, 70, 78, 101

Tatto, M.   151, 160
teacher(s), novice   57–8, 70, 75, 78, 79, 122
  interviews   119, 121
  longitudinal research   110, 115
  powerful disciplinary knowledge (PDK)   63, 64, 68, 81
  purpose of education   77
  visual representation   82
teacher-centred methods   45, 56
teacher competencies   14, 33, 36, 149
teacher education, organization of   2, 5, 10, 11, 235, 239
  academicization   233
teacher education institutions (TEIs)   3, 24, 28, 239

teacher education programmes, pre-service   111, 121, 122, 151
teacher educator(s)   45, 53, 56, 58, 115, 181
   commitment   101, 102
   experience   28, 208, 214
   judgement, professional   81
   reforms   29, 38, 50
teachers, pre-service   112, 213, 215
teacher training schools   46, 53, 56, 58
teaching practice   29, 49, 55–9, 75, 173, 238
   academization   52, 53
   capabilities of students   130, 140
   elementarization   198
   mathematical thinking   215
   reforms   24, 29, 50, 51
   subject-specific educational content knowledge (SSECK)   238
   theoretical frameworks   47
   theoretical perspectives   25, 239
technology   64, 65, 92, 146, 153, 163. *See also* online environment
tensions   64, 99, 114, 122, 128, 221
tertiary education   109, 113, 115, 118, 122. *See also* higher education; postgraduate education
themes, emerging   17, 114, 159, 160, 163, 236
theology   90, 94, 99
theoretical frameworks   47–8, 145, 146–8, 152, 154, 155
theoretical insights   206–7
theoretical perspectives   24, 25–7, 31, 37, 179, 239
theoretical syntheses   24, 25
theorizing. *See also* Weniger, Erich
   analytical frameworks   56
   habitual practices   59
   personal practical theory (PPT)   52, 57
   practical   151, 225, 232–3
   professional   46, 48
   traditions, persistent   58
theory, tyranny of. *See* tyranny of theory
'thinking geographically'   74, 76
3-T model   186, 189, 201
tools. *See* analytical tools

traditions, persistent   47, 55, 56, 58. *See also* tyranny of experience
transformation processes   7–15, 134, 147, 168, 170, 196–200
   capabilities   130
   context-independency   57
   multidisciplinary subjects   129
   pedagogical content knowledge (PCK)   17, 226
   research questions   4
   semantic profiles   179, 180
   semantic shifts   170
   subject-specific educational content knowledge (SSECK)   17
transformative potential   2, 68, 81
transmission of knowledge   26, 36, 47, 112
   substantive knowledge   45, 53, 54
transposition   8, 9, 147
trust   113, 129, 135
   between group members   138
   learning environment   160, 163
   professional judgement   24
   between teachers   139, 181
tyranny of experience   51, 52, 53–5, 59, 233
   traditions, persistent   47, 55, 56, 58
tyranny of theory   47, 52, 233

UCL Institute of Education (IOE)   63, 65, 66, 76
unintended consequences   133, 134, 136, 138
university-based teacher education   3, 46, 58, 102
University of Dundee   145, 153
University of Helsinki   46, 51
unpacking concepts   162, 168, 169, 172, 175, 176
UN Sustainable Development Goal 4   146

vision I and II   135, 136
visual representation   70, 74, 81, 209
vocational education   5, 11, 239
Vygotsky, Lev   69, 70, 91

Wasserman, N.   210, 211, 214–15
waste   130, 131, 132, 134, 135
'ways of knowing'   97, 101, 113, 114

Webster, K.   129, 131, 136, 140
Weniger, Erich   47–8, 50, 55, 56, 69. *See also* tyranny of experience; tyranny of theory
  and personal practical theory (PPT)   51
  tensions   233
'what' questions   9, 231
what to teach   64, 81, 130–2, 137, 171, 180
  and how to teach   7, 135, 139
Wheelahan, Leesa   5, 68, 72, 239
Whitty, G.   151, 201, 225, 229, 233, 239
  advanced mathematics knowledge (AMK)   222
  integrated knowledge traditions   97
  powerful professional knowledge (PPK) focus   11, 12, 14
  social context   226, 237
  transformation processes   134

Winch, C.   9, 71, 75, 147, 150, 232
workshop, professional development   206, 214–15, 216, 221
World Commission for Environment and Development (UN)   128
worldviews   89, 97–8, 102
writing   120–1
  and reforms   28, 31, 33, 34, 38

Young, Michael   9, 36, 69, 100, 113, 117
  assumptions   116, 121
  context-independency   48, 57, 68, 133
  curriculum principle   187, 202
  entitlement, students'   1, 26, 91
  futures, curriculum   5, 6, 7, 52
  knowledge form(s)   48, 110, 151, 229
  purpose of education   68, 77, 109
  transformation processes   14, 134

Zazkis, R.   210–11

www.ingramcontent.com/pod-product-compliance
Lightning Source LLC
Chambersburg PA
CBHW062123300426
44115CB00012BA/1788